Naked Is the Best Disguise

By Samuel Rosenberg

THE COME-AS-YOU-ARE MASQUERADE PARTY

SAMUEL ROSENBERG

NAKED IS THE

BEST DISGUISE

The Death & Resurrection
of Sherlock Holmes

THE BOBBS-MERRILL COMPANY, INC.
Indianapolis   *New York*

For permission to reprint, acknowledgment is made to the following:

Grover Smith for an excerpt from "T. S. Eliot and Sherlock Holmes," *Notes and Queries,* Vol. 193, October 2, 1948.

Harcourt Brace Jovanovich, Inc., for an excerpt from EMINENT VICTORIANS by Lytton Strachey.

Chatto and Windus Ltd. for excerpts from DUBLIN'S JOYCE by Hugh Kenner.

The Viking Press, Inc. for two poems from THE POETRY OF CATULLUS, translated by C. H. Sisson, copyright © 1966 by C. H. Sisson, reprinted by permission of the Orion Press, Grossman Publishers.

Prentice-Hall, Inc., for excerpts from THE COME-AS-YOU-ARE MASQUERADE PARTY by Samuel Rosenberg, copyright © 1970 by Samuel Rosenberg, published by Prentice-Hall, Inc., Englewood Cliffs, N.J.

A. P. Watt & Son for excerpts from OSCAR WILDE by Hesketh Pearson.

The Society of Authors for excerpts from AFFILIATIONS by Havelock Ellis, the Society of Authors as the literary representative of the Estate of Havelock Ellis.

ISBN 0-672-51914-3
Library of Congress catalog card number 73-11802
Designed by Winston G. Potter
Manufactured in the United States of America

First printing

For
My Father Jacob
and My Mother Fanny,
With Love
and Gratitude

No mask like open truth to cover lies,
As to go naked is the best disguise.

—WILLIAM CONGREVE, *The Double Dealer*, 1694

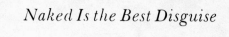

Naked Is the Best Disguise

CHAPTER ONE

1.

IF ANYONE WERE TO ASK ME, "What was your most embarrassing moment?" I would probably answer, "Sorry, but I can't tell you about *that one*. We prefer to keep it a dark, dark family secret!" (Pause) "But, if you wish to hear it, I will tell you about another humiliating experience. It occurred on a train leaving Meiringen, Switzerland—at precisely 8:15 A.M. on the 24th of June, 1954."

Then, like the Ancient Mariner (patron of all compulsive talkers), I would quickly add, "Yes, that was a very unhinging moment, but I will always be glad it happened. It was one of several unforgettable chance encounters which aroused my curiosity and led, finally, to this book of totally new and revolutionary discoveries about Sir Arthur Conan Doyle and his fabulous detective, Sherlock Holmes."

Now, in retrospect, I see that these "discoveries" were made during slowly developing phases, the first of which began with the sudden traumatic recognition that Conan Doyle had not only molded his best and worst villain, "Professor Moriarty," from the distorted contemporary image of Professor Friedrich Nietzsche, but that he had also actually, if deviously, informed his readers that he had done so!

This astonishing and hitherto-unsuspected "recognition" then led in turn to the further discovery that Conan Doyle was a

1

highly compulsive, self-revealing allegorist who had artfully implanted a large number of "purloined letter" clues among his stories. These clues profoundly associate Doyle and Sherlock Holmes and his companions with the following real-life, fictional, legendary, and Biblical figures:

1. *Friedrich Nietzsche:* the man himself and several of his works.
2. *Oscar Wilde:* as a character in *The Sign of Four* and *The Adventure of the Empty House,* and three of Wilde's friends.
3. The Greek Olympian god *Dionysus.*
4. *Jesus Christ:* as the Superstar of the Easter celebration of his Death and Resurrection.
5. *Gaius Valerius Catullus:* the bisexual poet of ancient Rome.
6. *John Bunyan:* two characters from his Christian allegory *The Holy War.*
7. *Robert Browning:* his masterpiece *The Ring and the Book.*
8. *Giovanni Boccaccio: The Decameron.*
9. *Napoleon Bonaparte:* his image in gold.
10. *Rachel,* the tragedienne, in the title role of *Phèdre.*
11. *Jean Racine:* his dramas *Phèdre* and *Mithridate,* and himself in a non-Sherlockian novel written by Doyle.
12. *Dr. Victor Frankenstein and his Monster:* together with several scenes borrowed from Mary Shelley's *Frankenstein.*
13. *Gustave Flaubert:* as the author of a letter quoted in French by Sherlock Holmes, and as the friend of George Sand.
14. *George Sand* (Madame Dudevant), author and transvestite. (Her connection with Sherlock Holmes is most remarkable.)
15. *Plato* and *Socrates.*
16. *Edgar Allan Poe* and his pioneer detective *Auguste Dupin.*
17. *Sarasate* and *Norman Neruda,* concert violinists of the day.
18. *The Old Testament:* (a) a scene from the destruction of *Sodom and Gomorrah* and two of its characters, and (b) an incident from *The Book of Joshua* involving the harlot *Rahab.*
19. *Antony* and *Cleopatra,* from the Shakespearean play.
20. The twin *Sebastian* from Shakespeare's *Twelfth Night,* and the play itself.
21. The mythological characters *Theseus, Ariadne,* and the *Minotaur,* in two Sherlock Holmes adventures.
22. *General George Gordon,* the martyred hero of Khartoum, and his private army of *"ragged street arabs."*

23. *Reverend Henry Ward Beecher,* the American clergyman, almost defrocked, with a hidden reference to his sister *Harriet Beecher Stowe,* author of *Uncle Tom's Cabin.*
24. Herman Melville's *Redburn* and *Benito Cereno.* And others. . . .

Sherlock Holmes and Friedrich Nietzsche? The mythological Theseus, Dionysus, Ariadne—and Sherlock Holmes? Oscar Wilde? Gustave Flaubert and George Sand? Sodom and Gomorrah? Plato and Jesus and Socrates? General Gordon of Khartoum? What possible connections, profound or trivial, could there be between such a motley group of saints and sinners—not to mention the ultralewd Catullus—and that Victorian duo, Conan Doyle and Sherlock Holmes?

When I first stumbled upon these hidden-yet-visible links or "identifications," so utterly alien to the established public images of Holmes and his shadowy father-creator, they seemed unbelievable, totally impossible. But taking my operational cue from the great detective's own words: "Whenever you have eliminated the impossible, whatever remains, however improbable, *must* be the truth," I continued with my captivating hunt of the seeming impossible.

Then, gradually, as the flagrantly visible clues generously given by Doyle were explored, there emerged, as from an archeological "dig," a fascinating new image of a hidden "second Conan Doyle" and of his alter egos: Sherlock Holmes, Dr. Watson, Professor Moriarty, and others.

The surprising "new Conan Doyle" who then became visible was a very brilliant, highly underestimated writer who created many of his heroes and villains in his own image, who recognized the startling self-revelations on view in his pre-Freudian psychodramatic confessions called "detective stories," and who then recoiled in fear that others might recognize them, too. But, at the same time, he was compulsively honest and, with both conscious and unconscious deliberation, he left clues to his personal allegory for some Sherlockian reader to find and interpret sympathetically.

2.

IF YOU ARE WONDERING, as I did at first, if Conan Doyle actually read, remembered, assimilated, and consciously utilized this great range of books, many very advanced, mentioned in his detective stories, I refer you first to Mrs. Jean Conan Doyle:

My husband was intensely thorough in his literary work. He took enormous pains to get everything right. For instance, before writing *The White Company* he soaked his brain with a knowledge of the period he intended to portray. He read over sixty books dealing with the heraldry—armour—falconry—the medieval habits of the peasants of the time—the social customs of the higher folk of the land, etc. Only when he knew those days as though he had lived in them—when he had got the very atmosphere steeped in his brain—did he put pen to paper and let loose the creations of his mind.*

(Not to mention that Doyle, who read history passionately on a scholarly level, also read most of the chronicles, memoirs, biographies, and journals of the periods he wrote about.)

In *The True Conan Doyle*, Adrian Conan Doyle first attests to his father's "omnivorous reading" and then adds:

Conan Doyle's memory was so extraordinary that it entered the realms of the freakish. For instance, if one examined him on any book which he had not read for as many as twenty years, he could give a fair outline of the plot and the name of every principal character. I have tested him on this on many occasions. Again, meeting any ex-serviceman, he could, and would, immediately inform the astounded recipient not only the name of his former brigade and division but the principal actions in which it took part!

The picture of Conan Doyle as a prodigious reader of Racine, Shakespeare, Goethe, Browning, Poe, Flaubert, Catullus, Bunyan, Plato, Boccaccio, etc., who could recall perfectly even the tiniest details in their writings, is completed by Doyle himself. While expressing his great admiration for Robert Louis Stevenson (from whose story *The Dynamiter* he took the "inner story" for *A Study in Scarlet*), Doyle speaks of Stevenson's *A Pavilion on the Links* and, in passing, tells us about his own phenomenal memory:

---

* Intro, *The Complete Sherlock Holmes,* Doubleday.

That story stamped itself so clearly on my memory when I read it in *Cornhill* [magazine] that when I came across it many years afterward in volume form, I was able instantly to recognize two small modifications of the text—each very much for the worse—from the original form.*

Conan Doyle's awestruck friends and relatives also testify that in addition to the more than two million words he published, he also found time to write a gloss or synopsis of most of the vast number of books he read.

3.

THE CONCEPTION of an Arthur Conan Doyle who concealed himself behind an opaque public *persona* has been put forth by Pierre Nordon in his biography:†

Every writer who cares about his posthumous reputation, or is merely interested in his own inner life, feels the need to orient himself by means of memoirs or confession—the special domain of introspection. In this respect Sir Arthur Conan Doyle's two autobiographical works, *The Stark-Munroe Letters and Memories and Adventures* are equally deceptive.

"Conan Doyle," says the perceptive Nordon, "hesitates to draw the reader into purely autobiographical regions. . . . He is not concerned with exposing his own personality or trying to interest his readers in it." Nordon concludes:

It is no exaggeration that Conan Doyle deliberately concealed the more intimate and important parts of his personality from posterity, and from his contemporaries.

Professor Nordon is only partly right. It is true that Conan Doyle "deliberately concealed the more intimate and important parts of his personality" in his "autobiographical works." But, as my more than one hundred discoveries will testify, there was a compulsively honest *second* Conan Doyle—an allegorist who left an abundance of clues which, when decoded, reveal a fascinating segment of his concealed personality.

---

* *Through the Magic Door* (1915), pg. 117, quoted by Pierre Nordon, *Conan Doyle,* London, 1966.
† *Conan Doyle,* John Murray, London.

4.

A BACKGROUND NOTE: When the author of a "popular" book beloved by the masses—a John Bunyan or Daniel Defoe or Conan Doyle—does finally receive the scholarly critical attention his genius deserves, much posthumous time has elapsed. *Robinson Crusoe,* as an example, was dismissed by most of the university intellectuals in Defoe's time as a narrative fit only for the barely literate working class. Many of the established critics who did respond to its magic flatly refused to believe that so irresistible a book could be the work of Defoe, the "literary hack," a man who had been "stood in the pillory." "Before the end of the Eighteenth Century," writes Professor Frank Ellis, "the authorship of *Robinson Crusoe* was successively attributed to Robert Harley, Earl of Oxford; Dr. John Arbuthnot, the Queen's physician; and Sir Richard Steele."

Several Earls of Oxford have been associated with such arcane literary controversy. Edward de Vere, an earlier holder of the title, has been nominated as the true hidden author of the plays and poems of William Shakespeare, a theory based (partly) on the same elitist premise that no "butcher's boy" could have written so understandingly about aristocrats and kings! But such expressions of snobbery are perennial. During the first performance of *Hamlet* in Boston in the eighteenth century, a gentleman was heard to exclaim, "This *Hamlet* is a fine play! Why, there are not ten men at Harvard who could write a better one!"

The extreme condescension toward the plebeian author of *Robinson Crusoe* has persisted well into the present. Sir Leslie Stephen (Virginia Woolf's father) wrote:

. . . for people not too proud to take a rather lowly order of amusement, *Robinson Crusoe* will always be the most charming of companions.*

But this attitude toward Defoe and his masterpiece has recently undergone a revolutionary change. Now, more than 250 years later, as the enchanting tale of the castaway mariner is still entertaining its millions of readers in many languages, it is being

---

* *Twentieth Century Interpretations of Robinson Crusoe,* Prentice-Hall, 1969.

rediscovered as a spiritual autobiography with many layers of profound meaning. Scholars like J. Paul Hunter, G. Starr, and Maximilian Novak have written fascinating studies of the *intentional* Puritan, sociopolitical, and psychological allegories found lurking below the surface of the book previously belittled as "entertainment for children of all ages."

Part of the credit for the change of attitude toward this and other demotic writings belongs to certain societal and psychic analysts who look for and recognize the hidden personal and social forces which direct even the "simplest" actions, decisions, jokes, dreams, and accidents of "ordinary people." Such insights bestow profundity on every one of us.

But these ennobling insights have not been utilized often enough for the understanding of "popular" literature like the Sherlock Holmes adventures. Even though the same cultural and personal forces operate in "serious" and "popular" literary works alike (their differences lie mainly in their declared goals and the fashionable criteria of "quality" applied to them), most critic-biographers have chosen to apply their skills and insights to the more "serious" writers.

5.

IF YOU ARE reluctant to believe that *Robinson Crusoe*, the "escapist" book of your childhood, was *also* intended to be an allegory of sin, punishment, suffering, expiation, and deliverance, I refer you to its opening paragraph. There, with the help of my pointing finger, you will discover what millions upon millions of readers have read and then promptly ignored: Daniel Defoe's clue to his allegorical intentions.

First he tells the reader that his hero is not really a typical Englishman: He is the son of a German immigrant! Then, even more surprisingly, Defoe informs us that Robinson's baptismal name was not Crusoe, and he offers his key to the profound allegory of *Robinson Crusoe*:

I was born in 1632, in the city of York, of a good family, tho not of that country, my father being a foreigner of Bremen, who settled first at Hull. He got a good estate from merchandise, and leaving off his trade lived afterward at York from whence he married my mother, whose relations were named Robinson, and from whom I was called *Robinson Kreutznaer;* but by the usual corruption of words in England, we are called, nay we called ourselves, and write the name, Crusoe, and so my companions always called me.

The key to the allegory of Robinson Crusoe? It is in the family name—Kreutznaer—for, as any good German-English dictionary will tell you, a *Kreutznaer* is a crucified fool.

6.

ANOTHER BACKGROUND NOTE: Ordinarily, "good-bad" popular writers like Conan Doyle are read for entertainment only and do not receive the serious critical appreciation some of them deserve. Of course the charming, worshipful, and ingenious "Baker Street Irregulars" have written a great many books and articles about Sherlock Holmes and his companion characters, but many of them are resolutely indifferent, even hostile, to his father-creator (perhaps they have never forgiven him for killing his "son" Sherlock and keeping him in cryogenic storage for nine years) : the articles about Holmes, Watson, and Moriarty in *The Annotated Sherlock Holmes* bibliography outnumber those about Conan Doyle 925 to 4!

But this form of oedipal discrimination is a very familiar, even banal, fact of life in the literary arena. Most of us know and love the immortal characters Romeo and Juliet, Don Quixote, Alice (in Wonderland), Frankenstein's "Monster," and Robinson Crusoe—but how many readers know or give a damn about the literary parent of each of these immaculately conceived, even parthenogenic brainchildren?

As an example of the curious manner in which Conan Doyle has been relegated to the status of a nearly invisible holy-ghost-writer by the Baker Street Irregulars, I offer the recent *A Sherlock Holmes Commentary* by D. Martin Dakin. Except for a mention of the Conan Doyle estate and the titles of the several biographies of Doyle, he is never once referred to in the entire 306-page text. The "Irregular" Mr. Dakin accomplishes this remarkable feat of suppression by designating Dr. Watson as the author of the Sherlock Holmes adventures. The result of this unique phenomenon in literature has been a denial of Conan Doyle's profound genius as a detective-story writer.

7.

Yes, I remember that embarrassing—and farcical—"train experience" vividly: After finishing a fascinating magazine assignment on the hidden glacial shelf high above the Hasli Valley (in eastern Switzerland), I taxied down to Meiringen and boarded the train for Zurich at precisely 8:13 A.M.

I entered the train's second-class compartment and found a window seat opposite a Japanese tourist half-buried in maps. I was busy stowing my luggage in the overhead rack—when it happened.

The Japanese tourist turned to the man across the aisle and said, "Excuse me, preez. I cannot find Meilingen on my maps. But I see many peeper coming and going here in Meilingen. It is a famous prace?"

The man, obviously a Swiss commuter on his way to work, looked up from his paper and answered enthusiastically: "Oh, yah, Meiringen iss a very famous place! From all over the vorld people they come to climb on the Rosenlaui Glacier. Also, from here you cannot see it, but up there behind zat mountain there iss the famous Reichenbach Falls where Sherlock Holmes und Professor Moriarty they hat their bick fight und both falled down to their deaths!"

The eyes of the Japanese gentleman opened wide in astonishment. He hissed like a leaky tire-valve, leaped to his feet, ran to the window of the now-moving train, made wild camera-shots in all directions, and shouted happily: "Leichenbach Forrs! Shulrock Horrms! I lead Shulrock Horrms in Engrish when I smorr boy! Thank you! Thank you!"

Of course everyone in the compartment laughed at his charming "Shulrock-Horrmsian" frenzy. Everyone but me, that is. Unnoticed by my train companions, I was having a conniption fit that almost forced me to leap off the train and return to Meiringen.

Caught completely by surprise, I gasped inwardly: "*Reichenbach Falls!* Sherlock Holmes and Professor Moriarty! Three long days at Rosenlaui *within a mile* of Reichenbach Falls and I, a lifetime Sherlock Holmes addict, never realized that I was on hallowed ground! How could I have been so incredibly stupid!"

At first my embarrassment was mainly professional. For many

years I'd worked as a literary consultant for major motion-picture studios which hired me when they were sued for plagiarism. I analyzed the embattled scripts, and when the resemblances between "theirs" and "ours" were too close for comfort, I tried to get my employers off the litigious hook by searching for the common literary ancestors of both properties. It was fascinating work, I received much praise, and one employer even dubbed me a "literary Sherlock Holmes" when I sometimes ferreted out important correlations undetected by other "experts." As a result, I'd developed a degree of professional conceit as an intellectual "private eye"—which now had been shattered by my humiliating failure to recognize the great roaring waterfall I'd gaped at four times—as the death arena of Sherlock Holmes and Professor Moriarty!

Seeking someone to share my shame, I turned primitively on Conan Doyle: "Dammit! It's all his fault! Why did he have to drag his characters . . . his *victims* all the way from England to this very remote Swiss boondock? He could have murdered Holmes and Moriarty with much less trouble by tossing them off a building in London. Or from a cliff in the Scottish highlands. Or in Timbuktu. Why did Doyle choose to kill his characters in this particular place? *No one ever associates Sherlock Holmes with Switzerland!*"

At that exact instant I experienced my moment of illumination. Suddenly the place names Switzerland, Rosenlaui, Reichenbach Falls, and the names Conan Doyle, Sherlock Holmes, and Professor Moriarty all became incandescently fused in my mind with that of Professor Friedrich Nietzsche.

As the train glided through the exquisite Alpine country, I ruminated: "Friedrich Nietzsche? Out of what strange cave of memory did *that* one emerge? What has Nietzsche to do with Holmes or Moriarty? There's a weird coupling of names: Conan Doyle and Nietzsche . . . it's exactly like those satirical *Imaginary Interviews* painted by Miguel Covarrubias in the old *Vanity Fair* magazine: Mae West flirting with Mahatma Gandhi . . . Greta Garbo and Calvin Coolidge . . . King Kong being seduced by Shirley Temple. What possible connection could there be between Sir Arthur Conan Doyle—extrovert, superpatriot, big-game hunter, amateur boxer, cricketeer, robust man of the world—and the fragile Nietzsche—poet-philosopher, celebrant of the orgi-

astic Dionysus, and the self-proclaimed antichrist who horrified
the pious Victorians by writing, "God is dead!" Impossible to
imagine the timid and sickly Nietzsche anywhere near the arena
where Holmes and Moriarty fought to the death . . . and later
Conan Doyle following in *his* footsteps. Did either Doyle or
Nietzsche relate to this precise location in Switzerland? Was Nietzsche known to Conan Doyle in the early 1890s? Did he ever
encounter the ghostly image or presence of the German philosopher at Reichenbach Falls? I suspect that he must have done so,
because my sense of connection between these two men seems far
too strong to dismiss. It is more than a coincidence that all of these
thoughts and associations have come together in such a tiny,
remote Alpine area so far from their normal scenes of action in
England and Germany. Two "evil" ex-professors—Moriarty and
Nietzsche—both at war with, and hated and feared by, the bour-
geois Victorians.

But, dammit, I won't be able to find my answers to these
tantalizing questions until I get to London. Get to London—that
phrase recalls one of my favorite bits of dialogue from *The Adventures of Sherlock Holmes:*

"You suspect someone?"
"I suspect myself." [said Holmes]
"What?"
"Yes, for coming to conclusions too rapidly."
"Then go to London to test your conclusions."
"Your advice is excellent, Miss Harrison," said Holmes, rising. "I
think, Watson, that we cannot do better."

Yes, like Holmes, "I cannot do better." I shall have to go to
London to verify my overly rapid suspicions and conclusions.
Meanwhile, trapped on this damned train, I'll just have to sit and
try to work up a face-saving alibi for my humiliating mental lapse.

But then, as the train raced through an Alpine village, I
remembered. "Wait a minute! I *did* encounter the image of Friedrich Nietzsche recently. When I arrived at Rosenlaui, the hotel
manager told me all about Nietzsche's visit, showed me his name
in the hotel register, and gave me the excerpt from his sister's
biography . . . and now all these images of Nietzsche and Moriarty have collided in some mysterious way."

8.

> But Sir Arthur Conan Doyle, the
> eminent spiritualist of whom we read
> in the Sunday papers . . . what has *he* to
> do with Sherlock Holmes?
> —T. S. Eliot, *Criterion*, April, 1929

WHENEVER I TRY to reconstruct the dramatic incidents and idea-associations that led to my discovery of the "Conan Doyle Syndrome" and his personal myth or allegory which the syndrome reveals—my thoughts always return to Mrs. Andrews (not her real name), the spiritualist medium who rented us her London flat.

These haunting (!) thoughts never reach finality, but I continue to pry and poke at them. I sense that it was her arresting, eccentric personality, her occult library and séance parlor, and her brilliant remarks about Conan Doyle that helped precondition me to see the Conan Doyle–Friedrich Nietzsche connections.

With my wife, Angela, and daughter Ruth, aged ten, I arrived in London four weeks before the Rosenlaui assignment for an indefinite stay as a European photographer-correspondent for *Collier's* magazine. Our plan seemed simple enough: Before accepting any assignments, we would quickly find a school for Ruth and an apartment near the school. But finding either proved very difficult, and after many weeks of fruitless search we grew anxious, pessimistic, and sick of our cramped (but expensive) quarters in the little hotel off Cromwell Road.

Then one day, in the *London Times,* we saw an ad for a flat in Maida Vale (scene of the Hitchcock film *Dial M* [Maida Vale] *for Murder*). We leaped into a cab and raced to the address listed in the "advert." As we approached it we asked the cabbie to drive slowly so that we could evaluate the neighborhood. What we saw was disappointing. Our weeks of search had taught us a few things about London neighborhoods, and it was obvious that Maida Vale had seen better days. Designed and built during the opulent eighteenth century by architects influenced by Robert Adam, the neighborhood and its houses had now become sadly run down.

But when we arrived at the advertised "private home" we were encouraged: It was freshly painted, well cared for, and had a pretty little garden at its front door.

We dismissed the cab and advanced to rap three times. There was no response for more than a minute. Then we heard an unearthly whining and the sound of something clawing frantically on the inside of the door. Finally, as in a Bela Lugosi film, the door opened slowly to reveal the most slovenly woman I'd ever seen outside the Gin Lane caricatures of William Hogarth. This sad wreck of a woman booted a weird-looking dog away from the door and, without looking at us, said dejectedly, "Yuv come about the flat, have yuh? Well, I guess yuh can come in."

She led us to a large sitting-room entirely filled with books. "Mrs. Andrews"—her tone conveyed loathing for her employer— "will see yuh in a few minutes." Then, grinning evilly, she said, "Mrs. Andrews is—uh—medicatin'. I mean she's—uh—meditatin'," and, cackling fiendishly, she left the room.

Eager to learn something about our prospective landlady, I began a quick survey of the library and was surprised to see that it was an exact duplication, book for book, of an occult collection I'd seen recently in Durham, North Carolina. There were books by and about Sir Oliver Lodge, Daniel Home, Annie Besant, Madame Blavatsky, and Sir Arthur Conan Doyle. There were many hundreds of books about monsters, druids, devils, fairies, ESP, astrology, the "lost continents" of Mu and Atlantis, ghosts and poltergeists, vampires, werewolves and werewolverines, witches and warlocks, flying saucers and flying sorcerers. There was a large section of books about Eastern wisdom (and Western stupidity) —and shelf after shelf lined with bound volumes of the Psychical Research Society's journals.

My furtive inspection was interrupted by the sudden and startling materialization of Mrs. Andrews, a remarkable person. She appeared to be in her eighties, was tall, once beautiful, still handsome, vigorous, and aggressively masculine in dress, manner and hairstyle. As I stared at her a strange thing happened. When startled, I sometimes hallucinate briefly. Now I thought I saw standing before me Warren G. Harding in drag!

But the uncanny resemblance disappeared as, with great charm, she introduced herself, heard a few words from us, and then said, "Americans! Well, that's all right. I've had good luck with you Yankees!" Turning to me she said, "Are you interested in books about the occult? Or in learning something about their owner? Well, sir, I shall put your mind to rest at once. They all belong to me. My former husband never bought or read a spiritual book in his entire lifetime."

Caught in the act of snooping, and exposed, I answered, "Guilty on both counts. I'm not a believer in the occult, but I've always been fascinated by those who *do* believe in—uh—unorthodox theories."

Mrs. Andrews nailed me again. " 'Unorthodox theories' indeed! If you mean crank theories, why don't you *say* so? I've been called a crank a thousand times and it doesn't bother me in the least!"

"Okay, crank theories. I also looked at your books because I am fairly familiar with occult literature. Your library is very similar to the collection of books I saw at Duke University last year when I visited and talked with Dr. J. B. Rhine."

She was impressed. "You've talked with Dr. Rhine, have you? How very interesting! You must give me your impressions of the man and his Parapsychology Institute one day. I've never met Rhine, but I did know Sir Oliver Lodge, Alfred Russell, and Conan Doyle quite well. Met them many, many times at the meetings of the Psychical Research Society."

It was my turn to be impressed. "You knew Conan Doyle? The creator of Sherlock Holmes? He must have been a remarkable man! Did he ever talk to you about Holmes and Watson and Professor Moriarty . . . ?"

She snorted indignantly: "Conan Doyle *hated* Sherlock Holmes and *hated* to be reminded of him. He would grow very angry when, inevitably, some person in an audience would ask him about his detective stories when he was talking about the occult or something else he considered far more important. Very angry. Y'know, he preferred his rahther juvenile romances like *Micah Clarke* and the *Brigadier Gerard* nonsense. I sometimes got the strong impression Doyle thought himself the reincarnation of Sir Walter Scott. He wrote the Sherlock Holmes things only because the public adored them and made him rich and famous. But, y'know, despite the money and the adulation he *killed* Sherlock Holmes. Got rid of him!"

"But he resurrected him. Why did he do that?"

"He needed the money. Doyle spent a quarter of a million pounds sterling promoting the cause of spiritualism. I admired him for *that,* but despised him—and told him so—when he expressed his Tory political and social views. Like Kipling, he was an archaic defender of imperialism. And he was a nahsty anti-feminist."

Turning to my wife she said even more angrily, "I never could read his Sherlock Holmes stories. Holmes dislikes and fears women and says so repeatedly. Treats them like helpless idiots. Except for Irene Adler, of course, and when she stood up to him and outwitted him he crumbled and expressed a vague infatuation. The cowardly man! He knew that she had gone out of his life forever and that it was *safe* to yearn for her in absentia! Actually, Holmes had no interest in women except as clients or victims. That was Doyle's antifeminist doing. And," she sniffed, "I've had me doubts about Holmes and that adoring chum of his—Dr. Watson."

Then, impulsively, she said, "I like you both and would be pleased to have you occupy my flat. But you haven't seen it. Why don't you go up now and look at it? It's the first door at the right at the top of the stairs."

As we walked toward the stairs, she added, "Oh, by the way, there is one thing you should know to help you decide about living here—I use this room for my Thursday evening séances."

Pleased with our decision to rent her flat, Mrs. Andrews said, "Splendid! Yes, you may move in this evening." Then, summoning her maid, she ordered tea and began a rapid, fascinating, and totally uninhibited monologue about herself, shrewdly mixed with darting questions about us: our interests, my work, our reasons for coming to England, our future plans, etc.

In a few minutes we learned that she was eighty-five, was retired with a barely adequate pension, and that she rented her flat "as a public service because of the scarcity of accommodations for transient families, but mainly to stave off the horrors of lonely old age." She had been a public school administrator, a Fabian Socialist "very close to Bernard Shaw and the Webbs," an antivivisectionist, a suffragette (imprisoned three times), a vegetarian, a prison-reformer (she hinted that her maid was a former prison inmate), a Hyde Park orator (all topics), a still-practicing spiritualist medium, and a former editor and writer on occult subjects.

After the maid noisily brought in a tea-wagon, dropped a few things, leered at us, and clumped out, her mistress served tea and biscuits. Ignoring me, she asked my wife her opinion of England, its weather, its people, its styles, and its foods. Choosing the last category, Angela said, "We find the food, especially the desserts much blander here than in America. Our Jell-O, for example, is much more tart than the Jell-O sold here. The packages are the same, but yours tastes rather flat. Why is that?"

This bit of small-talk seemed to derange our hostess. In the great voice that must have silenced generations of hecklers in Hyde Park, she boomed: "Your observation is accurate, my dear! The foods we serve our men are made less tart—a happy choice of word—because we try to control their brutish sexual cravings by denying them spicy aphrodisiacal foods. But, alas, we do not always succeed. I put saltpeter into my husband's food for years, but it had an inverse effect upon him. It intensified his lust, and, when he persisted in his efforts to force himself upon me every evening after dinner and several times on weekends and holidays, I finally got rid of him. Divorced him in 1907!"

When I later asked about the strange dog we'd seen at the door, Mrs. Andrews told us: "His name is Rameses. He is a barkless Basenji. You can see his remote ancestors in the hieroglyphic paintings at the British Museum. The ancient Egyptians bred Basenjis to be silent for hunting and military purposes. He's been very unhappy since I had him sterilized, and now the sullen beast spends all his time frantically digging up all the cellar tiles in search of God only knows what!" Then, looking straight at me for the first time, she asked with mock innocence: "Do you suppose he is trying to escape from *me?*"

Thinking "I won't touch that question with a ten-foot pole— my uncensored answer would lose us this badly needed flat," I quickly changed the subject. "Mrs. Andrews, you said that Conan Doyle spent more than a million dollars promoting spiritualism. Yet there is not a trace of occultism in any of the Sherlock Holmes adventures. How come?"

She answered without hesitation. "I've often asked meself the same question and have concluded that Doyle, a canny Scotsman— he was born in Edinburgh, y'know—and a shrewd commercial writer, understood that once having cast Holmes in the role of a scientific materialist adored by the public for his ability to solve mysteries by means of physical trivialities 'invisible' to others: cigarette ashes, the mud on boots, carriage tracks, the calluses on hands, he could not intrude his occultist ideas without offending his materialist readers. But, y'know, he *did* write an early story . . . I forget its title . . . read it so long ago . . . about a young writer, obviously based on Doyle himself, who experiences a prolonged writing block. In desperation he contacts the spirits of famous writers and, as in a control-medium's séance, they take turns dictating—a perfectly *dreadful* story for him to publish under his own name."

Mrs. Andrews laughed. "Of *course* it was dreadful! No author, even one who has passed on to the Highest Sphere of the Beyond would ever give a *good* story to another author!"

Recently, while reading a collection of very early nondetective stories* by Conan Doyle I recognized and read the one mentioned by Mrs. Andrews—*Cyprian Overbeck Wells*—and found her memory of it fairly accurate. The young writer—Smith—is Doyle himself, but the great English writers who come to help him cheat by ghost-writing a story for him are not occultly contacted: they arrive in the form of a daydream.

The story dictated by Defoe, Swift, Smollett, Bulwer Lytton (Dickens and Laurence Sterne refuse) consists merely of a series of brief self-parodies written, of course, by "young Smith." Doyle's habit of borrowing heavily from other writers is indirectly confessed to by "Smith-Doyle":

. . . in my strait I determined to devote my leisure to running rapidly through the works of the leading English novelists, from Defoe to the present day, in the hope of stimulating my latent ideas and getting a good grasp of the general tendencies of literature. For some time I had avoided opening any work of fiction because one of the greatest faults of my youth had been that *I invariably and unconsciously mimicked the style of the last author whom I happened to read.*   [my italics]

---

* Conan Doyle, *Captain of the Polestar,* London, 1894.

9.

> I should like to ask that Shedlock Homes
> person who is out for removing the roofs
> of our criminal classics. . . .
> —James Joyce, *Finnegans Wake*

THERE IS A MARKED resemblance between *Cyprian Overbeck
Wells* (1880s) and the *Oxen of the Sun* chapter in James Joyce's
Ulysses composed entirely of parodies of old English writers. The
interested reader who compares the two will find that Joyce has
written parodies of several of the same authors mentioned in the
earlier Doyle "daydream." Later I shall offer the evidence which
shows that Joyce, who biographer Richard Ellmann* says "read
pell-mell Tolstoy, Conan Doyle . . ." and who mentions Sherlock
Holmes and Doyle in his letters and in *Ulysses* and *Finnegans
Wake* many times—that Joyce, another great borrower, took an
important part of the basic skeletal plot of his *Ulysses* from the
work of Conan Doyle's first detective adventure, *A Study in
Scarlet!*

10.

THE "ADVENTURE of the murdered and resurrected Sherlock
Holmes" actually began when I cabled: "All set. Willing and
eager" to my editor in New York and received the following reply:

PROCEED IMMEDIATELY ROSENLAUI SWITZERLAND VIA ZURICH TO CHECK
UNITED PRESS REPORT EVEREST CONQUEROR TENZING NORKAY NOW STUDENT
REPEAT STUDENT MOUNTAINEERING SCHOOL THERE STOP ROSENLAUI HOTEL
ADVISED YOUR ARRIVAL THERE TOMORROW STOP IF REPORT TRUE PHOTO-
INTERVIEW TENZING AND OTHER NEPALESE SHERPAS STOP CABLE SITUATION
YOU FIND THERE SOONEST REGARDS

Hastily, I booked a seat on an early plane for Zurich where I
learned that Rosenlaui could be reached only by bus or train. On
the train next morning, I traveled for nearly three hours through

---

* *James Joyce*, Oxford, New York, 1959.

many spectacularly beautiful Alpine valleys to the remote town of Meiringen. There a taxi whisked me up a long winding road through dense pine forests and past several waterfalls to my destination.

Rosenlaui was not, as I'd imagined, a medieval village sitting atop a picturesque crag. It was a sparsely settled hamlet with one very large Victorian hotel at the base of a vast cliff, the top of which was hidden in low-hanging clouds. Above the hotel is the great Rosenlaui Glacier. Melting glacial ice feeds a wild torrent that races down the steep hill past the hotel. Then, continuing its mad slalom for another half mile, it flings itself into a deep chasm as the Reichenbach Falls.

When I signed the hotel register and casually asked the room clerk about the presence there of Sherpa Tenzing Norkay, he answered irritably, "I'm sorry, sir, but only the manager can tell you about the Indian party. If you wish to speak to him now, you will find him in the kennel—that building out there on the lawn."

Kennel? As I walked across the lawn, remembered images from children's books, comic strips, and Walt Disney cartoons prepared me for the sight of huge, shaggy, jolly Saint Bernards, each with a cask of schnapps slung under his chin. But instead the kennel swarmed with the smallest dogs I'd ever seen.

One of the popeyed critters, who weighed no more than eight ounces, became wildly hysterical as I approached the table where its master was grooming it with a toothbrush. It bared its tiny teeth and went into a yelping, spitting, frothing, pissing paroxysm of ridiculous miniaturized rage.

The hotel manager calmly wiped up after the trembling beast. "Don't mind Carmelita. Chihuahuas are a very jealous breed. The Latin temperament, you know."

"I expected to see Saint Bernards."

"A banal expectation. Everyone does. But they are now obsolete for mountain rescue work. Replaced by helicopters and motorized sleds. A pity. Everyone simply adores them."

"You seem to have gone to the other extreme."

"You've noticed that, have you? Well, I'm rather fond of these little rascals. Besides, they make the mountains around here look much larger."

I thought: This man is witty, interesting—and sarcastic. Will he tell me why Tenzing Norkay is here? I'll bet he won't.

My guess was right. "Look," he said, "I must respect the privacy of all my guests. The Indian party—Mr. Norkay, Major Jayal (he's in charge of them all) and the others—will be back at lunchtime. One o'clock. You can talk to *them* and ask *them* all your questions. Okay?"

He then smiled and said, "But you are also my guest! Have you had your breakfast? You haven't? Well, then, come with me. I'll get you something, tell you about the hotel, and show you something that I'm sure will interest you, something you may wish to include in your story."

As we walked back to the hotel he explained. "The Rosenlaui Hotel was built more than seventy years ago over the curative springs that are still in use. But later, when the English invented and introduced the *metaphysical* sport of mountain-climbing (he looked to see if I had noted his use of the word 'metaphysical'), people came here from many countries to climb the great Rosenlaui Glacier and the rock-faces you see all around us. And," he grinned, "of course we've always had all the business, because there is no other hotel up here."

In the huge old library and music-room he opened an old hotel register. "We are very proud of this book and show it to everyone who comes here." He pointed to a shaky, almost illegible signature. "Many very famous people have been our guests, but this is the signature of the most famous of them all: Professor Friedrich Nietzsche. He was a guest here during the summer of 1877 while on sick leave from the University of Basel, only a hundred kilometers (60 miles) from here. He was a professor of classical philology."

He gave me a mimeographed press-release. "You may keep it. It is copied from the biography of Nietzsche written by his sister Frau Elizabeth Förster-Nietzsche. It tells a fantastic story that was acted out in this hotel—in *this room*—in 1877."

The quoted passage really was fantastic:

> In a letter to [Ernst] Rohde from Rosenlaui, my brother wrote: "That same evening I played my song (Hymn to Solitude) and succeeded—so that all the angels would have listened, especially the human angels. But it was a dark room, with no one to hear, thus I had to keep my happiness and tears to myself."
> My brother's remark that his improvisations on the piano had not been heard was, however, a mistake; he did not know that a very

remarkable listener had been listening on the other side of the door, namely, the Emperor of Brazil, who is said to have been deeply moved by the wonderful playing.

Some days later, they met on a tour of the mountains, without my brother having any idea who his acquaintance was. The unknown expressed his thanks for the wonderful playing, and this gave rise to a wonderful conversation. My brother noticed that the stranger was treated with the greatest respect, but it was not until they separated that he learned he had been talking with Dom Pedro.

The hotel manager was ecstatic. "Just think, it happened right here in this room where we are sitting! Isn't that dramatic?"

I agreed wholeheartedly and thought: "It could be a beautiful, haunting scene in a film or drama about either man: Nietzsche, the very great but still-unknown philosopher-poet, expressing his agony of loneliness and neglect in a musical *Hymn to Solitude,* unaware that the tragic Emperor of Brazil is standing alone in the dark, deserted corridor, deeply moved by Nietzsche's performance."

My host continued. "But one thing bothers me about her story. The Emperor of Brazil, who was, by the way, the direct descendant of Louis XIV of France, William the Conqueror, Ferdinand and Isabella, Alfred the Great, and Charlemagne—did not sign the hotel register. And there is no trace of his visit here. But—who knows—perhaps one of the former employees kept it as a souvenir."

This dramatic anecdote, so loaded with sisterly "wonderfuls" has troubled me, too, perhaps because of its spurious tone, and also because of the unsavory reputation of Elizabeth Förster-Nietzsche. Dr. Karl Jaspers, Walter Kauffman, and other Nietzsche scholar-biographers now agree that she was a habitual liar who took advantage of Nietzsche's helpless insanity to further her own right-wing ambitions. As his literary executor she censored, deleted, rewrote, and even added her own reactionary ideas to his manuscripts. As a final act of betrayal she placed the Nietzsche Archives at the disposal of the Nazis and was photographed with Adolf Hitler in front of a bust of her brother—an act that would have horrified Nietzsche, a deadly enemy of German nationalism and anti-Semitism. Her actions created a tangled mass of mistaken ideas about Nietzsche and his philosophy that has taken scholars more than a decade to set straight.

Recently, while still hopeful that Frau Förster-Nietzsche's enchanting story about her brother and the eavesdropping emperor *might* be true, I read the leading biographies of both men and found that none of them mentions the melodramatic meeting between Nietzsche and the romantic "secret listener" whose full name was Pedro de Alacantara João Carlos Leopoldo Francisco Xavier de Paula Leocardio Miguel Gabriel Rafael Gonzago, His Sovereign Majesty, Emperor of Brazil!

Elizabeth Förster-Nietzsche's very touching tale about her brother and Dom Pedro at Rosenlaui *may* be true despite her reputation as a chronic fibber; liars do sometimes tell the truth! But my recent research tells me that her embellishments upon the actual letter written by Nietzsche to Rohde seem to be plagiarized from a highly publicized incident of the *very same Dom Pedro:* his very similar remote-auditory encounter with yet another genius on the verge of world fame: Alexander Graham Bell.

According to his biographers, the wandering Brazilian emperor visited the Philadelphia Centennial Exhibition (1876) exactly thirteen months before his alleged meetings with Nietzsche at Rosenlaui. At the exhibition, in the company of the scientist Lord Thomson, Dom Pedro participated in a demonstration of the newly invented "electromagnetic voice" or "tele-phone."

Bell handed His Sovereign Majesty an earphone; then from another room, he recited the entire soliloquy from Hamlet:

> To be, or not to be, that is the Question:
> Whether 'tis nobler in the mind to suffer
> The slings and arrows of outrageous fortune . . .

Later, according to contemporary news accounts, "Dom Pedro sought out Bell, expressed his astonishment at the remarkable demonstration, and promised to purchase a number of the instruments when they were placed on the market."

The Dom Pedro encounters in Philadelphia and later at Rosenlaui bear an obvious two-part resemblance. In each of these extraordinary encounters the *same unseen Emperor listens* ecstatically to something wonderful—a *"soliloquy"* and a *"Hymn to Solitude"*—being performed in *another room* by a genius who is soon to become world-famous.

In the follow-up scene, the omnipresent Dom Pedro seeks out

the unseen performer to express his great pleasure and appreciation.

Also, I have found another probable source—uh—borrowed—by Frau Elizabeth for use in her romantic sibling fantasy. As she tells it, the incident of the imperial eavesdropper takes place in a building that can be reached only through dense forests in mountainous Switzerland. At night, *inside* a room of this building, there is a man who plays music so beautifully that it evokes mingled "happiness and tears" from someone inside the room (himself). And *outside* there lurks an *unseen, unknown* "very remarkable listener" who becomes deeply moved by the performance.

Now why, as I read her account of the Rosenlauian incident, did it seem so familiar to me? The answer: Because I have recently published a long essay* about Mary Shelley's *Frankenstein* (1818), and I remember that the "eavesdropping" details of this story are *identical* with the "eavesdropping" scenes from Mary Shelley's classic.

In *Frankenstein,* the De Laceys are a politically exiled French family who have taken refuge in a secluded part of a forest on the Swiss-German border about 100 kilometers (65 miles) from Rosenlaui. One *night* the elder De Lacy *plays music so beautifully* that it evokes a response of "mixed pain and pleasure" from someone *inside* the room (his daughter). But *outside, unseen by the musician,* there is *a very remarkable listener* who becomes "deeply affected" by the beautiful musical performance. However, it is not till later that this extraordinary secret listener feels impelled to seek out the musician, express his appreciation, and reveal his identity.

Mary Shelley's "secret listener" is none other than Dr. Victor Frankenstein's misbegotten Monster, who has escaped from his natal laboratory in Geneva, Switzerland, and is now hiding in the dense forest. (Please note that these two scenes are staged in the same tight geographical arena: Switzerland is a very small country; Geneva is about 50 miles from Basel, where Nietzsche taught, and about 75 miles from Rosenlaui.)

We know Dr. Frankenstein's Monster from the various falsifying films as a creature who has not yet learned to use his vocal

---

* *Confessions of a Trivialist*, Penguin Books, 1972.

chords; who expresses himself with ghastly, strangulated sounds and primitive gestures. But Mary Shelley's original "creature" speaks French perfectly, learned from eavesdropping on the De Laceys through a chink in the wall of their cottage. In a few months he becomes sufficiently well educated to express himself in the best oratorical style of the period:

> But I was enchanted by the appearance of the hut: here the snow and rain could not penetrate; the ground was dry; and it represented to me then as exquisite and divine a retreat as Pandaemonium appeared to the daemons of hell after their sufferings in the lake of fire.

This articulate Monster describes his eavesdropping scene—so similar to Doyle's copy of it—in these terms:

> The young girl . . . sat down beside the old man who, taking up the instrument, began to play sounds sweeter than the voice of the thrush or nightingale. He played a mournful tune which, I perceived, drew tears from the eyes of his amiable companion . . . of which the old man took no notice until she sobbed audibly . . . I felt sensations of an overpowering nature . . . they were *a mixture of pain and pleasure* such as I had never experienced before.   [my emphases]

I believe that, through this devious association of her brother with Dr. Frankenstein and his Monster, Frau Förster-Nietzsche has betrayed her own inner agreement with the (mistaken) popular belief that Nietzsche's insanity was a Frankensteinian punishment for his hubris. Most consumers of the Frankenstein tale have falsely assumed that the "madness" of Dr. Frankenstein and his Monster were punishments for the doctor's Promethean attempts to make mankind immortal, thereby challenging God's preordained cycle of life and death. Similarly, the majority of Nietzsche's contemporaries, his sister as well, were convinced that he had been punished for having written, "I am the Anti-Christ!" and "God is Dead!"

11.

IN HIS *Uncle Bernac,* the historical romance written during the period of Holmes's prolonged immersion in the Reichenbach Falls (1893–1902), Conan Doyle also "borrows" this very same eavesdropping scene from Mary Shelley's *Frankenstein,* detail for detail. He even fashions a hideous homicidal giant named "Toussac," an obvious copy in some respects of Dr. Frankenstein's assembled man-turned-Monster. Did Conan Doyle copy these dramatic ingredients from Mary Shelley because he too had created a "Frankenstein's Monster" he hated and wished to destroy? I shall have more to reveal about this very important resemblance in the pages that follow.

12.

AFTER LEAVING the Nietzsche-haunted library and music-room I went up to my room, unpacked, and then walked downstairs to check my cameras with the hotel clerk. When I said, "I know where the Indian party is, but where are all the other guests?" he answered, "They are all out. Looking at the glacier. Hiking. Shopping in Meiringen. Or climbing on the cliff facing the front of the hotel." Then, pointing at a huge brass telescope mounted on a stand, he said, "If you wish to see them climb you will find that very helpful."

After peeping at a party of umbilically tied climbers inching their way down the vertical cliff, I wandered about the hotel, bought some picture postcards of the glacier and the hotel, and had more coffee and croissants. Then, in the inevitable American Bar, I found a British reporter who laughed when I told him about the hotel manager's irritable and evasive response to my questions.

"Oh, he's all right. A very bright and helpful fellow, but he *is* embarrassed by the silly farce that is being enacted in his little bailiwick. You won't believe it, but Tenzing Norkay, the world-famous conqueror of Mount Everest—the highest peak in the world—has failed to qualify as a Swiss guide!"

"*Tenzing* has failed to qualify . . . You're kidding!"

"Yes, the thick-headed fellow who runs the school, named Erwin Glatthard, won't hand over his bleeding diploma because, it seems, Tenzing can't climb vertical rocks and thinks it's *insane* to even try. I agree with him. Glatthard also says that Tenzing can't read and write French, German, or English well enough to meet his standards . . . can't read maps . . . and knows none of the niceties of dealing with tourists. But none of this really matters. Tenzing doesn't want to be a Swiss guide; his climbing days are over (he's more than forty years old), and he's going to be the headmaster of a new mountaineering school at Darjeeling."

(Many months later I learned the true story: The Indian government, alarmed by the Red Chinese sweep over the "impregnable" Himalayas into Tibet and their building of fortifications along the Indian-Chinese border, had sent Tenzing and some Indian army brass to Switzerland as part of a crash program for training mountain troops.)

The British reporter looked at his wristwatch. "Tenzing and the others will return for lunch in about a half hour. If you want to see something that will warm the cockles of your little heart, I suggest that you be at the front of the hotel at three minutes to one."

At 12:57 I stationed myself near the big brass telescope and waited for the unknown "cockle-warmer." Then, precisely on time, as in a dance choreographed by Martha Graham, women began to drift in from all directions: waitresses from the dining hall, hotel guests, office clerks, and chambermaids—all awaiting the return of the conqueror of Everest!

Soon, led by Tenzing, the Indian party came jogging down a steep path, across the rustic bridge spanning the glacial torrent, and over the front lawn. As he approached, grinned, and waved to the happy women, I saw that Tenzing Norkay was a very handsome, powerful, commanding personality. I understood immediately. "*Of course* Edmund Hillary invited Tenzing to share his great moment of glory! No one would *dare* treat this . . . this *superman* otherwise!"

After lunch I walked up to Tenzing, introduced myself, and began asking him some questions, but he became quite embarrassed and immediately referred me to a hovering Indian army officer, Major Jayal. The major said, "We are sorry, sir, but Mr. Tenzing and his companions are under exclusive contract with a publisher and newspaper syndicate and cannot grant unauthorized interviews. But, if you care to, you may accompany us to the 'practice climbing rocks' tomorrow morning and take all the photographs you wish."

Next morning I awakened with a start. My traveling alarm clock, set for 7:00, read 5:00, but it was already light outside. I arose and walked out onto the little balcony and saw that the rays of the rising sun had pierced the rain clouds at the top of a nearby mountain to form a perfect double rainbow.

I picked up my Leica and had begun taking some color shots of the spectacular sunrise when suddenly the entire hotel began to shake. "An avalanche!" I thought. "No, an earthquake! I'd better get out of this place fast!" But even as I began to throw on some clothes, the quake stopped. After a few minutes of anxious waiting, there were no further tremors, and I closed the shutters and went back to bed.

At breakfast the hotel manager walked from table to table, dry-washing his hands obsequiously, asking each guest, "And how did *you* sleep? Wonderful! Yes, the mountain air *is* wonderful for sleeping."

When it was my turn to perform in this daily charade, I said cheerfully, "I slept wonderfully well. Until 5:00. I usually get up at seven. So I assume that it was a preliminary earth tremor that awakened me. But when the earthquake ended, I found it rather hard to fall asleep again."

His smile vanished. "An *earthquake?* Did you say an *earthquake?* In *my* hotel? We don't *have* earthquakes in Switzerland!" He looked at me suspiciously. "It's very strange, but you are the only one in this hotel who has had this . . . this experience . . . this *earthquake.* Are you sure you didn't dream it? Perhaps you were ill."

His disbelief amused me. "Maybe I had an epileptic fit. Or hiccups. Or the dry heaves."

He continued to eye me warily as he retreated crablike, "If *you* say so, sir, if *you* say so."

After breakfast I attached a long telephoto lens to my camera, mounted it on a heavy tripod, and joined the Nepalese Sherpas and Major Jayal as they left the hotel and began to jog up the steep path to the practice rocks. But after a few minutes it became apparent that I couldn't keep up. As I began to puff and wheeze, the four youngest Sherpas, frisky as mountain goats, offered to push me up the hill. But this was too embarrassing, and I said, "No, you go ahead. I'll catch up with you later."

As I labored up the hill, stopping every two minutes to rest, my embarrassment increased as several old men and women, a group of British schoolgirls, and even two small children, all passed me. But an hour later (the Sherpas *ran* up the hill in fifteen minutes) I arrived at the outdoor schoolroom and began photographing Tenzing as he climbed a perpendicular rock about twenty feet high. Though attached by a rope to his friend Ang Tharkay (who had scaled Mount Annapurna with Maurice Herzog), Tenzing was visibly frightened, and he trembled as he clung to each piton.

When Major Jayal, standing next to me, noticed that I had noticed, he said, "The Sherpas have lived in the Himalayas for thousands of years and have always followed their cattle up the grassy slopes. They are far too sensible to enjoy climbing rocks as a sport."

Later, when we walked down the steep hill (even *that* was exhausting!), I was met by the hotel manager who ran up to me brandishing a newspaper. "Sir! There *was* an earthquake here this morning at 5:00! The first earthquake in this part of Switzerland in more than seventy-five years and *you* were the only one who witnessed it. Congratulations! Come, let me buy you a drink. You must accept my apology and tell me *all* about it!"

I accepted his apology and offer of booze (I needed a drink after my unheroic climb!). Then, after he had read and translated the newspaper account of the earthquake and ordered another round of martinis, I decided to tease this witty and intelligent man by telling him about an uncannily similar hotel and hotel-manager experience I'd had.

"You know, when I first told you about the earthquake, you said, "Not in *my* hotel! Well, I have heard those words before."

"You have? Someone said that to you after another earth-quake? In Switzerland?"

"Not exactly. It happened one night in Sulmona, Italy, ex-actly three years ago, during a photographic assignment on the Adriatic coast. After shooting a lot of scenic pictures of the stone houses of Alberobello, the cave city of Matera, and the bronze Colossus at Barletta, my chauffeur-interpreter and I finally headed for Sulmona, a town in the mountainous part of the Abruzzi."

"I know that part of Italy very well," said the hotel manager. "It's still very wild and beautiful."

"Yes, it is. Fatigued from the long day's drive I went to bed early. And then it happened. After some very frightening dreams I awakened at 4:30 with my worst asthma attack in years. Gasping for breath, I dressed quickly and walked down the four flights of stairs, through the deserted, unattended lobby and out into the empty streets of the town. The sightseeing distracted me, and the fresh air and exercise soon brought my asthmatic attack to a less frightening level.

"I was still breathing heavily but knew that I would soon be all right, and so I returned to the hotel and walked up the four flights to my room. But, as I turned a corner into a long dim corridor, I saw that a *wildcat*—about twice as big as an ordinary cat—had wandered into the hotel from the neighboring mountains and was trapped in the dead-end hallway. It snarled and spit at me and then raced down the corridor to the far end. There, like a performing circus cat, it leaped high onto a wall, ricocheted at high speed onto a second wall, and then came charging down the narrow corridor *right at me!*"

"Did you run?"

"I couldn't. It all happened too fast. Raging mad, the wildcat leaped at me, and, as I kicked it hard in the chest, it slashed my right leg through my trousers, ran past me, and disappeared around the corner of the hallway.

"I entered my room and found that the beast had ruined my trousers and left a foot-long scratch on my thigh. But, fortunately, it was a superficial wound and quickly stopped bleeding when I washed it with warm water.

"This very frightening experience left me shaken for several minutes. But then, when I realized that the shock had restored my breathing to normal, I laughed, relaxed, and finally was even able to go to sleep."

The hotel manager smiled. "Are you recommending *wildcats* as a treatment for *asthma?* It would be pretty difficult and expensive to arrange such nocturnal meetings with wildcats."

"No, I don't. I sure don't. Now we come to the hotel manager part of this experience: When I checked out next morning I told the *padrona* about my experience and she looked at me the same way *you* did when I told you about the earthquake, and she said exactly the same things: 'In *my* hotel? A *wildcat* attacked you in *my* hotel? Impossible! We don't have wildcats here, and I have never heard of a wild animal coming into Sulmona to attack people. How big did you say this cat was? Did anyone else see it? Are you sure you didn't *imagine* it?'

"I opened my suitcase and showed her the slashed trousers and said, 'Would you like to see the wound on my thigh?' but she turned down this intimate offer. 'No, thank you. How do I know when and where you tore your clothing?'

"I said, 'Look, *signora,* I'm not going to sue you, if that's what you are afraid of. But you had better believe that a dangerous animal came into your hotel last night and attacked me when he thought he was cornered. You have no toilets or baths in your rooms, so people leave their rooms to go to the toilets. If a small child met that wildcat in the hallway, he could be badly mauled or even killed.' But all she would say was, 'Not here. Not in *my* hotel.' "

The Swiss manager rose and said, "Very interesting. I must go now. Work to do. Sir, I assure you that you will *never* meet a wildcat in *my* hotel. But you might, with luck, meet another and more friendly kind of—ah—feline."

Next morning, the photographic part of my assignment finished, I checked out, entered the hotel taxi, and rode down the long road past the great waterfall to the station at Meiringen. There, on June 24th, 1954, I began my journey home to London by entering the waiting train for Zurich at precisely 8:13 A.M.

13.

NOT SO INSTANT REPLAY: I entered the train's second-class compartment and found a window seat opposite a Japanese tourist half-buried in maps. I was busy stowing my luggage in the overhead rack—when it happened.

The Japanese tourist turned to the man across the aisle and asked him about Meiringen. The Swiss businessman answered, "From all over the vorld people they come to climb on the Rosenlaui Glacier . . . and behind zat mountain there iss the famous Reichenbach Falls where . . . Sherlock Holmes und Professor Moriarty they . . . falled down to their deaths!"

CHAPTER TWO

IN LONDON, some quickly procured copies of *The Memoirs of Sherlock Holmes* and Conan Doyle's autobiography, *Memories and Adventures*, provided positive answers to some of the questions which had arisen in Switzerland. Yes, Conan Doyle had actually visited the scene of his crime against his own characters: he had, in fact, gone to Meiringen with the intention of putting an end to his phenomenally successful detective stories.

Here are some of the facts relating to the writing of *The Final Problem*, in which Holmes and Moriarty died "locked in each other's arms." Early in the spring of 1893 Conan Doyle and his wife went on holiday in Switzerland. About fifteen months earlier, on November 11, 1891, he had written to his mother:

Dearest Mam—

I have written five of the Sherlock Holmes stories of the new series. They are: 1. *The Adventure of the Blue Carbuncle;* 2. *The Adventure of the Speckled Band;* 3. *The Adventure of the Noble Bachelor;* 4. *The Adventure of the Engineer's Thumb;* 5. *The Adventure of the Beryl Coronet.* I think that they are up to the standard of the first series. The twelve ought to make a rather good book of sorts.

He then added:

I think of slaying Holmes in the sixth (The Final Problem) & winding him up for good and all. He takes my mind from better things.

[his own italics]

In his autobiography, Doyle wrote:

It was still the Sherlock Holmes stories for which the public clamoured and these from time to time I endeavoured to supply. At last, after I had done two series of them I was in danger of having my hand forced, and of being identified with what I have regarded as a lower stratum of literary achievement. Therefore as a sign of my resolution I decided to end the life of my hero. The idea was in my mind when I went with my wife to Switzerland, in the course of which we saw the wonderful falls of Reichenbach, a terrible place, and one which I thought would make a worthy tomb for Sherlock, even if I buried my banking account with him.

This answer to a question about Conan Doyle's visit to Meiringen and Reichenbach Falls raised another more important one. Did Conan Doyle, like countless others, actually travel up the mountain road past the Reichenbach Falls to the famous glacier and climbing rocks and then stop at the Rosenlaui Hotel, so haunted by the ghostly presence of Friedrich Nietzsche?

Conan Doyle's memoirs made no mention of any visit to the Rosenlaui Hotel, and I was about to settle for only an assumption, based on strong circumstantial evidence, that he had indeed been there—when I found exactly what I was looking for: Dr. Watson's crystal-clear reference to the only hotel at Rosenlaui.

In *The Final Problem,* Dr. Watson, as narrator, tells the reader that after a long zigzag flight from London, he and Holmes believe that they have finally eluded the murderous Moriarty.

For a charming week we wandered (from Geneva) up the valley of the Rhone, and then, branching off at Leuk, we made our way over the Gemmi Pass, still deep in snow, and so, by way of Interlaken, to Meiringen.

On the third of May [continues Watson] we reached the little village of Meiringen, where we put up at the Englisher Hof, then kept by Peter Steiler, the elder . . .

Then he tells us about a projected visit to the Rosenlaui Hotel:

On his advice, on the afternoon of the fourth we set off together, with the intention of crossing the hills and *spending the night at the hamlet of Rosenlaui.*

Now, at last I had pinpointed the needed proof of access: All of the characters, real and fictional, had actually gone or had intended to go to the Nietzsche-haunted hotel in that very remote hamlet in Switzerland.

2.

LIKE EVERY OTHER READER addicted to Doyle's great detective stories (my copy of *The Complete Sherlock Holmes* has been read to tatters), I am familiar with *The Final Problem,* in which Professor Moriarty first appears, and I have always assumed that he was a pure figment of Doyle's imagination. The suggestions that he based Moriarty on Adam Worth or Jonathan Wild are not convincing, because neither of these famous criminals was a "mad" Faustian genius with an academic background.

But now, alerted to the possibility that Doyle had Professor Nietzsche in mind when he created his own defrocked teacher, I reread *The Final Problem* and saw at once that Moriarty is clearly based on Conan Doyle's distinctly unfriendly attitudes toward the "notorious" German philosopher.

The story in which Moriarty is introduced begins with the arrival at Dr. Watson's office of a very agitated Holmes:

"Is Mrs. Watson in?" [asks Holmes]
"She is away on a visit."
"Indeed! Are you alone?"
"Quite."
"Then it makes it easier for me to propose that you should come away with me to the Continent."
"Where?"
"O, anywhere, it's all the same to me."

This worries Watson:

There was something very strange about all this. It was not Holmes's nature to take an aimless holiday, and something about his pale, worn face told me that his nerves were at their highest tension. He saw the question in my eyes, and putting his fingertips together and his elbows on his knees, he explained the situation.

Watson learns that for years Holmes has been closing in on a cabal of thieves and murderers and is now about to turn them in to Scotland Yard with the evidence which would put them all at the end of a rope. Now, perhaps too late to save himself, he realizes that they have learned his intentions and that they will try to kill him before he kills them. He then reveals the name of the leader of this terrible gang:

"You have never heard of Professor Moriarty?"
"Never."
"Ay, there's the genius and the wonder of the thing!" he cried. "The man pervades London, and no one has ever heard of him. That's what puts him on a pinnacle in the records of crime."

In response to further questions, Holmes then offers a brief background description of his dreaded adversary, which many readers will recognize as a biographical sketch of Friedrich Nietzsche as he would be viewed by a hostile and/or uninformed contemporary:

His career [says Holmes] has been an extraordinary one. He was a man of good birth and excellent education, endowed by nature with a phenomenal mathematical faculty. At the age of twenty-one . . . he won the mathematical chair at one of the smaller universities, and had, to all appearances, a most brilliant career before him. But the man had hereditary tendencies of the most diabolical kind. A criminal strain ran through his blood, which, instead of being modified, was increased and rendered infinitely more dangerous by his extraordinary mental powers. Dark rumours gathered about him in the university town, and eventually he was forced to resign. . . . So much is known to the world.

Sherlock Holmes increases Moriarty's resemblance to Nietzsche by endowing Moriarty with these "superman" characteristics: "He is a genius, a philosopher, and abstract thinker. He has a brain of the first order." Sherlock then bestows the accolade: "He is my intellectual equal."

Professor Moriarty's resemblances to Professor Friedrich Nietzsche are numerous and striking: Like Nietzsche, Moriarty achieved the very rare distinction of a professorship in a European university while still in his early twenties. Like Nietzsche, whose insanity was caused by paresis (the third stage of syphilis), Moriarty became criminally insane because of a (venereal) *"blood taint."* Both Nietzsche and Moriarty resigned from their "smaller universities" under duress because of their acute medical and personality problems. And both diverted their massive intellectual powers from respectable academic channels into forms of "criminality." Of course Nietzsche never committed any crimes against persons or property, as Moriarty did, but he *was* regarded by his pious contemporaries as a genius whose mind had been erased by God as punishment for his terrifying blasphemy.

Eleven years after he created his Professor Moriarty as a weirdly distorted caricature of the noble Nietzsche, the conservative Conan Doyle (there is "second and quite different Conan Doyle" whom we shall meet later) wrote in his journal:

One of the singular characteristics of the present age is a wave of artistic and intellectual insanity breaking out in various forms in various places. . . . Nietzsche's insanity in a purely mental way is symptomatic of what I mean. It is openly founded in lunacy, for the poor fellow died raving.

There are some obvious differences: Nietzsche was an academic philologist, while Moriarty taught mathematics. (Doyle probably took this detail, along with other major borrowings, from Edgar Allan Poe, whose intellectual villain in *The Purloined Letter* is also a mathematician.) But in a later story, Doyle increased the Nietzschean resemblances by giving Sherlock Holmes a profound involvement with branches of philology similar to those of Nietzsche: Holmes studies "the Chaldean roots of the great Celtic language," a field that requires a very advanced knowledge of linguistics.

Not only can Sherlock Holmes read "the great Celtic language" and Chaldean (as well as French, German, and Latin), but also:

The ancient Cornish language had . . . attracted his attention, and he had, I remember, conceived the idea that it was akin to the Chaldean and had largely derived from the Phoenician traders in tin. He had received a large consignment of books upon philology and was settling down to develop this thesis. [*Devil's Foot*].

And in *The Adventure of the Golden Pince-Nez* Doyle lets us know that Holmes, like Nietzsche, is also a paleographer. "He was *engaged in deciphering* the remains of the original inscription upon a palimpsest . . . an Abbot's account from the fifteenth century." (I have italicized the words "engaged in deciphering" for comparison with T. M. Kettle's words about Nietzsche. In his early biography of the German philologist, Kettle has Nietzsche "*engaged in deciphering* difficult Byzantine manuscripts.")

Also, in *The Adventure of the Golden Pince-Nez*, the vocation of arcane philological research is repeated: When we first meet Professor Coram (another intellectual villain), he is engaged in a similar study of *early Christian* manuscripts: ". . . that is my *magnum opus* . . . it is my analysis of the documents found in the Coptic monasteries of Syria and Egypt."

I surmise that Doyle, who seems to have been very familiar with Nietzsche's life and work, recognized the similarity between Sherlock Holmes's work as a detector of "unknown criminals"— and cryptographer—and that of Nietzsche, a philological "detective" who deciphered ancient, secret, and unknown languages. By borrowing such intellectual, esoteric elements from the field of philology Doyle sought, I suppose, to heighten the reader's respect for Sherlock Holmes and himself, and to enrich the text. As we shall see later, Conan Doyle also borrowed from various "profound" writers and philosophers and always felt compelled to leave clues to his use of their ideas.

Now, convinced that Professor Moriarty was a contorted likeness of Professor Nietzsche and aware of the manner in which authors love to repeat themselves, I looked for more Nietzschean resemblances in Holmes's "resurrection" story, *The Adventure of the Empty House,* published ten years after the tragic incident at the falls of Reichenbach.

In that story I found that not only had Conan Doyle molded his new character, Colonel Sebastian Moran, in the image of Friedrich Nietzsche, he had also copied many of the exact words used by F. Shuré to describe his friend Nietzsche when they met at the Bayreuth Opera Festival in 1876.

Shuré's description, translated into English by Havelock Ellis, may be seen in Ellis's *Affirmations* published in 1895, eight years before Conan Doyle wrote *The Empty House.*

As I talked to him I was struck by the superiority of his mind and the strangeness of his physiognomy. *A large forehead,* short hair brushed up off his forehead; the projecting cheekbones of the Slav. The *strong drooping mustache,* the sharp cut of the face, would have given him the *air of a cavalry officer,* had it not been for the indescribable something in his address that was at the same time timid and haughty. The musical voice, the slow speech, denoted the organism of the artist; the prudent and meditative *bearing was the philosopher's.* Nothing was more deceiving than the apparent calm of his expression. *The fixed eye* of a keen observer, and of a *visionary.* This double character added a disturbed and disturbing element, the more so because *it always seemed so riveted on one point.* In his effusive moments this look was moistened by the softness of a *dream,* but soon it became *hostile* again. . . . During the general performances, and the first three [Wagnerian] performances, Nietzsche appeared sad and dejected.

[words italicized for comparison]

In 1903, in *The Adventure of the Empty House,* Conan Doyle wrote the following description of Colonel Sebastian Moran:

He was an elderly man with . . . a *high* bald *forehead,* and a *huge grizzled mustache.* An *opera hat* was pushed to the back of his head, and an evening dress-shirt front gleamed out through his open over-coat.

When this would-be assassin of Holmes is captured a moment later, Dr. Watson gives us a very close look at him:

It was a tremendously virile and yet *sinister* face which was turned towards us. With the *brow of a philosopher* above and the jaw of a sensualist below, the man must have started with great capacities for *good and evil.* But one could not look upon his cruel blue eyes, with their *drooping* cynical lids, or upon the *fierce, aggressive* nose and the *threatening* deep-lined brow, without reading Nature's plainest danger signals. He took no heed of us, but *his eyes were fixed upon Holmes's face* with an expression in which hatred and amazement were equally blended. "You fiend!" he kept on muttering. "You clever, clever, fiend!"

Here for more convenient visual comparison are F. Shuré's description of Friedrich Nietzsche (1876), reprinted in Ellis's essay on Nietzsche (1895); and Conan Doyle's description of Colonel Sebastian Moran (1903):

Shuré: Nietzsche is seen at the Bayreuth *Opera* Festival.
Doyle: Moran is wearing an "opera hat," and has just come from an *opera performance.*

Shuré: Nietzsche has the *"bearing of a philosopher."*
Doyle: Moran has the *"brow of a philosopher."*

Shuré: Nietzsche has a *"large forehead."*
Doyle: Moran has a *"high . . . forehead."*

Shuré: Nietzsche has a *"strong mustache."*
Doyle: Moran has a *"huge grizzled mustache."*

Shuré: Nietzsche has *"drooping mustache."*
Doyle: Moran has *"drooping eyelids."*

Shuré: Nietzsche has the *"fixed eye* of a keen observer."
Doyle: Moran's *"eyes were fixed* on the face of Holmes."

(Common knowledge): Nietzsche was the author of *Beyond Good and Evil.*

Doyle: Moran "must have started with great capacities for *good and evil."* (He is beyond that choice now: he is evil.)

In a later chapter, I shall offer my evidence for the discovery that Conan Doyle also based Colonel Sebastian Moran, in part, on another notorious personality.

The inevitable question now arose: "Did Conan Doyle ever mention Friedrich Nietzsche in any of his Sherlock Holmes stories or in his other published work?" The answer: He did. Directly in several of his other writings, and indirectly in several of his detective stories.

Conan Doyle's first published mention of the German philosopher may be seen in his *The German War,* a pamphlet published at the outbreak of the First World War (1914):

Like Nietzsche, Trietschke was not a German at all. Both men were of the magnetic *Slav* stock, *dreamers of dreams* and *seers of visions* —evil dreams and dark visions for the land in which they dwelt. With their magic flutes *they have led the whole blind nation down that easy pleasant path which ends in this abyss.* Nietzsche was, as his whole life proved, a man on the edge of insanity, who at last went obviously mad. [my emphases]

This reference is exciting! It not only clearly establishes Doyle's sharp awareness of Nietzsche, but—have you noticed?—it also presents the precise image of *Nietzsche dragging a personified nation to its destruction in a* great chasm or *abyss.* This is an exact repetition by Conan Doyle of his earlier great scene: that of Nietzsche-Moriarty dragging Holmes to their mutual destruction in the falls of Reichenbach—which Doyle calls "a fearful place . . . a tremendous *abyss."* It substantiates, does it not, the discovery that Conan Doyle definitely had Nietzsche in his thoughts when he created Moriarty as the fatal wrestling partner for Sherlock Holmes?

In addition, I have found that several of the key words in the above quotation from *The German War* were taken by Doyle from F. Shuré's previously quoted description of Nietzsche. The three words or phrases borrowed from Shuré are: "Slav," "visionary," and "dream." (By themselves not important, of course, but when seen in the full context of Doyle's fascination with Nietzsche, they become highly significant proofs of access and copying.)

For comparison:

Shuré: *Nietzsche* has the "cheekbones of a *Slav.*"
Doyle: *Nietzsche* is "of the magnetic *Slav* stock."

Shuré: *Nietzsche* is a *"visionary."*
Doyle: *Nietzsche* is a *"seer of visions."*

Shuré: *Nietzsche's* "look was of . . . the softness of the *dream.*"
Doyle: *Nietzsche* . . . is a *"dreamer of dreams . . . evil dreams."*

The second direct mention of Friedrich Nietzsche by Conan Doyle may be found in his private and unpublished journal.*

One of the singular characteristics of the present age is a wave of artistic and intellectual insanity breaking out in various forms and in various places. If it stops where it is, it will be only a curious phenomenon. If it is a spreading movement it will be the beginning of vast human changes. It attracted Max Nordau's attention when he wrote 'Degeneration.' But look at the strides it has taken since. It is the difference between queerness and madness, between Pre-Raphaelites and Post Impressionists, between Wagner's operas and (Strauss's) *Elektra* or between the French symbolists and the Italian Futurists. *Nietzsche's philosophy in a purely mental way is symptomatic of what I mean. It is openly founded in lunacy, for the poor fellow died raving.* One should put one's shoulder to the door to keep out insanity all one can.

[my italics]

3.

AFTER SUBMITTING *A Study in Scarlet* to many publishers, Doyle finally sold it outright to *Beeton's Christmas Annual* for the paltry sum of £25. (Later he paid a fortune to buy back the copyright.) *Beeton's* held the story for more than a year and then published it

---

* July, 1912, quoted from Doyle's journal by Pierre Nordon, *Conan Doyle, a Biography.*

in its 1887 issue, where it was tepidly received and immediately forgotten. Little Sherlock Holmes, only one year old, seemed doomed to die of the dread malnutritive disease, reader's indifference.

But, as Conan Doyle learned later, Sherlock was unkillable. When shortly afterwards *A Study in Scarlet* was reprinted in America it became an instant success, and readers clamored for more stories about "that wonderful new detective Sherlock Holmes!"

In 1888, after *Lippincott's,* an American magazine, commissioned Doyle to write two series of six stories, the Sherlock Holmes boom accelerated, and the astonished, delighted—then enraged—author found himself the *unhappy* owner of a literary gold mine.

Mrs. Andrews (my London landlady) had correctly described his curious dilemma: "Conan Doyle *hated* to be reminded of his Sherlock Holmes and became angry when, inevitably, some person in the audience would ask him about his detective stories when he wanted to talk about the occult or something he considered more important. Very angry . . . he wrote the Sherlock Holmes stories only because they made him rich and famous. But despite the money and the adulation he *killed* Holmes. Got rid of him . . . and (resurrected) him only after he needed money badly . . . he spent a fortune in promoting the cause of spiritualism."

(During a visit to the Conan Doyle Museum at Lucens, Switzerland, in 1971, Mrs. Adrian Conan Doyle told me: "My late husband told me that once, when he violated the unspoken family rule *never* to mention Sherlock Holmes, his father became *livid* and shouted: 'Don't mention that *name* to me! I forbid it! I *hate* him!' ")

In November, 1891, Conan Doyle informed his mother in the letter (quoted above) that he intended to "slay Holmes for good and all" in the last story of the second series, *The Final Problem.* Then, early in 1893, Doyle, the premeditating murderer, went on a working holiday to Switzerland, where, his memoirs tell us, he traveled along the *very same route* (eastward from Geneva to a glacier) taken by Dr. Frankenstein and his unshakable Monster, the same route later used by him for the epic flight of Holmes from *his* pursuing demon. If Doyle also visited the glacier at Chamonix, he does not say so. (I think he did.) Instead, like his own characters, he says he turned northward, passed through

Meiringen, and then, while gazing in awe at the "wonderful falls of Reichenbach, a terrible place," he decided that "it would make a worthy tomb for Holmes," and his (Doyle's) "banking account with it."

Now that he had found his Swiss death-arena, and the exact route for bringing his intended victim to it from far-off London, only one story element was lacking: the character of the *executioner,* a personification of his own Holmicidal intention, an antagonist so powerful in intellect and body, so terrifying that even the dauntless Holmes would flee from him—all the way to this fateful and remote glacial shelf in Switzerland.

Continuing his journey up the mountain road, Conan Doyle soon arrived at the Rosenlaui Hotel, where, like every other visitor, he was brought face to face with the haunting presence of Professor Friedrich Nietzsche, whom he recognized at once as the prototype for his needed character: an antagonist worthy of Sherlock Holmes.

As I reconstruct this traumatic encounter: Threatened by his own distorted and prejudiced conception of the now-insane Nietzsche as a satanic theocide and an "enemy of society," the occultist Conan Doyle grappled with the "ghost" of Professor Nietzsche, conquered him, and finally disposed of him, by transforming him into Professor Moriarty, who, like Friedrich Nietzsche, was a "philosopher," and "abstract thinker," a "brain of the first order," whose "blood taint" had turned him into an enemy of society and God.

4.

AT AN INFORMAL GATHERING in London in 1956, my friend Julian Spiro introduced me to the eminent philosopher Mr. A. J. Ayre and said mischievously, "Professor Ayre has one of the toughest minds in England. I *dare* you tell him about your Conan Doyle and Nietzsche discoveries!"

I had heard of the formidable "Freddie" Ayre and was most reluctant to expose my still-unresolved hypothesis to such a great intellect; but, after a little arm-twisting by Julian, I did make a scattered presentation and was relieved when Professor Ayre said, "An amusing and quite plausible set of discoveries. Many writers were influenced by Nietzsche before the turn of the century. Bernard Shaw, for one, in his *Man and Superman*. If Shaw, why not Doyle?"

"Was Nietzsche known in England as early as 1893?"

"I don't know. But there is a man who was alive at the time and could tell you precisely what happened in that year—Bertrand Russell. He has a perfect recall and remembers even the smallest details."

"Would he answer a letter on such a lowly topic from a stranger?"

"He might. Tell him that Professor Ayre suggested you write and that I thought he, an ex-Professor, would be amused by your discovery that Conan Doyle modeled his 'good superman' Sherlock Holmes and his 'evil superman' ex-Professor Moriarty upon Friedrich Nietzsche and his conceptions."

To my surprise and delight, Lord Russell *did* answer my letter. He wrote:

You may deduce the answer to your question from the following facts: In the spring of 1893, several of us at Cambridge began the publication of a student journal. In a moment of generosity we invited a student at Oxford to contribute a paper. To our dismay he sent us a brilliant essay about a philosopher of whom we had never heard: *Friedrich Nietzsche!*

But even before Lord Russell's letter told me that Nietzsche's ideas arrived at Cambridge University in 1893, I found that the German philosopher was already well known throughout Europe, mainly through the praiseful Danish critic Georg Brandes and the vicious attacks of Max Nordau, a Lombrosian critic. In his *Degeneration* (1892), a book cited by Doyle in his notebooks, Nordau wrote:

From the first to the last page of Nietzsche's writings the careful reader seems to hear a madman, with flashing eyes, wild gestures, and foaming mouth, spouting forth deafening bombast, and through it all, now breaking into frenzied laughter, now sputtering expressions of filthy abuse and invective, now skipping about in a giddily agile dance, and now bursting upon the auditors with threatening mien and clenched fists. So far as any meaning at all can be extracted from the endless stream of phrases, it shows, as its fundamental elements, a series of constantly reiterated delirious ideas, having their source . . . in diseased organic processes.

Conan Doyle's image of the criminally insane Moriarty-Nietzsche as physically threatening may have been inspired by Max Nordau's image of Nietzsche as, "bursting upon the auditors with threatening mien and clenched fists." (See the first confrontation between Holmes and Moriarty in *The Final Problem* for a portrait of Moriarty that seems to be taken directly from Nordau's hysterical attack on the alleged hysteria of Nietzsche.)

5.

Friedrich Nietzsche and The Adventure of the Speckled Band

WHILE SEARCHING FOR (and finding) these Nietzschean needles in the Holmesian haystack, I have also found that Conan Doyle probably borrowed an incident in *The Adventure of the Speckled Band* from one of Nietzsche's major works.

In that adventure, a young woman named Helen Stoner hires Sherlock Holmes to save her from the kind of mysterious attack that killed her twin sister, Julia. From information given to him by Helen, Holmes deduces that Grimesby Roylott (what a great name for a villain!), the girls' Anglo-Indian stepfather, is seeking to kill them for their inheritance.

At night, Holmes and Watson secretly enter the country residence of Helen Stoner and her evil stepfather, and, without letting grimy Grimesby know, they occupy Helen's bedroom.

In the middle of the night, Holmes hears a whistle and a strange clanging sound and realizes that rotten Roylott is sending some small deadly creature through the ventilator connecting his bedroom with Helen's bedroom.

Holmes slams shut the ventilator cover on his side of the wall; a moment later a terrible scream is heard, and when Holmes and Watson enter Roylott's room they find him dead.

Dr. Watson narrates:

. . . his eyes were fixed in a dreadful rigid stare at the corner of the ceiling. Round his brow he had a peculiar yellow band, with brownish speckles, which seemed to be bound tightly round his head.

After Holmes whispers excitedly, "The band! The speckled band!" Watson continues:

I took a step forward. In an instant his strange headgear began to move, and there reared itself from among his hair the squat diamond-shaped head and puffed neck of a loathsome serpent.

"It is a swamp adder!" cries Holmes. "The deadliest snake in India. He has died within ten seconds of being bitten."

I believe that Conan Doyle, who borrowed his story ideas from many authors, probably found and used the unique image of a *person being stung in his sleep* by a particular snake—an adder—from Nietzsche's masterpiece, *Thus Spake Zarathustra,* published eight years before Doyle published *The Speckled Band.*

In *Zarathustra's* twenty-first chapter, *Of the Adder's Bite,* we find:

One day Zarathustra had *fallen asleep* under a fig tree because of the heat, and had laid his arms over his face. *An adder came along and bit him.* [my italics]

But Conan Doyle does more than copy this unique incident and verbiage from Nietzsche: he even *disputes* with Nietzsche about the moral he derived from it!

After Zarathustra forgives the adder and *spares its life* he explains the ironic meaning of the incident to his disciples:

My story is immoral. When you have an enemy, do not requite him good for evil, for that would make him ashamed. But prove that he has done something good to you. . . . And should injustice be done to you, then quickly do five little injustices besides.

Conan Doyle, possibly offended by Nietzsche's "immoral" anti-Judeo-Christian statements, has Sherlock Holmes, his defender of Victorian morals, flatly contradict the German philosopher. As Holmes imitates Zarathustra by *sparing the life of the adder* that killed Miss Stoner and Roylott (most people vengefully kill biting snakes), he offers in answer to Nietzsche these goody-goodies: "Violence does, in truth, recoil upon the violent, and the schemer falls back into the pit which he digs for another."

Though he contradicts Nietzsche-Zarathustra, Sherlock manages to sound just like him. Is Conan Doyle here indulging in conscious parody? I didn't think so at first, but now after a careful reading of the sixty Holmesian adventures and most of his non-Sherlockian stories, I am convinced that Doyle was fully conscious when he wrote parodies of writers one never expects to find in any

Victorian detective story: Plato, Shakespeare, Racine, Flaubert, Goethe, the New Testament—and even Oscar Fingall O'Flahertie Wills Wilde!

6.

Friedrich Nietzsche and Von Herder

> Holmes picked up the powerful air-gun from the floor. . . . "I knew Von Herder," [said he], "the blind German mechanic."
>
> —*The Adventure of the Empty House*

WHO DOES NOT REMEMBER the "wax bust" of Sherlock Holmes, set up by Holmes for Colonel Sebastian Moran to shoot at? Or the Tom Swiftian "airgun" used in that thwarted assassination?

After Holmes overpowers Moran and turns him over to Inspector Lestrade, he says,

"The man who shot the Honorable Robert Adair with an expanding bullet from an airgun through the open window of the second floor of No. 427 Park Lane upon the thirtieth of last month." [He picks up the weapon from the floor.] "An admirable and unique weapon," [said he], "noiseless and of tremendous power: I knew Von Herder, the blind German mechanic who constructed it to the order of the late Professor Moriarty."

Here, for the second time in the same story, Conan Doyle has one of his characters *pick up something from the ground,* describe it in detail, and attach importance to it. From what has gone before, we know that it is another "dropped clue" to a hidden meaning.

This prompts us to ask, Who *is* this German aristocrat-mechanic who, though blind, was able to construct such a remarkable weapon? Previously, I'd assumed that the name, like some others, was merely decorative, but now, with the images of Moriarty and Moran as villainous surrogates of Nietzsche still shimmering before me, I suspected that this blind German who made the weapon for "Nietzsche-Moriarty" and later used by "Nietzsche-

Moran" might also be related in some way to the German poet-philosopher.

The biographies of Nietzsche verified my intuitive guess. Conan Doyle's "Von Herder" was not a "blind German mechanic" at all. He was none other than *Johann Gottfried Von Herder,* the famous *blind* German philosopher and scholar, the teacher of Goethe, a leader of the *Sturm und Drang* movement— and a friend of the Nietzsche family. Nietzsche once wrote, "My grandmother was a member of the Schiller-Goethe circles at Weimar, and her brother succeeded Herder as General Superintendent of Schools in Weimar." Another most important link: About one hundred years before Nietzsche became known as "the teacher of the Superman," Von Herder coined the word and used the concept of the Superman in one of his best-known poems.

But though this evidence shows that the widely read Doyle (who remembered everything he ever read) had Von Herder (1744–1803) in mind when he invented his remarkable gunsmith, I pursued this matter further because the word "blindness" intrigued me. Remembering that Conan Doyle was an eye doctor before he turned writer, and hoping that, paradoxically, the word "blindness" might help me see more Nietzschean references, I went back to the various biographies.

Once again the hunch was accurate; it led not only to more allusions to the man I was looking for, but also to one of the first of the personal archetypal images in the Conan Doyle syndrome (sin-drome) and allegory.

Here are some of the strange eye images that cluster about Doyle's blind mechanic, Von Herder: The original Von Herder, we learn, was afflicted with an eye fistula which confined him in *darkened rooms* for long periods. Goethe records his visits to his old teacher at the Strasbourg Eye Hospital where he talked with Von Herder in a *dark and gloomy room.*

Nietzsche, it seems, also suffered from severe eye ailments and complained to a friend, "The doctor has ordered me to sit in *darkened rooms.*"* His discoverer and champion, Georg Brandes, adds to the picture: "Nietzsche's eyes were so weak that he was threatened with *blindness.*"

Within the mind of the former eye doctor Doyle, who exam-

---

* Quoted in T. M. Kettle's *Life of Friedrich Nietzsche,* 1911, pg. 360.

ined patients in dark rooms, there was, I feel, a profound medical and poetic resonance among his blind mechanic Von Herder, who makes guns in rooms perpetually dark; the blind philosophers Nietzsche and Von Herder; and the personal archetypal image, found in story after story, of a Sherlock Holmes who also *sits in darkened rooms* awaiting the arrival of a "man of violence."

The existence of this personal archetypal image (one of the major elements in the Conan Doyle syndrome and personal allegory) is revealed by Conan Doyle himself in his poem *The Inner Room*. After describing the "motley company" of men who comprise his "multiplex personality" (nowadays we would use the word "schizoid") Doyle refers to the *darkened room:*

> There are others who are *sitting*
> Grim as doom,
> In the *dim* ill-boding *shadow*
> Of my *room.*
> Darkling figures, stern or quaint,
> Now a savage, now a saint,
> Showing fitfully and faint,
> *Through the gloom.* [my italics]

7.

Friedrich Nietzsche in The Adventure of the Engineer's Thumb

> *"Fritz! Fritz!"* she cried in English.
> "You are mad, *Elise!"* he shouted.
> —Conan Doyle, *The Engineer's Thumb*

YOU, READER, may not believe it (I didn't at first) but the "Fritz! Fritz!" and "mad Elise!" in the above quotation are Doyle's caricatures of Friedrich Nietzsche and his sister Elizabeth.

This first indirect reference to the German philosopher-poet (who appears in Doyle's writings over a span of *thirty years*) may be seen in the surrealist—cuckoo would be a better word—story of Victor Hatherley, hydraulic engineer who comes to Dr. Watson for the emergency treatment of a severed thumb. When Watson learns that the hysterical young man has been the victim of a near-homicidal attack, he persuades Hatherley to consult Sherlock Holmes at once.

Hatherley tells Holmes how it happened. After working for a large engineering firm for some years, he had gone into business for himself as a consulting engineer. But (like Doyle) he spent many months waiting for the first client to appear and was about to quit and return to his former employer when a strange German named Colonel Lysander Stark appeared with the offer of fifty pounds. But the conditions the job imposed were as strange as this mad-looking German: Hatherley had to go to a house in a remote rural area and inspect a hydraulic press at midnight!

When he arrives at his job, he is met by a terrified German woman who begs him to leave. But he badly needs the fifty pounds and decides to stay. When he finally enters the room-size press, his suspicions of the German are confirmed when he sees evidence that the press is being used for counterfeiting silver coins. When he unwisely voices his opinion, the colonel turns into a raving maniac and tries to crush him to death in the press. But Hatherley escapes by smashing through a thin wall at the side of the press. The German woman reappears, guides him to a second-floor bedroom window, and tells him to jump. But as he hangs from the windowsill ledge, he hesitates (something about not wishing to leave the woman in such a crazy house), and the mad colonel rushes at him with a meat cleaver.

Then, as Hatherley tells Holmes:

. . . she threw her arms around him and tried to hold him back.

"*Fritz! Fritz!*" she cried in English. "Remember your promise after the last time [he had killed another young man], you said it should not be again. He will be silent! Oh, he will be silent!"

"You are mad, *Elise!*" he shouted, struggling to break away from her. "You will be the ruin of us. He has seen too much. Let me pass, I say!" He dashed her to one side . . . when his blow fell . . . and I fell into the garden . . . and saw that my thumb had been cut off.

The connection between the mad German Lysander Stark, his woman companion, and the "mad" German philosopher-poet Nietzsche lies in their names: "Fritz" is the German nickname for "Friedrich," and "Elise" is "Elizabeth." There are other similarities, but they will become visible in due course when the Doyle syndrome and allegory is unveiled. They will show that this adventure, like many of the others, is a personal psychodrama in which Doyle cast *himself* in the part of Victor Hatherley.

8.

Sherlock Holmes and "nitsky"

AFTER NOTING AND ENJOYING Conan Doyle's mischievous conversion of Nietzsche and his sister into the macabre comedy team of "Fritz and Elise," I was now prepared for *any* form of reference to the tragic philosopher, profound, trivial—you name it. And, of course, as anticipated, I found a trivial one in *His Last Bow*.

In that propagandistic adventure published during the First World War, Holmes, pretending to be "Altamont," an Irish-American spy, has brought some top-secret British "naval secrets" to the German master spy Von Bork.

But, before he hands over the "papers" to the enemy, Holmes, disguised to look like the caricatures of Uncle Sam, asks for his payment in advance:

> The American [Holmes] held the small parcel in his hand, but made no motion to give it up.
> "What about the dough?" he asked.
> "The what?"
> "The boodle. The reward. The £500. The gunner turned damned nasty at the last, and I had to square him with an extra hundred dollars or it would have been *nitsky* for you and me. . . ."

"Nitsky"? The word, listed in many English and American slang dictionaries, is defined as "nothing," but it also closely resembles the original Polish version of the Nietzsche family name, "Nietzky." (Nietzsche was proud of his Polish origins.)

9.

A journey through the mind of Conan Doyle

THE TOTALLY UNSUSPECTED DISCOVERY of Friedrich Nietzsche's pervasive presence in the mind and writings of Conan Doyle soon led me to an entirely new conception of Doyle as a writer and of Sherlock Holmes as a character—a massive breakthrough that occurred as I read *The Adventure of the Empty House*.

But first I shall set the stage. One morning, while still mourning for Holmes, Dr. Watson reads that the Honourable Robert Adair has been killed in a classical "locked-room" situation. He goes to the scene of the crime, stares futilely at the home of the deceased, and wonders how the late and great Holmes would have solved the mystery. Finally, sad at heart, he turns to leave and enters into a most revealing incident:

As I withdrew, [he says], I struck against an elderly, deformed man who was behind me, and I knocked down several books he was carrying. I remember that as I picked them up I observed the title of one of them, *The Origin of Tree Worship,* and it struck me that the poor fellow must be some poor bibliophile, who, either as a trade or a hobby, was a collector of obscure volumes.

I endeavoured to apologize for the accident, [says Watson], but it was evident that these books which I had so unfortunately maltreated were very precious in the eyes of their owner. With a snarl of contempt he turned upon his heel, and I saw his curved black and white sidewhiskers disappear among the throng.

Watson continues:

. . . I returned to [my home], and I had not been in my study five minutes when my maid entered to say that a person wished to see me. To my astonishment it was none other than that strange old book collector, his sharp, wizened face peering out from the frame of white hair, and his precious volumes, a dozen of them, wedged under his arm.

After explaining that he had come to apologize for his crankiness, the old man tells Watson that he owns a bookshop nearby and tries to sell the books to the bewildered doctor.

"Here's *British Birds,* and *Catullus,* and *The Holy War*—a bargain, every one of them. With five volumes you could just fill that gap on that second shelf. It looks untidy, does it not, sir?"
"I moved my head [says Watson] to look at the cabinet behind me. When I turned again, Sherlock Holmes was standing smiling at me across my study table. I rose to my feet, stared at him for some seconds in utter amazement, and then it appears that I must have fainted for the first and last time in my life."

After reviving Watson (a second symbolic resurrection) Holmes explains his reasons for his long and secret exile (only his brother Mycroft and his enemies knew he was alive). At Reichenbach Falls he had thrown Moriarty to his death, but immediately afterwards Colonel Moran, now Moriarty's successor (a third resurrection!), tried to kill him.

Holmes tells his friend that after escaping from Moran he had found his way over the mountains to Italy. Then, incognito, he traveled to the Himalayas (Nietzsche-Zarathustra country) where he visited the "head lama." (An odd coincidence [?] Nietzsche's nickname for his sister Elizabeth was "Lama.")

Now, in my own Nietzsche-haunted mind, an analytical reverie began to revolve around a single peculiar aspect of the "resurrection incident" as it is reported by Dr. Watson.

What's all this about *books?* Why is Conan Doyle so insistent, so repetitious in his associating the "return from the dead" of Holmes with *books?* When we first see the disguised Holmes he has *books* knocked out of his arms. Watson picks up the *books.* Not only picks them up but makes a dramatist's point of *reading the title of one book and reciting it.* Watson characterizes the man he has jostled as a "bibliophile" and a collector of *obscure volumes* who is angry because his *precious books* have been maltreated. Five minutes later the strange old *book collector* reappears with a *dozen volumes,* explains his rudeness and tells him that he "is obliged for his picking up" the *books.* He says that he owns a *bookshop* nearby and tries to sell the *books* to the bewildered Watson. He points to the *bookshelf* behind the doctor and says that there is room for *five volumes.* Watson turns to look at the *bookshelf,* then turns again to find that the weird old bookseller is really the long-lost Sherlock Holmes magically restored to life.

My Sherlockian rumination flowed on. With these numerous *book references* Conan Doyle is trying strenuously to draw the attention of the reader to the objects being carried by Holmes at the moment of his resurrection. But why? I must investigate this great insistence. In that huge pile of books there's got to be a pony!

Then my train of thought shunted itself onto another track, one that offered some convincing answers to Conan Doyle's obvious challenge. Eventually that track carried me all the way to Rosenlaui and to Friedrich Nietzsche. Finally, it ended with the discovery of the Conan Doyle Syndrome and the self-revealing allegory or myth hidden by Conan Doyle behind the lustrous and delightful façade of his great detective stories.

But now my attention was riveted on the "obscure" and "precious" volumes thrust at Watson and the reader: Where have I read about an author whose character picks up some books from the ground, recites their exact titles, and then explains their profound significance and effect on him?

After racking my fevered brain, I suddenly remembered where—and laughed. It was my own long essay about *Frankenstein, or The Modern Prometheus.** The author I was trying to think of was, of course, Mary Shelley. The character who *picks up books from the ground* and explains the "greatness" of the books and their profound impact upon him is: the Monster created by Dr. Frankenstein!

I now opened my copy of Mary Shelley's novel to the incident of the picked-up books and found that Conan Doyle had taken a great deal more from the author of *Frankenstein* than this curious business about books.

Earlier, on the train en route from Meiringen to Zurich, I asked the questions: Why did Conan Doyle drag his characters . . . his *victims* all the way from England to this remote Swiss boondock? He could have slain Holmes and Moriarty by tossing them off a high building in London. Or from a cliff in the Scottish highlands. Why did Doyle choose Switzerland? No one ever associates Holmes with Switzerland!

Now, as I read the melodramatic episode in *Frankenstein*— in which the incident of the picked-up books is a small but significant part—some convincing answers to these questions emerged. Sherlock Holmes had been dragged all the way from England to Switzerland because of Dr. Conan Doyle's passionate (and secret) identification with a character in a Gothic novel, one that becomes dramatically visible when the actions of the real-life Doyle are compared with those of monster-creating Dr. Frankenstein.

10.

CONAN DOYLE'S FAMILIARITY with Mary Shelley's novel has already been noted. He borrowed the voyeurist and eavesdropping scenes from *Frankenstein* for his historical romance *Uncle Bernac,*

---

* In my *The Confessions of a Trivialist*, Penguin Books, 1972.

in which his enormous, ugly, and homicidal Toussac is an obvious imitation of *Frankenstein's Monster*. Both are described as noble and kindly idealists who have been transformed into killers by the cruel and humiliating acts of ignorant people. They have several common traits, including the rare talent for dismembering men or wild animals with their bare hands!

11.

MIDWAY THROUGH MARY SHELLEY'S Gothic romance, we find a Dr. Frankenstein who is in a state of extreme agony because of the catastrophic failure of his noble experiment. In my essay I have explained:

The films derived from Mary Shelley's book have given us a morally corrupt, even deranged, scientist whose creature—through the mistake of a half-witted lab assistant—is given the brain of a murderer instead of the genius's brain selected by the doctor.

But Mary Shelley's original Dr. Frankenstein failed, not for God-punishing reasons, as most people think, but because of two terrible *human* mistakes made by the doctor himself. The first was technical and forgivable. He aspired to build a superman, beautiful in mind and soul, with the finest bodies and organs and attributes he could obtain. But the extreme complexities of the task slowed him down, and his biological materials deteriorated.

When he finally succeeded in vitalizing his assembled man, he found that instead of a radiant superman, he had created an incredibly ugly monstrosity. He then made the second and worst of his mistakes: He revealed his disgust and horror to the sensitive newborn creature and then fled from its presence. That reaction—which overlooked the fact that *inside* the loathsome frame was a beautiful and noble human being—was Dr. Frankenstein's kiss of death.

This newly created being later becomes a Monster because of this massive rejection and the additional brutalities inflicted upon him by the ignorant peasants who try to exterminate him because of his surface ugliness.

At the height of his torment, Dr. Frankenstein prescribes a holiday for himself! As he later describes his feelings at the time:

Sometimes I could cope with the sullen despair that overwhelmed me; but sometimes the whirlwind passions of my soul sought me to seek, by bodily exercise and by change of place, some relief from my intolerable sensations. It was during an access of this kind that I suddenly left my home, and bending my steps towards the near Alpine valleys, sought in the magnificence, the eternity of such scenes, to forget myself and my ephemeral, because human, sorrows.

Unaware that the maddened and vengeful Monster is pursuing him, the agonized doctor leaves Geneva, the birthplace of the abortive creature, and travels eastward along a river valley until, as he says, "I arrived at the village of Chamonix." Later, when Holmes and Dr. Watson follow the exact same route from Geneva eastward along a river valley, Watson (Doyle) uses the same language: "We reached the village of Meiringen."

Then, after a night in Chamonix, Dr. Frankenstein hikes through a desolate, uninhabited area. He passes through dense forests, sees several glacier-fed waterfalls and comments on "the particularly dangerous paths down which stones continually roll from above." Finally, he reaches his destination: the great glacier above Chamonix. (There are only two glaciers in Switzerland. The other, about 150 miles to the east, is at Rosenlaui.)

Suddenly, Dr. Frankenstein is overtaken by the Monster. After a heated exchange of words, the enraged doctor, screaming that he would "extinguish the spark which [he] had so negligently bestowed," leaps upon the creature with murderous intent. But the superhumanly powerful creature eludes his wrestling hold, subdues him, and forces him to listen to a marathon recital of his great sufferings—all caused by the scientific, moral, and psychological blunders of his father-creator. It is in the midst of this uninterrupted monologue (when a monster talks, you listen!) that the doctor—and the reader—are told how the Monster became educated by eavesdropping on the De Lacey family and of the curious bit of luck that enabled him to complete his voyeuristic training:

One night [he says] during my accustomed visit to the neighboring wood . . . where I gathered my food . . . *I found upon the ground some books.* I eagerly seized my prize and returned with it to my hovel. Fortunately, the books were written in the language (French) which I had learned (from the De Laceys) ; they consisted of *Paradise Lost,* a volume of *Plutarch's Lives,* and the *Sorrows of Werther.* The possession of these treasures gave me extreme delight: I continually studied and exercised my mind upon these histories. . . . They produced in me an infinity of new images and feelings, that sometimes raised me to ecstasies. . . .

From *Plutarch's Lives,* the Monster learns about the noble and evil men of history. He weeps for Goethe's suicidal Werther, and he identifies completely with Satan, the fallen angel of *Paradise Lost,* which teaches him that he too has been rejected by God; that he is a misfit Adam forever denied admission to human society.

12.

The haunted road to the falls of Reichenbach

REPLAY: In 1886 an obscure young eye specialist named Dr. Arthur Conan Doyle opened an office in Southsea—and failed to attract a single patient. To meet his bills, he sold some short stories to small magazines. He soon learned that he was potentially a very fine storyteller and began a lengthy historical romance. But when he realized that his ambitious project would require about two years for completion, he decided, though contemptuous of the lowly genre, to dash off a detective story (*A Study in Scarlet*) for quick sale.

It was then, thinking perhaps that an obscure story written by an obscure writer would go unnoticed, Conan Doyle made a grave mistake, the error in judgment that, I believe, became a decisive factor in his later decision to "slay" Sherlock Holmes: He carelessly copied the pioneer detective tales of Edgar Allan Poe.

From Poe's three stories featuring the first private detective, Auguste Dupin, Doyle took the following major ingredients: (a) the character of Dupin, who is (b) an advanced intellectual who solves baffling crimes by means of his almost superhuman analytical powers; (c) the detective who sees things that are unnoticed by others; (d) who is able to read the inner thoughts of people by observing "trivial" surface indications; (e) who has a double, almost schizophrenic personality, and who (f) lives the sexless life of a bachelor whose emotional and sexual energies are entirely sublimated in his philosophical and criminological pursuits. (g) The detective is a musician, (h) a tobacco addict (i) who is addicted also to long self-congratulatory explanations to his entirely platonic male roommate, (j) a mental inferior and (k) the narrator of Dupin's exploits in which he (Dupin) solved the crimes which (l) completely baffled the stupid police detectives. (m) The detective is an omnivorous student of profound books, science, literature, mathematics, and philosophy who frequently (n) quotes from them in the original Latin, German, and French. Doyle also borrowed the basic concept and several of the plot devices from Poe's *The Purloined Letter.*

Some apologists for Conan Doyle have excused his plagiarism, arguing that Sherlock Holmes is a much more interesting charac- ter than Poe's Dupin and that Doyle improved Poe's ideas and devices when he used them. I agree in part with these opinions and prefer the Sherlock Holmes stories. But I find this line of defense as unconvincing as the similar argument that a thief de- serves to keep stolen money if he invests it more wisely than the person he stole it from.

13.

DURING MY VISIT to the Conan Doyle museum in Lucens, Switzer- land, Mrs. Adrian Conan Doyle conducted me to the marvelous reconstruction of Sherlock Holmes's study and said, "My husband made explanatory tapes in more than fifty languages, including Bulgarian and Swahili. Which language would you like to hear?"

After sampling a bit of Swahili, I switched to English and listened to the late Adrian Conan Doyle as he described every familiar object in the room, including the Persian slipper in which Holmes kept his tobacco, the famous hypodermic needle, the pic- tures of General Gordon and Henry Ward Beecher on the wall, the wax dummy made for Colonel Moran to shoot at, the "re- markable and unique" airgun made by Von Herder, the blind German mechanic, etc.—a fascinating reconstruction.

When Mrs. Doyle returned, I pointed to the bookshelf inside the room and said, "The narrator said that *every* book mentioned in the Sherlock Holmes stories was on display."

"Yes, my husband went to great trouble and expense to find them."

"Well, I'll bet there is *one* book, mentioned in *The Adven-*

ture of the Empty House, that isn't in there: it's called *The Origin of Tree Worship."*

Amused, Mrs. Doyle said, "I'll take that bet! Why don't we look?" After some delay in finding the key ("This room is sacred; no one has entered it for more than a year") we entered the magical room jointly occupied by Holmes and Watson, a spine-tingling, eerie experience.

The bookshelf on which rested the unframed portrait of Reverend Henry Ward Beecher held books mentioned in every story. There was the *Encyclopaedia Britannica* which had been used to lure the gullible pawnbroker Wilson away from his shop (*The Red-Headed League*); the volumes of Catullus and John Bunyan's *The Holy War* carried by Holmes when he "returned from the dead"; the copy of Boccaccio's *Decameron* found in the pocket of Drebber, the murdered Morman (*A Study in Scarlet*) ; a copy of Gustave Flaubert's *Letters* (Holmes quotes from it in French in *The Red-Headed League*) ; and the novel *La Vie Bohème* (read by Watson when he waited for Holmes to return from his pursuit of the transvestite actor, in *A Study in Scarlet*)— but there was no copy of *The Origin of Tree Worship.*

When Mrs. Doyle paid her bet by inviting me to talk with her, I explained, "There was no copy of the book about tree worship because it is one of the many mythical books, places, and objects invented by Conan Doyle as a part of the personal allegory he wove into the fabric of his detective—and other—stories."

14.

The Origin of Tree Worship
Sherlock Holmes and Nietzsche-Dionysus

WONDERING where all this would lead, I accepted Conan Doyle's challenge in *The Adventure of the Empty House* and, like Dr. Watson and the self-educating Monster, also (mentally) picked up one of the books that had been knocked out from under Holmes's arm and looked at it through a Sherlockian magnifying glass.

A half-hour's reading at the British Museum established that *The Origin of Tree Worship,** a book as mythical as its subject,

---

* For further reference to this book, see *The Annotated Sherlock Holmes*, W. S. Baring-Gould, vol. 2, pg. 331.

was intended by Doyle as a connection between Sherlock Holmes and the worship of the Greek god Dionysus. In *The Golden Bough,* published three years before Doyle placed this book under Holmes's arm, Sir James Frazer wrote:

The god Dionysus or Bacchus is best known as the personification of the vine and of the exhilaration produced by the juice of the grape . . . he was also the god of trees in general.

Then, more relevant to Sherlock Holmes, we find Frazer saying, "Dionysus was believed to have suffered a violent death, but to have been brought back to life again; and his suffering, death and resurrection were reenacted in sacred rites."

Obviously, with this invented book and book-title "clue" which he had so strenuously thrust at the reader, Conan Doyle tells us that at the very moment of his resurrection, his own legendary hero is carrying a book about Dionysus, who symbolized resurrection and eternal recurrence. Dionysus died each winter and was reborn in the spring.

Conan Doyle's conscious identification of Holmes with the Dionysian cycle of death and rebirth is verified by the facts contained in the death and resurrection stories. Though Holmes and Watson fled from England to Reichenbach Falls in April, they saw *winter* conditions in Switzerland. Watson says:

We made our way over the Gemmi Pass, *still deep in snow,* and so, by way of Interlaken, to Meiringen. It was a lovely trip, the dainty green of spring, below, *the virgin white of the winter above.*

[my emphases]

The Dionysian parallel is completed in the opening words of the resurrection story, *The Adventure of the Empty House.* "It was in the *spring* of 1894 that all of London was interested, and the fashionable world dismayed, by the murder of the Honorable Robert Adair."

The alert reader has already anticipated my next move and is thinking, "Nietzsche was the Dionysian philosopher! Obviously all of this is leading to a demonstration of the further connections between Doyle's characters, especially Holmes and Friedrich Nietzsche."

Yes, Nietzsche was the apostle of Dionysus. His first book, *The Birth of Tragedy* (1872) —in letters he called it *The Origin of*

Tragedy—was a discourse on the origin of tragedy in the cult of Dionysus. In his *Will to Power* he wrote:

Dionysus versus the 'Crucified One': there you have the contrast. . . . The God on the cross is a curse on life, a pointer to seek redemption from it; Dionysus cut to pieces is a *promise* of life: He is eternally reborn and comes back from destruction.

Sherlock Holmes and Nietzsche and Dionysus, a summary

The very real Friedrich Nietzsche and the fictional Sherlock Holmes have much in common:

Item: They are both philologists and paleographers. Nietzsche was a professional philologist and is described by T. M. Kettle as *"engaged in deciphering* difficult Byzantine manuscripts."* Sherlock Holmes, Doyle tells us, was similarly *"engaged in deciphering* the remains of the original inscription upon a palimpsest . . . an Abbot's account."* Holmes also studied "the Chaldean roots of the great Celtic language."

Item: Nietzsche and Holmes were amateur musicians with similar tastes in music. Nietzsche, a pianist, and Holmes, a violinist, are both mentioned as inveterate concert-goers, and both are specifically mentioned as lovers of *Wagnerian operas*. Nietzsche was, of course, the intimate friend and disciple of Richard Wagner. (It was to Wagner's wife, Cosima, that the insane Nietzsche wrote, "I love you, Ariadne," and signed it "Dionysus.")

Conan Doyle's consciousness of the relationship between the two famous Germans is attested to in his journal entry (quoted above) in which his mentions of "Wagner's operas" and "Nietzsche's philosophy" are only eight words apart.

Item: Both Nietzsche and Holmes used hard drugs. Nietzsche was a chronic user of the dangerous *chloral hydrate* and wrote to someone, "I have begun to sleep again (without narcotics) ." The significance of this common addiction to narcotics is, I find, Dionysian, since hallucinogens and other drugs were used by worshipers of the Greek god to escape dull reality and to seek the heights of Dionysian ecstasy. Nietzsche suffered acutely and complained of the "nullity" of existence; Holmes complained of the "banality of existence" and explained that when he was not engaged in the exciting intellectual and physical pursuit of dangerous criminals he found it impossible to exist without recourse to morphine and cocaine.

Item: A poetic possibility: It may be that, by placing the mythical book about the worship of Dionysus under the arm of the disguised Holmes, Conan Doyle was hinting that Holmes had somewhere along the line abandoned his fiercely rational position to flirt, like Doyle, with esoteric religions. (How else can his pilgrimage to the Buddhist Dalai Lama in Tibet be explained?)

I mention Holmes's dalliance with the Eastern religion which was for several reasons connected with his worship of Dionysus, because:

Item: Dionysus (or Bacchus) was the symbolic god and transformation of all vegetation and of all the ecstasy-producing plants held sacred by his worshipers. This may, in part, explain Sherlock Holmes's marked fondness for what Frazer calls "the exhilaration produced by the juice of the grape" and, more significantly, his addiction to the alkaloid derivatives of the poppy and coca plants.

Item: To convert the people of Asia, Dionysus traveled through Persia to India. Nietzsche, the Dionysian philosopher, traveled mentally to Persia and the Himalayas to stage his *Also Sprach Zarathustra.* And our man Holmes also, while fleeing from Professor "Nietzsche-Moriarty," passed through Persia on his way to visit the "head lama" in Himalayan Tibet, just north of India. And who knows, there may be some connection even between these Persian-Dionysian-Bacchic-vegetation links and the fact that Sherlock Holmes kept dried and cured leaves of the tobacco plant in a "Persian slipper."

Final and perhaps most important item: The above comparisons convince me that Professor Moriarty as Doyle's "evil" superman and Holmes as his "good" superman are both the result of Doyle's endless fascination with Friedrich Nietzsche. Again, as Professor A. J. Ayre said to me when told of the possible influence of the German philosopher upon Doyle, "Many writers were influenced by Nietzsche at that time. Bernard Shaw, for one, in his *Man and Superman.* If Shaw, why not Doyle?"

Conan Doyle's intense preoccupation with Nietzsche as a mad professor, his concept of the superman, and the mountainous heights that inspired Nietzsche to create *Zarathustra* are all implied in a comment made by Hesketh Pearson in his excellent biography of Conan Doyle. Pearson, who has also observed Doyle's frequent literary use of professors who are either demigods or demidevils attributes this to the great impression made on Doyle by two professors at Edinburgh University. (I agree with the demigod influence but disagree with the demidevil influence, since Doyle had no diabolical teachers at the university. Professor Nietzsche was his demidevil.)

Pearson singles out "Professor Maracot, who appears in *The Maracot Deep*. We are told that he lives on a mountain-top out of the reach of ordinary mortals." Pearson then quotes Doyle: "The quiet scholar [Maracot] had been submerged, and here there was a *superman,* dominant soul who might mold mankind to his desires."

All of this evokes for me the image of *Zarathustra,* who lived in the *Himalayas* for ten years and who came down from his mountain to cry: "I teach the Superman!" It also evokes Nietzsche, whose "ghost" still haunts the mountainous heights at Rosenlaui, where Conan Doyle (and I and others) encountered it.

It seems entirely fitting and proper, does it not, that when Conan Doyle finally decided to rid himself of his incubus "good superman," he did so by having him grapple with and "die locked in the arms of" the "evil superman" Moriarty, surrogate of Friedrich Nietzsche.

A simple synoptic comparison of the last episodes of *The Final Problem* with the pursuit and confrontation scenes in *Frankenstein* shows quite plainly that Conan Doyle copied from Mary Shelley's novel: the exact geographical arena, the exact "flight plan" for reaching it, and some of the details of the fatal wrestling match between Sherlock Holmes and Professor Moriarty.

The Final Problem: Convinced that Professor Moriarty will certainly kill him if he remains in London, Sherlock Holmes flees to Switzerland. Accompanied by his Boswell, he enters that country at Basel (where Nietzsche lived and taught). Then, as a map shows, he turns southward to Geneva, the birthplace of the Monster, when Frankenstein, unaware that his vengeful creature is following him, also starts his journey to the glacier at Geneva.

Similarly mistaken in the belief that they have shaken off the homicidal Moriarty, Holmes and Watson leave Geneva, following in the footsteps of Dr. Frankenstein. First, as he did, they travel *eastward along a river valley.* But then, unlike the doctor, who turns *right* to reach the *village of Chamonix,* they turn *left* to arrive at the village of Meiringen. (How similar!)

After they spend the night at *Meiringen,* Holmes and Watson then begin their hike up the long mountain road to the Rosenlaui Hotel (where Nietzsche met the Emperor of Brazil)—their base for climbs up the *Rosenlaui Glacier.*

But, as we know, they never reached their final destination, for as they approach the Falls of Reichenbach, Holmes realizes that Professor Moriarty, a mathematics genius and master of topology, has anticipated their every move, passed them, and is in fact waiting for them at the Falls of Reichenbach, midway between Meiringen and their intended goal, Rosenlaui.

Upon their arrival at the fatal waterfall, Sherlock Holmes saves the life of Watson by sending him back to Meiringen to attend a nonexistent sick woman and goes on to his final confrontation with Moriarty, his awaiting demon and alter ego.

The final showdown that follows also borrows its essential details from Mary Shelley's fight on the glacier scene. The two antagonists meet alone at the foot of a glacier and exchange words. Then the enraged Moriarty lunges at Holmes (as Frankenstein lunged at the Monster), but, like the Monster, Holmes easily eludes his grasp and throws him over the cliff to his death in the abyss.

15.

Dionysus in The Adventure of the Speckled Band

I WAS NOT TOO SURPRISED to find the first implied mention of Dionysus in this "adventure"; since, as the reader will recall, we have already found that Conan Doyle borrowed the unique image of an adder biting a sleeping person from (Dionysus) Nietzsche's masterpiece, *Thus Spake Zarathustra.*

The ultimate image in *The Speckled Band* is that of the very dead Anglo-Indian Grimesby Roylott:

. . . his eyes were fixed in a dreadful rigid stare at the corner of the ceiling. Round his brow he had a *peculiar yellow band,* with brownish speckles, *which seemed tightly bound round his head.*

"The band! The speckled band!" whispered Holmes.

I took a step forward. In an instant *his strange headgear* began to move, and there reared itself from among his hair the squat diamond-shaped head and puffed neck of a loathsome serpent.

"It is a swamp *adder!*" cried Holmes. "The deadliest snake in India!"   [my emphases]

In his admirable *The Annotated Sherlock Holmes,* W. S. Baring-Gould has offered the opinion that the snake that killed Julia Stoner and Grimesby Roylott could not have been an Indian snake because there are no such adders in India; Conan Doyle, while borrowing Nietzsche's image of the biting adder from *Zarathustra,* also borrowed Nietzsche's mistaken idea that there were adders in the part of Asia through which Zarathustra traveled.

But the idea of a snake as a "yellow headband" or "strange headgear tightly bound round" someone's head was probably suggested to Conan Doyle in contemporary books and from published pictures of art objects relating to the ancient cult of Dionysus.

The reader who opens Miss Jane Harrison's classic *Prolegomena to the Study of the Greek Religions** (a magnificent book!) to page 398 will find a striking picture of a wild-eyed Dionysian priestess who is striding along carrying a live tiger and wearing a very strange head decoration. Miss Harrison explains:

The beautiful, raging *Mænad,* in figure 123, from the center of a *cylix* (drinking cup) is a fine example. She wears the typical *Mænad* garb, the fawn-skin over her regular drapery; she carries the *thrysos* (staff), she carries in fact the whole gear of Dionysus. For *snood in her hair the Mænad has twined a great snake.*   [my italics]

Thus we see a most remarkable fusion of images: Both the raging destructive Maenads (who tore their own children to pieces while honey and drug intoxicated) and the Victorian Grimesby Roylott, murderer of his own stepdaughter, are both "wearing" exactly the same speckled snake band wrapped about their heads.

Earlier in *The Speckled Band,* the filthy Grimesby is described as a "fierce old bird of prey." Now we find that predatory old bird dead with a snake wrapped about his head. This is another image probably borrowed from Nietzsche, since Zarathustra, like Roylott, is very friendly to wild creatures, especially a rapacious eagle which flies about with a snake coiled around its neck.

---

* Reprinted by *Meridian Books,* N.Y., 1955.

16.

Sherlock Holmes and Dionysus in His Last Bow

EVERYONE ACQUAINTED with the long and uneasy oedipal relationship knows that Sherlock Holmes has already survived his creator and would-be assassin by more than forty years (Doyle entered the spirit realm in 1931) and that the immortal detective is now in retirement on a farm on the South Downs. There, according to Conan Doyle, the unkillable Sherlock Holmes devotes himself to philosophy and agriculture and the *cultivation of bees*—the last and perhaps most poetic link in the Doylean chain of images and ideas that bind Sherlock Holmes to the cult of the undying Dionysus.

Here, once again, in *His Last Bow,* we find that it is a book carried by Holmes and read by an "amazed" character that reveals the hidden allegorical reference. This clue, significantly, comes immediately after Holmes utters the word "nitsky," a reference to "Nietzky," the ancient family name of "Nietzsche-Dionysus."

After Holmes, disguised as Altamont, a double agent, extracts the "dough," the "boodle," the advance payment for his promised "British Navy secrets," he hands a brown parcel to Von Bork, the German master spy:

Von Bork undid a winding of string and two wrappers of paper. Then he sat gazing for a moment of silent amazement at a *small blue book* which lay before him. Across the cover was printed in golden letters *Practical Handbook of Bee Culture.* Only for an instant did the master spy glare at *the strangely irrelevant inscription.* The next he was gripped at the back of his neck with a grasp of iron, and a chloroformed sponge was held in front of his writhing face.   [my italics]

The Dionysian reference? It is contained, profoundly, in the book itself, its subject matter, its "strangely irrelevant" title, and the fact that its author was Sherlock Holmes, an expert beekeeper, for *the honeybee was the sacred insect of Dionysus.* The honeybee fertilized the Dionysian flower as it stole the nectar and pollen from the reproductive organ of the plant. It then metabolically transformed the fertilizing material into honey, which, when fermented, became the intoxicating mead used by the Dionysian celebrants to ascend the emotional heights to ecstasy. (When Dionysus was an infant he was fed mostly *honey*.)

In the great processionals honoring the god of eternal recurrence, the "nurses of Dionysus," called the *Thriae*, personified and imitated the sacred bees. In her *Prolegomena*'s fascinating chapter on Dionysus, Miss Harrison writes:

The Thriae are . . . like the Mænads, they rave in holy madness . . . but their inspiration is not from Bacchus, the wine-god; or from Bromios, Sebazios, or Baraites, the beer-gods: it is from an intoxicant yet more primitive, from honey. They are 'Melissae,' honey-priestesses, inspired by a honey intoxicant, *they are bees,* their heads white with pollen; they hum and buzz, swarming confusedly.

How profound and poetical and secretive and persistent Conan Doyle was! In 1892 in *The Speckled Band* he presented the dramatic image of the Dionysian Mænad who wears a snake as a headdress; in 1903, eleven years later, he put a book about the worship of Dionysus into the hands of Sherlock Holmes; and then, twenty-five years after the first such mention, we find that Holmes once again carries a book which announces his eternal kinship with the unkillable god.

17.

THE TIRELESS MYTHOGRAPHER Doyle repeats the visual metaphor of the Dionysian bee in a singular detail of *The Adventure of the Empty House:* The famous wax dummy of himself set up by Sherlock Holmes for Sebastian Moran to shoot at could have been fabricated from many materials, but Doyle, thinking perhaps of the figures in Madame Tussaud's Museum on Baker Street, chose also to mold it from beeswax, a detail verified and explained by the *Britannica*'s article on wax figures.*

"Beeswax," says the encyclopedia, "is possessed of properties which render it a most convenient medium for preparing figures and models, either by modeling or by casting it in molds. At ordinary temperatures it can be cut or shaped with facility; it melts to a limpid fluid at low temperatures; it mixes with any coloring matter and takes surface tints as well . . . the practice of wax

---

* 11th edition, 1911.

modeling can be traced through the Middle Ages, when the votive offerings of wax (effigies) were made for churches. . . ."

How very consistent of Conan Doyle to mold an invulnerable perfect facsimile of the Dionysiac Nietzsche-Holmes from the bodily wax secretions of the sacred insects of Dionysus!

CHAPTER THREE

. . . and yet I dare call nothing trivial
when I recall that some of my most
classic cases have had the least promising
commencement. You will recall, Watson,
how the dreadful business of the Aber-
netty family was first brought to my attention by the depth to which the parsley
had sunk into the butter upon a hot day.
—Sherlock Holmes

1.

The Conan Doyle Syndrome (sin-drome) and personal allegory

Syndrome, n., a group of related
things, events, or actions, etc. From *syn*
(together) and *drome* (to run)
—*Random House Dictionary*

THE "CONAN DOYLE SYNDROME" was discovered serendipitously
during my search among the Sherlockian adventures for book-title
clues like *The Origin of Tree Worship,* which might allude to
Friedrich Nietzsche and Dionysus. My procedure was a simple
one: When a book was mentioned, I read the book, something
about its author in various reference works, and then wrote a brief
gloss of the story and scene in which the book was mentioned.

Soon, after I had repeated this process with the books mentioned in fourteen stories, a very strange phenomenon began to loom up out of the pages of *The Complete Sherlock Holmes*. My accumulated notes had revealed that in almost every story I'd synopsized, the *printed or written word in any form*—books, book titles, magazine or newspaper articles, advertisement, signs, diaries, manuscripts, letters, words scribbled on scraps of paper, words written on the wall (even in blood) or in the floor dust of a murder chamber, or even expressions read in a person's face—was always accompanied by an allusion to some form of forbidden sexual expression, either heterosexual or homosexual, or both. This allusion was usually associated in turn with images of draconian punishment in the form of the murder of individuals or of masses of people in Sodom and Gomorrah, Khartoum, Jericho or Milan, or in the English and the American Civil Wars.

Astonished by the discovery of this rigid and repetitive constellation of images secretly revolving about one another within so many of Doyle's "simple detective stories," I continued my study of these exciting obsessive idea and image clusters, and I found that they usually appeared in an obligatory or climactic scene in tandem with other obsessive elements, all of which were irrelevant to the stories in which Doyle had implanted them!

It was now obvious that this observed pattern was far from random. It was a syndrome of compulsively linked images, ideas, persons, and actions which functioned like any other medical or philosophical syndrome: If any single element of the pattern appeared, I could now accurately predict that every other element in the constellation would, like "Mary's little lamb," be sure to follow.

Yes, Conan Doyle thought in "syndromic" terms: In *A Study in Scarlet,* he has his great explainer Holmes, while defining his philosophy of crime detection, speak of the "logician" who could:

From a drop of water . . . infer the possibility of an Atlantic or a Niagara without ever having seen or heard of one or the other. So all life is a great chain, the nature of which is known whenever we are shown a single link of it.

And, in *The Five Orange Pips,* Conan Doyle, as Sherlock Holmes, expands upon the same syndromic philosophy:

The ideal reason, he remarked, would, when he had once been shown a single fact in all its bearings, deduce from it not only all the chain of events which led up to it but also all the results which would follow from it. As Cuvier could correctly describe the whole animal by the contemplation of a single bone, so the observer who has thoroughly understood *one link* in a series of incidents *should be able to state all the other ones,* both before and after. [my italics]

This "sin-drome," so called because of its central theme of illicit love or sexuality linked to a set of unique Doylean images and ideas, is expressed with the following elements:

(A) After using his superlative reasoning and detective powers to penetrate the mystery brought to him, Sherlock Holmes generally anticipates the criminal's plan of action and goes to the scene of the intended crime. In other instances he sets a trap for the suspected malefactor.

(B) There, with Watson and sometimes others as well, he conducts a vigil at night or in a dark room for the

(C) arrival of the unknown person (or one known only to Holmes) or of a dangerous criminal or murderer.

(D) Before or after, sometimes before *and* after, the arrival of the expected "man of violence" one or more printed or written word references will be made (books, words written on paper, walls, etc.), usually by the all-revealing Sherlock Holmes, which evoke the already mentioned heterosexual or deviant sexuality, which is then linked to some form of drastic punishment and the private and legal murder of individuals and of masses of people.

(E) When the expected "unknown violent man" does finally appear after the long night vigil, another uniquely Doylean surprise will occur: There is a sudden reversal, switching or confusion of the sexes. Instead of a man, a woman will appear, or a man dressed as a woman. Or he will prove to be effeminate or weak. Conversely, a suspected woman will appear as a man, or disguised as a man (Irene Adler in *A Scandal in Bohemia*). In one story (*The Yellow Face*) a "hideous man" who is seen in a second-story window turns out to be a pretty little black girl who has been wearing a mask!

Sometimes the confusion or switching of the sexes is expressed by Doyle in verbal terms: by the verbal manipulation of names or by means of allusions to literary works in which transvestism plays a very important part.

(F) A hand-to-hand combat will follow the arrival of the awaited villain or criminal. Alone or with the help of Watson and others Sherlock Holmes will overpower him (usually) and turn him over to Scotland Yard for arrest and punishment. In the few stories where the "unknown person" who appears in the "syndromic" dark room proves to be a woman, there is no hand-to-hand combat or wrestling match, and she usually goes unpunished. (Again, Irene Adler in *A Scandal in Bohemia.*)

(G) Perhaps the most important element of the *Doyle Syndrome* and allegory: In every story Sherlock Holmes is the unquestioning, incorruptible guardian of the Victorian criminal and moral codes. As such his unvarying role is that of the detector, preventer, judge, and punisher of every larcenous or immoral act, especially those that are sexually deviant.

2.

The arena

WITH VERY FEW EXCEPTIONS (*His Last Bow* is one) Conan Doyle stages his syndrome and allegory in a curious architectural setting: the "second story" of a residence or in a "two-storied house." The significance of this unique arena of action? I have verified and now believe that any description in a Sherlock Holmes story of a house as "two-storied" means that Doyle has consciously or unconsciously created a theater of allegory in which an actual house with two floors or stories is also a house with *two stories to tell,* or a house with *stories on two levels of meaning.*

We find this remarkable stage-setting first and most importantly in the fact that Sherlock Holmes's residence and office is on the second floor of the mythical house on Baker Street.

Before W. S. Baring-Gould* proves with maps and records that there never was a 221B on Baker Street when Holmes lived there, he says: "Christopher Morley cited Leonard Merrick's *Conrad in Quest of His Youth* (1903), where a young woman gives her address as:

> Miss Tattie Lascelles
> care of: Madame Hermiance
> 42 bis, Great Tichfield Terrace, W.

---

* *The Annotated Sherlock Holmes,* London, New York, 1968.

Baring-Gould explains: "Madame Hermiance ran a laundry on the ground floor, and Miss Tattie had rooms one flight up—on the English *first,* and on the American *second* floor—just as Holmes and Watson did."

Even the famous house number "221B" may be read as an allegorical clue. Taken literally it reads and means: "two-twenty-one." Or, if regarded as a play on words, it can be read as the number of a mythical house with two stories to tell since "221" can be interpreted as "two-to-one," or two meanings in one place.

Similarly the letter "B," or "bis": *The Oxford Unabridged Dictionary* defines "bis" as the French word meaning twice, encore, or repetition. We see, therefore, that every troubled or mystified client who arrives at the mythical house numbered "221B" climbs to the second story, where he/she sets in motion a Doylean story (mystery or allegory) with several layers of meaning for Sherlock Holmes and the reader to unravel.

The next stage of Conan Doyle's unique use of this architectural place symbolism occurs whenever Sherlock leaves his study to inspect the scene of the reported crimes or place of eventual showdown with the suspected criminal or villain.

This second theater of allegory is frequently described by Dr. Watson (Dr. Doyle, of course) as a "two-storied house." I have found these symbolic settings in many stories including *The Sign of Four, The Man with the Twisted Lip, The Yellow Face, The Adventure of the Empty House,* and *The Red-Headed League.* (I am not a selfish man and leave the many others for the reader who wishes to play the serious Doyle Syndrome game with me. As we traverse the fascinating maze of Doyle's imagination I shall point out each of these allegorical stage-settings and offer my interpretations of their related meanings.

3.

"I wrote no *letter.*"
"The cunning demons! But you?"
"I came in answer to *your letter.*"
"Lucia, I wrote no *letter.*"
"*They have trapped us with the same bait.*" [my italics]
—Conan Doyle, *The Adventures of Gerard*

I DO NOT CALL IT the "Sherlock Holmes Syndrome" because Conan Doyle employs the same set of mutually enchained images, ideas, and other story elements in his *Brigadier Gerard* novels.

In *How the Brigadier Lost His Ear,* a Freudian gem, we find the heterosexual "crime," the drastic punishment of the lovers, and the unique Doylean images of individual and mass murders all associated with their acts of forbidden sexuality. We also find two people waiting in a pitch-dark room for an expected man of violence, and, then, a surprising switching of the sexes and transvestism.

Brigadier Gerard loses his ear during Napoleon's occupation of Milan. Enraged by Gerard's conquest of Lucia, the Doge's granddaughter, the defeated and enraged men of Milan use the syndromic trick of forged notes to trick, capture and imprison the fornicating pair. Gerard is sentenced to death.

But during the night before the execution, he breaks into the adjoining cell, where he finds Lucia and learns that an executioner will arrive shortly to cut off her ear for fraternizing with a French soldier. While they are waiting in the syndromic pitch-dark cell for the syndromic expected man of violence, Gerard has a brilliant idea: He will accept her punishment. To do so, he shoves Lucia into his cell, puts on her cloak (transvestism) and waits in her bed. The executioner turns out to be soft-hearted and compassionate, and, believing in that dark room (he works in the dark because he cannot bear to look at the beautiful woman he is about to mutilate) that Gerard is Lucia, he cuts off the lobe of Brigadier Gerard's ear. Just then, before the switching of the sexes is discovered, Napoleon's soldiers arrive to rescue Lucia and Gerard. The soldiers then complete the syndromic requirement of mass murder associated with sex by killing all the Milanese sexual avengers. Gerard leaves Milan, and the "guilty" Lucia spends the rest of her life as a sequestered nun.

4.

ONE SUPERB EXAMPLE of the syndrome in action: In *His Last Bow,* we recall, the German master spy Von Bork is given a handbook of bee culture instead of the volume of British naval secrets he had been promised by the disguised Sherlock Holmes, who is acting as a double agent. (The alias used by Holmes is Altamont, a Doyle family name: another fact identifying Sherlock Holmes as one alter ego of Doyle.)

Like every other book mentioned by either Watson or Holmes, this bee book, written by Dionysus-Holmes himself and bearing the subtitle, *With Some Observations upon the Segregation of the Queen,* fulfills Doyle's strange need to associate sexual intercourse with mutilation and murder with a book-title. After a queen bee is fertilized by the drone, she kills him in a manner revealed in the ancient Greek myth cited by Robert Graves:*

Aphrodite Urania ("queen of the mountain") or Erycina ("of the heather") was the nymph-goddess of midsummer. She destroyed the sacred king, who mated with her on a mountain top, as the queen-bee destroys the drone: by tearing out his sexual organs.

Also, the required syndromic metaphor of the murder of great masses of men tied "irrelevantly" to the homicidal sexual act (of bees) is conveyed by the fact that the book Von Bork *thought* he was getting contained top military secrets he would have used to kill many thousands of British sailors, soldiers and civilians.

5.

LATER, WHILE ALTERNATING between the many stories in which Doyle implanted his "sexual sin-drome," and his *Memoirs,* I discovered also that he had habitually used his detective stories as personal psychodramas in which Sherlock Holmes *and* the villains were actually personified fractions of his own inner psyche and imagination. It now became apparent that each story was a "double feature" that could be read either as a brilliant tongue-in-cheek entertainment or as a segment of Conan Doyle's personal allegory.

These discoveries, though conjectural at first, were later confirmed by three confessional statements made by Conan Doyle. The first, from his *Memories and Adventures* (1924), was his answer to the question often put to him about the origin of his great detective. "If anyone is Sherlock Holmes" he wrote, "I must confess that it is I." His second answer, concerning the origin of

---

* *The Greek Myths* (Penguin Books), London, Batmore, 1955.

his villains (like Professor Moriarty or Grimesby Roylott) was equally explicit and informative:

A man cannot spin a character out of his *inner consciousness* and make him really life-like unless he has the possibility of that character within him—a dangerous admission for one to make who has drawn as many villains as I.

But Conan Doyle's most illuminating confession of his characters as projections of his inner consciousness is his remarkable self-revealing poem *The Inner Room*. Published in 1893, many years before Dr. Carl Jung introduced his theories of racial memory and archetypal images, *The Inner Room* describes in almost clinical terms Doyle's sharp recognition of his fragmented, even schizoid, personality and imagination, complete with racial memory and his personal archetypes.

Here with some of my underscorings and interpolations is:

The Inner Room

It is mine—the little chamber,
    Mine alone.
I had it from my forbears
    Years agone.
Yet within its walls I see
A most motley company,
And *they all claim it for their own.*

There's *one who is a soldier*
    Bluff and keen,
Single-minded, heavy-fisted
    Rude of mien.
He would gain a purse *or stake it,*
He would win a heart or break it,
He would *give a life or take it,*
    Conscience-clean.
[Colonel Moran was a soldier, gambler, and murderer.]

And near him is *a priest*
    Still *schism-whole:*
He loves the censer-reek
    And organ roll.
He has *leanings to the mystic*
Sacramental, eucharistic.

And dim yearnings altruistic
    Thrill his soul.
[Holmes disguised himself as a priest. Doyle quit Catholicism
    but admits to a secret residual belief in it.]

There's another who with doubts
    is overcast;
I think him younger brother
    To the last.
Walking wary stride by stride,
Peering forwards anxious-eyed,
Since he learned to doubt his guide
    In the past.

Now some syndromic images:

And 'mid them all, alert,
    But somewhat cowed,
There sits a *stark*-faced fellow
    Beetle-browed.
Whose *black soul shrinks away*
From a *lawyer-ridden day*
And *he has thoughts he dare not say,*
    Half-avowed.
[The last echoes Oscar Wilde's homoerotic "love that
knows no name."]

The Inner Room holds more syndromic images:

There are others who are sitting
    Grim as doom
In the dim, ill-boding shadow
    Of my *room*
Darkling figures, stern and quaint,
Now a savage, now a saint
Showing fitfully and faint
    Through the gloom.

This is Conan Doyle's personal archetypal image of the con-
gregation of men who wait in a dark and gloomy room for an unknown man of violence. The poem concludes with the sad
admission that the personified fragments of his multiplex (schizoid) personality use him (his mind, imagination, stories) for their
eternal battleground:

And these shadows are so dense,
　　There may be more,
Many—very many—more
　　Than I see.
They are *sitting* day and *night*
Soldier, rogue, and anchorite;
And they wrangle and they fight
　　Over me.

If the stark-faced fellow win
　　All is o'er!
If the priest should gain his will
　　I doubt no more!
And if each shall have his day,
I shall swing and I shall sway,
In the same old weary way,
　　As before.

All of these dramatic, even melodramatic characters, all fis-
sional components of Doyle's soul or psyche, emerge from his
inner dark room to become the characters in his *Sherlock Holmes*
and other stories. In *The Final Problem*, for example, Sherlock
Holmes disguises himself as a priest in order to escape from another denizen of his inner asylum (stanza 5) whom he calls Professor Moriarty. Moriarty strongly resembles the poem's "stark-
faced fellow, beetle-browed, whose black soul shrinks from a
lawyer-ridden day" and who has Oscar Wildean "thoughts he dare
not say."

6.

But this (cipher) is different. It is clearly
a reference to the words in a page of a
book.
　　　　—Sherlock Holmes, in *The Valley of Fear*

CONAN DOYLE's conscious use of written and printed word references, especially to books, as his clues to secret meanings and
hidden stories-within-stories (allegories) is openly displayed in
The Valley of Fear (1915). Though this completely syndromic
tale was published twenty-eight years after the first, which revealed

his unique set of fixations, it was not the last. That honor belongs
to *The Adventure of Shoscombe Old Place,* published in 1927.

In *Shoscombe* the printed and written word clues, in the form
of heraldic inscriptions on buildings and words engraved on tomb-
stones and coffin plates, are linked to the story of an allegedly
murdered old woman who is impersonated by a male actor wearing women's clothes. Doyle's curious preoccupation with transvestism and male and female impersonation, first seen in his first
story (1887), is last seen in a story published forty years later. I
call that a compulsion!

To show how consciously Conan Doyle used his syndromic
elements: A cryptogram scribbled on paper, a letter from a mysterious man "whose name is not his own" and who "can never be
traced," and a "book with double columns" (two meanings) to
which the cryptogram refers, I herewith reprint an excerpt from
The Valley of Fear:

"Let us consider the problem in the light of pure reason. This
man's reference is to a book. That is our point of departure."

"A somewhat vague one."

"Let us see if we can narrow it down. As I focus my mind upon it,
it seems rather less impenetrable. What indications have we as to this
book?"

"None."

"Well, well, it is surely not quite as bad as that. The cipher message begins with a large 534, does it not? We may take it as a working
hypothesis that 534 is the particular page to which the cipher refers.
So our book has already become a *large* book, which is surely something gained. What other indications have we as to the nature of this
large book? The next sign is C2. What do you make of that, Watson?"

"Chapter the second, no doubt."

"Hardly that, Watson. You will, I am sure, agree with me that if
the page is given, the number of the chapter is immaterial. Also that
of page 534 finds us only in the second chapter, the length of the first
must be really intolerable."

"Column!" I cried.

"Brilliant, Watson. You are scintillating this morning . . . so
now, you see, we begin to visualize a large book, printed in double
columns . . . have we reached the limits of what reason can supply?"

"I fear we have."

"Surely you do yourself an injustice. One more coruscation, my dear Watson—yet another brain-wave: Had the volume been an unusual one he would have sent it to me. Instead of that, he had intended, before his plan was nipped, to send me the clue. He says so in his note. This would seem to indicate that the book is one he thought I would have no difficulty finding for myself—and he imagined I would have it, too. In short, Watson, it is a very common book."

"What you say certainly sounds plausible."

After eliminating various books, including the Bible, that are printed in double columns, Watson finally blurts out:

"An almanac!"

"Excellent, Watson! I am very much mistaken if you have not touched the spot. An almanac! Let us consider the claims of *Whittaker's Almanac*. It is in common use. It has the requisite number of pages. It is in double column. . . ." He picked the volume from his desk.

"Let us see what page 534 has in store for us. . . . 'There is danger—may—come—very—soon—one.' Then we have the name 'Douglas'—'rich—country—now—at—Birlstone—House—Birlstone—confidence—is—pressing.' There, Watson! What do you think of pure reason and its fruit? If the greengrocer had such a thing as a laurel-wreath, I should send Billy the page round for it."

When the amazed Watson gazes "at the strange message which I had scrawled, as he deciphered it, upon a sheet of foolscap on my knee," and says: "What a queer, scrambling way of expressing his meaning!" Holmes responds:

"On the contrary, he has done remarkably well. When you search a single column for words with which to express your meaning, you can hardly expect to find every thing you want. You are bound to leave something to the intelligence of your correspondent. The purport is perfectly clear. Some deviltry is intended against one Douglas, whoever he may be, residing as stated, a rich country gentleman."

Perhaps the most self-revealing incident in Conan Doyle's sixty Sherlock Holmes "fables" (Doyle's own word) occurs in *The Valley of Fear*. After deducing that the facially mutilated and therefore unidentifiable corpse found at Birlstone Manor is not that of "John Douglas," Sherlock further deduces that Douglas is in hiding, and in a climactic scene he smokes him out.

There (syndromically) emerges from a secret and dark room

of the ancient manor—a room associated by the compulsive Doyle with the English Civil War that cost the lives of great masses of soldiers and civilians—a man (supposedly killed by his wife and her lover) who, says Watson, "advanced to me and handed me a bundle of paper."

"I've heard of you," said he. . . . "You are the historian of this bunch. Well, Dr. Watson, you've never had such a story as that pass through your hands before. . . . Tell it your own way; but there are the facts, and you can't miss the public as long as you have those. I've been cooped up two days . . . in that rat trap—in putting the thing into words. You're welcome to them—you and your public. There's the [story-within-a-] story of *The Valley of Fear*."

My reasons for believing so cannot be given at this moment of my narration. They will, like Douglas, emerge from Conan Doyle's own secret inner room in the chapter of *The Red-Headed League* which follows, but take my word for it: The man who emerges from the hidden room of Birlstone (Rosetta Stone?) Manor is none other than—the hidden, disguised alter ego of allegorist Sir Arthur Conan Doyle!

CHAPTER FOUR

"... a study in scarlet, eh? ... It's our
duty to unravel it, and isolate it, and expose every inch of it."

—Sherlock Holmes

1.

The Doyle Syndrome in A Study in Scarlet (*1887*)

And so I had my puppets and wrote my
Study in Scarlet.

—Conan Doyle, *Memories and Adventures*

THIS, THE FIRST Sherlock Holmes adventure, is written by Conan
Doyle on two levels of narration: the detective story "written" by
Dr. Watson, and the story-within-a-story based on the history of
the crime told by the "avenger" Jefferson Hope after Holmes
captures him.

The story begins: One morning shortly after they meet and
begin sharing the flat at 221B Baker Street, Holmes and Watson
fall into an argument about a magazine article entitled *The Book
of Life.* (With this magazine article, Doyle begins his long series of
revelatory written and printed word clues scattered among all of
the sixty stories he wrote about his marvelous detective.)

Irritated by its dogmatic tone, Watson takes exception to the
claim of the anonymous author (Holmes later admits *he* wrote it)
that "an observant man could, by a momentary expression, a

twitch of a muscle or a glance of an eye, fathom a man's most inmost thoughts. Deceit, according to him, was an impossibility in the case of one trained to observation and analysis."

This sharp dispute between Watson and Holmes about the feasibility of reading a man's "most inmost thoughts" with "trivial" clues may be understood in two ways. The first is obvious. It is the author's introduction to the crime-solving theory and methods of Sherlock Holmes. But now, on the basis of my discoveries, I suggest that this sharp and lengthy dispute about inmost thoughts can be read as the author's invitation to us to look for even the smallest clues that will reveal the inmost thoughts of Arthur Conan Doyle.

A Study in Scarlet: Its surface, or conventional, story begins with the arrival of a letter (written-word signal of: "syndrome" to follow) from Scotland Yard's Gregson inviting Holmes to help solve the mysterious murder of "Enoch J. Drebber," of "Cleveland in Ohio," U.S.A.

By applying his analytical genius to many small clues that are invisible to or misunderstood by the bumbling police detectives, Holmes determines that Drebber and later Joseph Stangerson have been killed by a third American named Jefferson Hope. Holmes then captures Hope and turns him over to Scotland Yard, where Hope relates the history of the crime as a lengthy story-within-a-story.

In 1847 disaster befalls a wagon train of westward-bound pioneers in The Great American Desert, leaving only two survivors: John Ferrier and a little orphaned girl named Lucy, now both dying of hunger and thirst.

They are rescued, of course, but are first required to perform in a dying scene, a gem of unintentional humor that recalls Oscar Wilde's remark: "Anyone who fails to laugh at the 'death of little Nell' has a heart of stone."

When after much soul-searching John Ferrier finally decides to tell his little companion "There's an almighty small chance for us now," the five-year-old Lucy, "checking her sobs and raising her tear-stained face," asks:

"Do you mean we are going to die too?"
"I guess that's the size of it."
"Why didn't you say so before?" she said gleefully. "You gave me a

fright. Why of course, now as long as we die, I'll be with [my] mother again."

"Yes you will, dearie."

"And you too. I'll tell her how good you've been. I'll bet she meets us at the door of heaven with a big pitcher of milk and a lot of buckwheat cakes, hot, and toasted on both sides" [obviously Doyle never saw a buckwheat cake]. "Like me and [brother] Bob was fond of. How long will it be?"

"I don't know—not very long." The man's eyes were fixed on the northern horizon. In the blue vault of heaven there appeared three little specks which increased in size every moment, so rapidly did they approach. They speedily resolved themselves into . . . buzzards, the Vultures of the West, whose coming is a forerunner of death.

"Cocks and hens!" cried the girl, gleefully pointing at their ill-omened forms, and clapping her hands to make them rise. "Say, did God make this country?"

"Of course He did," said her companion, rather startled by her unexpected question.

"He made the country down in Illinois, and He made the Missouri," the little girl continued. "I guess somebody else made the country in these parts. They forgot the water and the trees."

"What would ye think of offering up prayers?" the man asked diffidently.

"It ain't night yet," she answered.

But they do pray, and God answers their prayer in exactly thirty minutes when they are rescued by the advance riders of the great Mormon party on its way to Utah.

Ferrier and Lucy are taken at once to Brigham Young himself. He lays down a brown book (syndromic announcement of sexually motivated murder to follow) and curtly offers Ferrier the either/or choice: "convert" to Mormon or "we leave you behind to die in the wilderness." The instant conversion of Ferrier to Mormonism, says the witty Doyle, "was made with such emphasis that the grave Elders could not restrain a smile."

When the Mormon party reaches Utah, Ferrier adopts Lucy, and, though secretly hostile to the religion and polygamy, he conforms outwardly and becomes a prosperous member of the community. But the inevitable conflict arises when Lucy grows up to become the beautiful "flower of Utah," and wishes to marry a non-Mormon named Jefferson Hope.

Brigham Young himself arrives one day to intervene. After quoting the Mormon bible (again a book is the announcement of sexual tragedy to follow) Young forbids Lucy's marriage to a Gentile and orders her to marry either Enoch J. Drebber or Joseph Stangerson within thirty days.

During the following month the Ferriers await the return of Jefferson Hope and are terrified each morning to find that some-one has (syndromically) written the numbers "29," then "28," then "27," etc., on the doors, on the ceiling, and even on the bed to remind them of the terrible consequences of noncompliance.

Finally, Hope does return and the three flee into the moun-tains. But one day, while Hope is out hunting for food, the Mormons overtake them, kill John Ferrier, and take his daughter back to a forced marriage with Drebber.

Unable to live with her grief and humiliation, Lucy soon dies of a broken heart. As she is lying in her coffin, Hope breaks into the room, kisses her cold forehead, snatches the wedding ring from her finger, and vows eternal vengeance against Drebber and Stangerson, who killed Ferrier.

This latter-day Count of Monte Cristo pursues the two "mur-derers" for twenty years and finally locates them in "Cleveland in Ohio." They recognize him and flee to England, where the un-shakable Hope finds them. To earn a living at a trade that will also enable him to continue his hot pursuit, Hope becomes a hansom-cab driver. The end of the epic chase finally arrives. One day after following Drebber through the maze of London streets from one "liquor-shop" (saloon) to the next, Hope finally lures the drunken Drebber into his cab and takes him to the "empty house" where, after showing his victim Lucy's wedding ring, he holds a knife to his throat and forces Drebber to take poison.

2.

Now the Doylean Syndrome and allegory: We have already mentioned the first such element: the letter from Scotland Yard inviting Holmes to help solve the murder mystery.

At the scene of the crime, Holmes is present when the ring and the book clues are found and presented to the reader. ("A ring and a book? Why, that reminds me of Robert Browning's masterpiece!" As we shall soon see, the finding of the ring and the book, in that order, is no coincidence.)

The *ring:* As the murdered villain is being carried out, a gold *wedding ring* falls from his body. ("There could be no doubt at all," writes Watson, "that this plain circlet of gold once adorned the finger of a bride.") Thus we see the *syndrome* appearing in its unique Doylean form: a ring, symbol of licensed sexual love and union, is physically associated with death, and, before the story ends, with a total of *four* murders: Ferrier, Lucy, and the two Mormons. Hope faces certain hanging but cheats the gallows with a heart attack. Later, as we shall see, this *ring,* and a *book* found at the same time, become the nuclei of *another* round of associations with sex-inspired murders.

The *book?* After Sherlock Holmes inspects the ring, he turns to Inspector Gregson and asks, "What did you find in [the victim's] pockets?" and is told that, along with various pieces of gold jewelry, there is a copy of Boccaccio's *Decameron.*

The choice of this particular book as the one to be carried by Drebber during his drunken round of saloons en route to his own death was not a random one. The *Decameron* is filled with stories in which severe punishment, torture, even capital punishment are inflicted upon lovers who seek fulfillment in sexual union.

In one story, for example, a nobleman discovers that his wife and his best friend truly love each other. One day he entraps his friend and kills him. That night, after he and his wife have enjoyed a delicious *ragout* he tells her:

"This that you have eaten was in truth the heart of Sir Guillaume de Huardestaing, whom you, disloyal wife as you are, so loved, and know for certain that it is his very heart, for that I tore from his breast with these hands before my return."

The wife responds to this terrible disclosure by "throwing herself through a window that was exceeding high above the ground wherefore she fell, she was not only killed, but well-nigh broken in pieces." The husband lives out his long life in utter misery.

But now, guided by my knowledge of Doyle's unique imperatives, I read on and found, as expected, that many of the tales featured some form of *sexual deviation* (usually transvestism) *associated with the murder of a leading character.*

In *Bernabo of Genoa Wagers on His Wife's Honesty,* Ginevra, a virtuous and loving wife, is falsely accused of infidelity by the villainous Ambroglioulo. Bernabo believes him and hires a wife-killer. But the kind-hearted "contractor" believes in Ginevra's innocence and allows her to escape. After spending six years disguised as a man, Ginevra meets her husband and proves that she was the falsely accused. The story's villain is tied to a stake, anointed with honey and devoured by insects. (As I wrote the last words, another even stronger example of sexual ambivalence from the *Decameron* came vaguely to mind: something said by Stephen Dedalus in James Joyce's *Ulysses.* After a little search, it was found: "Boccaccio's Calandrino," said Dedalus, "was the first and last man who felt himself with child."

3.

"*Rache*": *the graffito written in blood*

". . . the *fatal thread,*" Racine's *Phèdre*
". . . the *scarlet thread* of murder"
A Study in Scarlet

THE SYNDROME set in motion by the ring and the book accelerates when Inspector Lestrade, who never gets *anything* right, finds a false clue to the murder. Pointing to a corner of the syndromic dark apartment, he shouts triumphantly: "Look at that!"

Dr. Watson explains, "In this particular corner of the room a large piece [of wallpaper] had peeled off, leaving a yellow square of coarse plastering. Across this bare space was written in blood-red letters a single word: RACHE."

When he is asked what the mysterious word means, Lestrade answers, "Mean? Why, it means that the writer was going to put the female name Rachel, but was disturbed before he or she had the time. You mark my words, when this case comes to be cleared up, you will find that a woman named Rachel had something to do with it. It's all very well for you to laugh, Mr. Sherlock Holmes. You may be smart and clever, but the old hound is still the best when all is said and done."

As Sherlock is leaving he neatly egopunctures the inept Scotland Yard detective who misreads the blood graffito: "One more thing, Lestrade: 'Rache' is the German word for 'revenge,' so don't waste time looking for Miss Rachel."

4.

THOUGH SHERLOCK HOLMES proved to be *right* when he told Inspectors Lestrade and Gregson that there was no "Miss Rachel" directly connected with the execution-slaying of the evil Drebber, Holmes was, in a sense, wrong in telling them it would be a "waste of time" to look for her.

My investigation of *A Study in Scarlet* convinces me that Lestrade was unknowingly on the right track when he told Holmes defensively, "You mark my words, when this case is cleared up you will find a woman named Rachel had something to do with it."

I shall explain. Since becoming aware of Doyle's singular insistence on using written or printed word references—even those written in blood on a wall—as clues to some unknown conflict within himself, I have carefully examined every such allusion. Now, after applying his proffered keys to this story, I believe that with his playful use of the word "Rache," or "revenge," Doyle was, first, being syndromist, since the word written on the wall as a false lead by Jefferson Hope fulfills Doyle's formula: it links the bloody word with the revengeful murder of the man who sexually violated the innocent Lucy Ferrier. Second, my probe tells me that with this wall inscription, Doyle was telling himself— and the reader who might decipher his word clues—that he had taken some elements of *A Study in Scarlet* from Jean Racine's *Phèdre* and *Mithridate*. They are:

1. The thematic title *A Study in Scarlet*—from *Phèdre.*
2. The theme of murderous revenge for thwarted love—from *Phèdre.*
3. The image of hand dipped into blood—from *Phèdre.*
4. *Poison* as a final resolution of sexual deprivation—from *Mithridate.*

Here, from textual material garnered from the Sherlock Holmes adventures and from a historical novel written by Doyle, are the links in the chain of observation and analysis which led me to these conclusions: First of all, there really was a "Miss Rachel." She was Elizabeth Felix (Rachel), who was called the greatest tragedienne of the nineteenth century and was world-renowned for her performances in Racine's dramas, especially *Phèdre*.

At the beginning of *A Study in Scarlet* Doyle hints subliminally of Rachel's presence when, through Watson, he tells us that Holmes was once visited by a "Jew Peddler," a possible link between the actress and the story that follows, because, as her biographers reveal, she was the "daughter of a Jew peddler." Biographer Louis Barthou, ignorant of the fact that many intellectual Jews—who as a group have always revered learning—were forced to earn their living as lowly itinerant peddlers, has written:

One marvels at the explicable decree of destiny which made the almost illiterate daughter of a Jew pedlar high priestess in the temples of Corneille, Racine, and Voltaire.

Another Doylean link between the two "Miss Rachels" and Sherlock Holmes: In *A Scandal in Bohemia,* written shortly after *A Study in Scarlet,* Sherlock is actually outwitted by Irene Adler, the actress with a similarly Jewish name. Some Holmesians hold that Miss Adler was based on Lola Montez because, among other reasons, she bedded with aristocrats. Others, with whom I agree, believe that Rachel, the mistress of at least one nobleman, was the original of Irene Adler.

Further, the title *A Scandal in Bohemia* may have been suggested by the fact, probably known to Doyle, the omnivorous reader, that Rachel was half Bohemian. James Agate, another biographer, has written: "Her mother was Esther Haya Felix, a Bohemian dealer in second-hand clothes." (In a figurative sense Doyle seems to have bought some of Mrs. Felix's second-hand clothes.)

I was amused to see that, ironically, the first Racinean clue connecting the nonexistent "Miss Rachel" with the real "Miss Rachel" is offered by Doyle immediately after Sherlock deflated the two policemen by telling them that Drebber was poisoned, that "Rache" means "revenge," and that they would be wasting their time looking for anyone named Rachel. Doyle's words were: "With which *Parthian shot* [Holmes] walked away, leaving his two rivals open-mouthed." [my italics]

A Parthian shot, as every Parthian knows, refers to the

mounted Parthian (Persian) archers who, while galloping forward, turned rearward and shot with deadly accuracy.

The Racinean link between the words: "poison," "revenge," "Miss Rachel" and the phrase "Parthian shot" which immediately follows them? It lies in the fact that one of Rachel's greatest successes was in the role of the Parthian princess in Racine's *Mithridate*. Mithridates was the Parthian monarch whose dread of poisoning was so great that he constantly drank antidotes. Dr. Doyle, a medical man and former student of pharmacology, knew that a "mithridate" was a sovereign remedy for all poisons. (Jefferson Hope, Doyle tells us, learned all about poisons while working as a janitor in a medical school. Significantly, the poison used to kill the monstrous Drebber came from arrows, which in the *sindromic* context may be read as "Eros" or Cupid: a psychic transformation of love into murder.) *

A further comparison between Racine's *Phèdre* and *A Study in Scarlet* offers a plausible source for the graffitian word "RACHE" (revenge, or Rachel) which Inspector Lestrade said may have been written by a "Miss Rachel" with blood into which she had dipped her hand.

This precise image comes from a scene in *Phèdre* in which the revengeful Phèdre, played by Rachel, declaims:

> My *homicidal hands* . . .
> In *innocent blood* burn to *plunge themselves!*

My literary sleuthing has also uncovered the possibility that Doyle may even have taken the thematic title and its language from some other lines spoken by "Miss Rachel" in Racine's tragedy. When Phèdre reminds Hippolytus of his father Theseus's murder of the Minotaur with the help of the maze-penetrating thread given him by Ariadne, her sister, she calls it "the fatal thread."

How very similar these words are to those used by Holmes when he explains the thematic title of the story to Dr. Watson:

. . . a study in scarlet, eh? . . . there's a scarlet *thread of murder* running through the colourless skein of life . . .   [emphasis mine]

---

* In addition to the enormous fee he paid to Holmes for ridding him of the blackmailing Irene Adler, the King of Bohemia also gave Holmes a splendid "gold snuffbox with a great amethyst in the center of the lid." Doyle probably selected this particular gem because the warheads of Cupid's phallic arrows are made of *amethyst.*

But the proof that Conan Doyle was an allegorist who had Racine's version of the Phaedra myth in mind when he wrote *A Study in Scarlet* was revealed later by Holmes himself in *The Final Problem,* in which he alludes to himself as a Theseus who uses Ariadne's thread to penetrate the Cretan maze of London's underworld to find and kill the criminal Minotaur named Professor Moriarty:

. . . and at last the time came when *I seized the thread and followed it,* until it led me, *after a thousand cunning windings, to Moriarty.*

[my italics]

Yes, the scarlet thread and the fatal thread are the same thread which, when unraveled, enabled Theseus-Hope to traverse London's maze, kill the Minotaur and escape. (I now ask the unanswerable question: "What terrible Minotaur lay hidden in the darkest corner of Conan Doyle's psychic 'inner room,' whose allegorical presence is syndromically hinted at in so many stories, and even in those stories in which Sherlock Holmes does not appear?")

But the clear proof of Doyle's conscious use of Racine's *Phèdre* is displayed in his historical romance *The Refugees.* In this novel, begun a few weeks after he passed his death sentence upon Sherlock Holmes (see letter to his "Mam," November 11, 1891), Doyle wrote a lengthy scene which includes Racine himself, his *Phèdre,* and a partially syndromic discussion in which Madame de Maintenon is compared to the doomed antiheroine of Racine's tragedy.

In Chapter 2 of *The Refugees, The King in Deshabille,* Louis XIV has just arisen, breakfasted, and is being dressed by his courtiers. After comparing this strange ritual to "the dressing a favourite doll by a knot of children," Doyle names all the politicians, priests, architects, soldiers, artists, etc., present in the King's chamber. Among them is the author of *Phèdre* and *Mithridate:*

Close to the door, Racine, with his handsome face wreathed in smiles, was chatting with the poet Boileau and the architect Mansard. . . .

Said Racine ". . . I am to be at Madame de Maintenon's room at three o'clock to see whether a page or two of the *Phèdre* may not work a change [in the King's mood]."

"My friend," said the architect, "do you think that Madame herself might be a better consoler than your *Phèdre?*"

[Racine answers:] "Madame is a wonderful woman. She has brains, she has heart, she has tact—she is admirable."

This concludes my case for the belief that Conan Doyle, a man with an encyclopedic brain and phenomenal memory, knew a great deal about Racine and his plays, especially the *Phèdre* as performed by Rachel. He fully integrated that knowledge and his power of minute recall in the writing of his *A Study in Scarlet* and *The Refugees.*

So it does seem that Inspector Lestrade was right after all when he defensively told the vastly superior Holmes, "When this case comes to be cleared up, a woman named Rachel will be found to have something to do with it."

5.

I AM VERY GRATEFUL to Sir Arthur Conan Doyle for enabling me to identify two nineteenth-century advertising paintings I bought at the Flea Market in Paris in 1962. These paintings, about twenty by thirty inches in size, offer the products of a "Sarah Felix," a French manufacturer of cosmetics and patent medicines.

One painting shows a beautiful young woman dressed in a Turkish costume. She is pointing to a green glass flask which contains, the French words over her head tell us, "Elixir Ottoman," a "sovereign remedy for sterility, heart ailments, and pallid color." In the other twin painting, another turbaned beauty offers "Baume Ottoman," a "lotion for bleaching, clarifying, and making the skin transparent," and guaranteed "will never turn rancid."

While searching for the "nonexistent Miss Rachel," I found, in the James Agate's biography of *Rachel (Elisa Felix)*, that my unknown Sarah Felix was not only the great Rachel's sister but a fine actress who performed with her in all of the plays of Racine. During Rachel's tour of America in the 1850s, Sarah played Queen Elizabeth to Rachel's Mary, Queen of Scots.

When Rachel died of tuberculosis at the age of thirty-eight, she left much of her estate to Sarah, who then promptly left the theater to manufacture perfumes, cosmetics, and patent medicines.

A comparison of my Sarah Felix advertising paintings with contemporary prints of Rachel has revealed that the turbaned beauty who offers the "Baume Ottoman" is none other than Rachel in her role as the Ottoman Princess in Racine's *Bajazet.*

Thanks to Conan Doyle, the paintings bought at the Paris Flea Market have suddenly become magically charged—and two lost objects related to a great actress have been recovered.

6.

> . . . this *scarlet thread.*
> —*The Book of Joshua,* Chap. 2 (Old Testament)

> . . . *the scarlet thread*
> —Sherlock Holmes, *A Study in Scarlet*

WHEN I WORKED FOR WARNER BROS. as a literary consultant on plagiarism cases, my legal supervisor gave me some advice which has been of great value in all my idea investigations: "Don't be fooled by the sometimes astonishing resemblances you will find when you compare *any two* films, plays, stories, books, or film scripts. During the past twenty-five years we have made hundreds of such comparisons in preparation for court trials, and in a great many cases we have found that *both* of the quarreling authors— each convinced that *he* was honest and that the other writer was an idea-thief—had copied their plots, ideas, sequences from an *earlier* literary classic or from the Bible or some 'forgotten' childhood story. So—always look for the *common literary ancestor!*"

Now, applying this wisdom to the problem at hand, I thought: "Yes, it does appear that Doyle, following the train of linked ideas I've found, did get the idea of the fatal thread from Racine's *Phèdre.* But even as I wrote these words I, and probably others, was thinking of Nathaniel Hawthorne's *The Scarlet Letter* and the punitive badge of shame worn by Hester Prynne:

. . . on the breast of her dress, in *red cloth,* surrounded with an elaborate embroidery, and fantastic flourishes of gold thread, appeared the [scarlet] letter A.   [emphasis mine]

A letter made of scarlet cloth would, of course, be woven from scarlet threads, but did Hawthorne merely report an historical instance of a "scarlet woman" who was branded with such a scarlet letter, did he invent the phrase himself, or did he copy it from an earlier literary source?

I followed an intriguing Ariadne-thread through many "mythologies" and concordances, and, after rejecting the thread of life woven, measured and cut by the Three Fates (their thread is not scarlet), I finally found the scarlet thread which most closely fulfilled Conan Doyle's syndromic requirement of carnal passion linked to the image of mass murder: It was in the biblical story of Joshua's two spies and their covenant with the harlot Rahab.

This Old Testament tale, which supplements the Racinean image of Ariadne's fatal thread and which (who knows?) may also have been in Racine's mind when he wrote his *Phèdre,* is beautifully relevant to several Sherlock Holmes stories.

Joshua, directed by Jehovah to conquer the city-state of Jericho, kill all its inhabitants, and occupy the city, begins his campaign of conquest by sending two spies to appraise Jericho's vulnerability. This God-directed action is a curious heterosexual replay of His earlier and similar action of sending two spying (androgynous) angels into the sodomitic city of Sodom as his genocidal agents.

The two spies infiltrate Jericho with the help of the harlot Rahab, ferret out the weak spots in the city's defenses, and are about to leave when Rahab stops them. She knows, she tells them, who they are, why they have come, how the Israelites killed all the inhabitants of other cities they conquered, and begs them to spare her life and that of her entire family.

Grateful for her help, Joshua's spies agree and tell her:

Behold, when we come, thou shalt bind this line of *scarlet thread* in the window which thou didst let us down by, and thou shalt bring thy father, and thy mother, and thy brethren, and all thy father's household unto thee.   [my emphasis]

The delighted and relieved Rahab asks them to swear they will keep their promise and says:

According unto thy words, so *be* it. And she sent them away, and they departed, and she bound the *scarlet line* in the window. (*Book of Joshua,* Chap. 2)   [my emphasis]

Later the promise was kept: when all the inhabitants of Jericho were massacred, Rahab and her family were spared. (Racine and

Hawthorne probably knew that in addition to her sexual services Rahab was also engaged in the manufacture and dyeing of linen cloth. It would not have attracted undue attention if scarlet or other colored threads she used for weaving hung from her window.)

John Watson responds to Sherlock Holmes's jovial disquisition on "the scarlet thread of murder" in "this finest study in scarlet" by observing:

"Leaning back in the cab, this amateur bloodhound* carolled away like a lark while I meditated upon the manysidedness of the human mind."

And I, reading this multileveled scene, meditated upon the manysidedness of Conan Doyle's psychic hang-ups and imagination and wondered why, in so many of his stories like *The Red-Headed League, The Cardboard Box, The Empty House, The Illustrious Client,* etc., Doyle associates love and carnal knowledge with individual murder and with the legal or divine murder of large masses—even entire populations.

7.

A "found" and "picked-up book" entitled "De Jure inter Gentes" (1642)

"Do you see this Ring? 'T is a figure, a symbol."

"Do you see this square old yellow book . . . Secreted from a man's life?"
                    —Robert Browning, *The Ring and the Book*

ON THE DAY AFTER the ring and the book, the bloody graffito and the meanings of the data printed in the dust, and "Norman Neruda" were given overt and hidden attention, an advertisement appeared in every London newspaper, an ad written by Holmes to lure and entrap the unknown murderer of Enoch Drebber:

In Brixton Road, this morning, a plain gold wedding ring, found in the roadway between the White Hart Tavern and Holland Grove.

---

* Sherlock Holmes began as an "amateur bloodhound," but turned professional very quickly. He received more than $25,000 for ending Irene Adler's blackmailing presence and threat in *A Scandal in Bohemia.*

Apply Dr. Watson, 221B, Baker Street, between eight and nine this evening.

That evening, as Sherlock Holmes and Watson wait for the possible arrival of the unknown man of violence (suspected murderer) to respond to the written and printed ad, all of the other "automatics" in the Doylean formula appear in a quantity and density that can only be called *phenomenal!*

After ensuring that Watson has his old army revolver in his pocket, cocked and ready, Holmes says: "Yes, [it is eight o'clock]. He will be here in a few minutes. Open the door slightly. That will do! Now put the key on the inside."

Then, in the very midst of this crisis of apprehensive waiting, Holmes utters one of his seeming irrelevancies: He hands Watson a book (always a *sin-dromic* warning) and says:

> This is a *queer* old *book I picked up* at a stall yesterday—*De Jure inter Gentes*—published in Latin at Liege, in the Netherlands, in 1642. (King) Charles's head was still firm on his shoulders when this little brown-backed *volume was struck off.*   [my italics]

Like all of the other books mentioned in the Holmes stories, this one, mentioned during this crisis of waiting in a clearly *sin-dromic* scene, interested me. Previously, during my commentary on the ring and the book (found in that order on the dead man), I'd wondered if this juxtaposition of words and symbolic objects had any connection with Browning's poem about a "ring and a book." Now, after an intensive comparative study of *A Study in Scarlet* (1887) and *The Ring and the Book* (1868–69), I am convinced that the book in Holmes's possession (*De Jure inter Gentes*) is *really* Robert Browning's *The Ring and the Book* and that it derives some of its important images and ideas and sometimes even the exact words from Browning's masterpiece.

First, the book itself: According to Madeleine Stern, a bibliographer and scholar,* the book as described by Holmes is nonexistent, or mythical. Miss Stern says that there was a *De Jure inter Gentes,* but never one printed in Liege in 1642.

My assumption that Conan Doyle was thinking of *The Ring and the Book* while writing his first Sherlock Holmes adventure rests on more than a dozen facts found in the two books, and

---

* *The Annotated Sherlock Holmes,* vol. 1, pg. 344.

especially from the data offered by Sherlock Holmes, who, I now know, is always the "great exposer" on both levels of story meaning.

The book's provenance: Sherlock Holmes tells Watson that he "picked up the book at a stall yesterday." Apart from the fact that every move he made on that busy day is fully accounted for, and precludes *any* leisurely visit to bookstalls, I believe that this image of finding a queer old book at a stall was taken by Doyle from *The Ring and the Book:*

Do you see this *square old* yellow *book?* . . . Examine it for yourself! I found this book . . . across a square of Florence crammed with *booths* . . . With this one glance at the *letter-back* of which, and *"Stall!"* cried I: a *lira* made it mine.

(When I saw these striking similarities, I said to myself: "The leather-backed book found in a booth by Browning was a 'square old yellow book,' but the 'queer old book' found 'in a stall had a brown back.' How do you explain the difference in color?" And "myself" answered: "Elementary, my dear I. With that choice of color Conan Doyle admitted, perhaps unconsciously, that he had taken the *brown* book from Robert *Brown*ing." ("I" has not talked to "myself" since.)

There are other similarities: In each the sexual desire of two men for one virtuous and innocent girl ends with the death of all three by murder or execution. Both stories are told by more than one narrator, including the murderer himself, who does so in the form of an extended flashback as a story-within-a-story. These are, of course, elements that exist in countless other stories told since the beginning of time, but the fact that they are expressed in somewhat the *same words,* and in concert with many other major similarities which follow, indicates to me that Conan Doyle consciously used *The Ring and the Book* as one of his models.

The notion that Doyle had Robert Browning and his poem in his thoughts when he wrote *A Study in Scarlet* is strengthened by his choice of naming a *town* and a *street.* When Jefferson Hope confesses to his murders of Drebber and Stangerson, he says:

It was some time before I found out where these two gentlemen lived, but I inquired and inquired until at last I came across them. They were living in a boarding-house in *Camberwell,* over on the other side of the river. . . . on *Torquay Terrace,* as the street was called in which they boarded.   [my italics]

Robert Browning was born in Camberwell and lived there until he was twenty-eight. Camberwell, disguised as "Wurzburg," is the scene of his first important poem, *Paracelsus* (1835). And "Torquay Terrace" is not a street at all. Torquay was the summer home of Elizabeth Barrett for many years before she married Robert Browning. It was at Torquay that Elizabeth's brother Edward was drowned during a mysterious boating accident.

8.

> Do you see this Ring?
> . . . 'T is a figure, a symbol, say;
> A thing's sign: now for the thing signified.
> —*The Ring and the Book,* Robert Browning

WHAT ABOUT THAT "Ring"? Does the lost and found gold wedding ring in *A Study in Scarlet* come from *The Ring and the Book,* too? The answer is, simply, "Yes, it does." Browning describes his ring as a *"circlet . . . of* pure *gold . . . found . . .* after a *dropping* in April at an Etruscan *grave*site." As described by Dr. Watson, the ring in *A Study in Scarlet* that *dropped* from the body of a *dead* man and was taken from a *dead* woman is described as "a *circlet* of *gold* that once adorned the finger of a bride." Thus both "circlets of gold" are associated with a bride long since dead, a ring separated from her finger and later found. It is the same ring.

But the gold wedding band advertised as "found" in the London papers is not the *original* ring worn by Lucy Ferrier. It is, Holmes says, "almost a *facsimile."* Even *this* detail comes from *The Ring and the Book,* since, as Browning explains:

> . . . this Ring?
>   'T is Rome-work, made to match
> (By Castellani's *imitative* craft)
> Etrurian circlets found . . .

Yes, in both the poem and the detective story, the ring is a symbolic object which recalls, very similarly, the catastrophic consequences of love that is destroyed along with all the men and women who strove for it.

Here for ready reference and more vivid visual comparison is a tabulation of the similarities between *The Ring and the Book* (1868–69) and the "found book" in *A Study in Scarlet* (1887):

Browning: It is titled *The Ring and the Book:* symbolic objects.
Doyle: Tells of a *ring* and a *book,* found in that order.

Browning: "a *square old* yellow *book*."
Doyle: "a *queer old book*."

Browning: "Found in an outdoor booth."
Doyle: "Picked up at an outdoor stall."

Browning: "This *book* . . . *secretes a man's life*."
Doyle: At the beginning of *A Study in Scarlet* we are told that Holmes wrote *A Book of Life,* which claims that the *secrets* of a *man's life* and his "inmost thoughts" can be read by tiny clues.

Browning: It is written in *Latin,* mixed with Italian, with a *Latin* title.
Doyle: It is a *Latin* book.

Browning: Printed in seventeenth century. (1698.)
Doyle: Printed in seventeenth century. (1642.)

Browning: It is a collection of *legal* documents and pamphlets.
Doyle: A book about international *law.*

Browning: Deals with the trial of a man who *killed his wife and her parents* and who, in turn, is *executed.*
Doyle: Enoch Drebber is "executed" for "killing" his *wife and her father.*

Browning: The *murderer* (Franceschini) *tells his version* of the tragedy.
Doyle: The *murderer* (Hope) *tells his version* of the tragedy.

Browning: The murdered girl is an innocent victim.
Doyle: Lucy Ferrier is an innocent victim.

Browning: She lives in *Lucina.*
Doyle: Her name is *Lucy.*

Browning: The *Ring* is called a *"circlet of gold."*
Doyle: The ring is called a *"circlet of gold."*

Browning: It is found at a place of *death:* Etruscan *tomb.*
Doyle: 1. Taken from a *dead* woman in a *coffin.*
2. Found after having fallen from a dead man.

Browning: The ring was once worn by a bride now long since dead.
Doyle: When Holmes sees it, Lucy Ferrier has been dead for twenty years.

Browning: The Ring is *not* the original worn by that bride; it is a *copy* made by *Castellani.*
Doyle: The ring used by Holmes to entice and entrap the murderer is "almost a *facsimile.*" The original ring is held by the police.

Browning: was born and lived in *Camberwell* until he was twenty-eight; his *Paracelsus* takes place in "Wurzburg" (*Camberwell*).
Doyle: Jefferson Hope finds his victims in *Camberwell.*

Browning: His wife, Elizabeth Barrett Browning, spent her summers in *Torquay,* the scene of her brother's death.
Doyle: Hope finds Drebber and Stangerson on *Torquay* Terrace.

Browning: In the foreword to *The Ring and the Book* (Penguin), Richard Altick calls Browning a "connoisseur of crime."
Doyle: Sherlock Holmes certainly qualifies as "a connoisseur of crime."

9.

"King Charles's severed head"

THE PLAGUING QUESTION that has accompanied each new example of Doyle's syndrome, "Was he aware of his highly obsessive reiterations?" is answered in part, I find, by a second irrelevance found alongside the description of *De Jure inter Gentes,* the first "irrelevance."

After giving the details of its publication, etc., Holmes, once again the "compulsive revealer," adds gratuitously, "(King) Charles's head was still firm on his shoulders when this little brown-backed volume was struck off."

This oddly digressive remark likening a book to a decapitated head puzzled me until I found that Doyle, speaking ventriloquially through Holmes, was reminding himself and his readers of Mr. Dick, the eccentric but lovable kite-flyer in *David Copper-*

field. Mr. Dick, perfectly normal in other respects, was obsessed with the image of Charles the Martyr's lopped-off head and could not stop himself from mentioning it, irrelevantly, in every conversation.

My accumulated observations suggest to me that Doyle, who mentions the *da capo* King Charles in several stories, saw, as he came to this moment of his story, that he was about to follow his mention of a book with more references to his sexual fixations. So, pausing for a moment, he alluded to the severed head as if to say:

"I am really talking to myself, reminding myself that I am another Mr. Dick and that the tragic sexual images that follow irrelevantly each mention of the *written or printed* are my own 'King Charles's heads.'

"But! If any probing Holmes-like reader should recognize my compulsive need to implant my private obsessions and fixations in almost every story, I hope that he will also recognize that by mentioning King Charles I show that I am aware of this process. I hope also that this ideal reader will see that by invoking the eccentric but charming Mr. Dick I am also asking myself and the reader not to take what follows, however perverse it may seem, too seriously.

"After all, these detective stories are intended to be fictional entertainments, mere escapist fantasies which should be read and forgotten immediately. And finally, the investigative reader will, I'm sure, never confuse the Conan Doyle whose imagination betrays him into implanting these perverse references with the true Sir Arthur Conan Doyle, who, as the world and I will assure you, is a remarkably well-adjusted normal and wholesome man, husband, father, citizen and writer."

In retrospect, Conan Doyle could also have added: "Any reader of the various biographies written about me, and of my own memoirs, will know that I was most uncomfortable about the Sherlock Holmes stories. On the basis of what has already been revealed about my stories in the present book, the perceptive reader may begin to understand that my uncontrollable allusions to certain 'obsessions' and 'compulsions' were partly responsible for my decision in 1891 to discontinue the writing of the detective tales. As I said at the time, '[I will] slay poor Sherlock . . . even if I have to bury my banking account with him.' "

10.

A concert violinist named Norman Neruda

WHILE EN ROUTE to interrogate the constable who found the body of Enoch Drebber, Holmes explains to Watson how he knows that no *woman* could have written "Rache" on the wall: his scrutiny of the showmarks imprinted in the dusty floors of the empty house has assured him that two *men* were there at the time of the murder. Summing up, Sherlock says: "I could *read all that in the dust.*"   [my italics]

The image of the great detective reconstructing a murder by reading clues printed in the dust recalled William Shakespeare's use of the same image, expressed in identical words.

Years ago, while exploring his highly reiterative imagery, I found that Shakespeare, deeply moved by the image of a person impelled by tragedy to write in the dust, used the image over and over again in his dramas. (I believe he probably found this image in Arthur Golding's 1565 translation of Ovid's *Metamorphoses:** When the mortal maiden Io was transformed into a cow by Jupiter after he had raped her [and Juno arrived on the scene], Io met her father, and, unable to speak, she *printed her name in the dust.*)

I first noticed this strange image in *Titus Andronicus:* Poor Lavinia enters the stage with "her hands cut off, and her tongue cut out, and ravished"—and is unable to tell who has done these terrible things to her.

Shakespeare's stage direction then gives us a book image that is already familiar to us because of its later use by Mary Shelley and Doyle. ("Enter Lucius's son and Lavinia running after him, and the boy flies from her with books under his arm . . ." [he drops them] ". . . Lavinia turns over with her stumps the books which Lucius has let fall.") You will recall that Mary Shelley's Monster picked up books dropped upon the ground and that Watson did the same thing. The similarity is intensified when we note that, from an infinity of books to choose from, the respective

---

* In his *ABC of Reading,* Ezra Pound writes: ". . . Golding's *Metamorphoses,* which is the most beautiful book in the [English] language (my opinion and I suspect it was Shakespeare's) ."

authors have their characters pick up and make much of a book by an ancient Roman author. Thus "Lavinia" chooses Ovid's *Metamorphoses;* the Monster picks, among others, a copy of *Plutarch's Lives;* and Watson picks up many books, one of which is by Catullus.

When Titus Andronicus sees Lavinia's frantic business with the books he realizes that she is trying to tell him something:

Titus: Lucius, what book is that she tosseth so?
  Boy: Grandsire, 'tis Ovid's Metamorphoses,
      My mother gave it to me.
Titus: . . . so busily she turns the leaves!
      Help her: what would she find? Lavinia, what shall I read?
      This is the tragic tale of Philomel
      And treats of Tereus' treason and rape;
      And rape, I fear, was at the root of thy annoy. [Act 4, 1]

Then, at the suggestion of Marcus, the speechless Lavinia takes a stick in her mouth and writes in the dust the names of the three men who raped and mutilated her. They are immediately killed.

The best-known Shakespearean image relating to murder and murderers that is written in the dust is beautifully expressed by the imprisoned Richard II shortly before his assassination:

                 . . . of comfort no man speak!
    Let's talk of graves, and worms, and epitaphs,
    Make dust our paper, and with rainy eyes,
    Write sorrow in the bosom of *the earth.*

            .   .   .

    And tell sad stories of the *death* of kings!
    How some have been deposed, some *slain* in war,
    Some haunted by ghosts they have deposed,
    Some *poisoned* by their wives, some *sleeping killed,*
    All murdered. (Act 3, 2, 146)   [my italics]

A third example of the many others in Shakespeare's plays offers an expression of revenge written in blood in the dust. Enraged by the perfidy of the Earl of Warwick, King Edward holds out his hand and shouts:

    This hand, fast wound about your coal-black hair,
    Shall, while thy head is warm and new cut-off,

Write in the dust this sentence *with thy blood:*
'Wind-changing Warwick now can change no more!'
(3rd Part, Henry IV) [my italics]

We return to the slightly less flamboyant melodrama of *A Study in Scarlet* with its words written in blood and in the dust. From previous experience I knew that Holmes's reference to the story of a murder he has found written in the dust would be followed by a mention of some variant of the switching of the sexes and/or other sexual deviations. But this time it proved to be a very innocent one.

After divulging to Watson the precise information he'd read upon the floor of the murder chamber, Holmes abruptly changes to a subject never previously mentioned:

I've told you all I know, the rest is all surmise and conjecture. We must hurry up, for I want to go to Halle's concert to hear *Norman Neruda* this afternoon. [my italics]

The fixated Doylean coupling of murder and confusion of the sexes is contained in the name "Norman Neruda" placed next to Holmes's explanation of the murder clues printed by the shoes. Norman Neruda was not, as the name suggests, a man; nor was she a woman who chose a man's name for her public career as a violinist. She was a Czech virtuoso of the first rank named Wilma Neruda, who, after her marriage to a Swedish musician named Norman, performed as Madame Norman-Neruda, a name quite different from "Norman Neruda" given her by the always meticulous Doyle. By simply removing the hyphen from her name, Doyle, tireless *syndromist,* switched her from woman to man—making of her another Madame Dudevant, who habitually appeared in public in drag as George Sand.

In my discussion of *The Red-Headed League,* written by Doyle at about the same time, I will show that he repeats this same verbal sex transplant with the name of another violin virtuoso whom he refers to simply as: Sarasate.

11.

Sherlock Holmes's "found" advertisement and "found book"

You know my methods, apply them.

—Sherlock Holmes

WE RETURN TO THE SCENE in which Holmes and his brave companion are nervously waiting for the murderer (or his messenger) to retrieve the advertised "found" wedding ring. We have already seen how the disguised mention of *The Ring and the Book* led to a prime example of the murderous consequences of heterosexual love. In Browning's poem nine men and women were privately or legally murdered as the result of one man's mad sexual jealousy, possessiveness, and revenge.

Now we come to the predicted companion references to the required compulsive associations with (a) the switching, reversal, or confusion of the sexes and (b) transvestism.

As we roll back the story to the "waiting scene" we find Sherlock Holmes telling Watson that he'd found a printed book-plate and a name written on the flyleaf of *De Jure inter Gentes* (*The Ring and the Book*). He interrupts these casual remarks with the excited announcement: "Here comes our man now."

Watson takes over:

As he spoke there was a sharp ring at the bell. . . . We heard the servant pass along the hall, and the sharp click of the latch as she opened it.

"Does Dr. Watson live here?" asked a clear but harsh voice . . . someone began to ascend the stairs . . . there was a feeble tap at the door.

"Come in," I cried.

At my summons, *instead of the man of violence* whom we expected, *a very old and wrinkled woman* hobbled into the apartment. . . . I glanced at my companion, and his face had assumed such a disconsolate expression that it was all I could do to keep my countenance.
                                                                    [my italics]

Then, after giving the reader the automatic reference to a surprise switching of the sexes (following a book reference), Conan Doyle performs a sexual reversal once more as we learn that the "very old and wrinkled woman" is not a *woman* at all: "She" is a young actor in women's clothes, a transvestite! Later, after the nearly infallible Holmes returns from a futile chase of this same "old woman," he admits (third reversal of sexes) that he had been completely taken in: "Old woman be damned! *We were the* old *women* to be so taken in. It must have been a young man, and an active one, too, besides being an incomparable actor. The get-up was inimitable." [italics mine]

Does any reader believe that the nearly infallible Holmes, himself a master of disguise, could have been fooled by a disguised man with whom he had talked "close-up" for nearly ten minutes? Yet, significantly, Holmes was fooled twice by a transvestite performance. In *A Scandal in Bohemia,* the actress Irene Adler, dressed as a "slim youth in an ulster" walked right up to him and said, "Good night, Mr. Sherlock Holmes," and walked away unrecognized. Taken in by her bold performance, Holmes looked about vaguely and said: "I've heard that voice before. Now I wonder who the deuce it could have been?"

The transvestite comedy continues. When Holmes asks this garrulous "old crone," who claims that the lost ring belongs to her daughter, to tell him her name, she croaks:

"My name is *Sawyer*—hers is [*Sally*] *Dennis,* which *Tom Dennis* married her. . . ." [my italics]

These italicized names seem irrelevant and innocent, but when slightly rearranged they read: Tom—Sawyer—Sally seems to be a reference to the transvestite scene starring Tom Sawyer's immortal buddy, Huckleberry Finn. At first the "Tom Sawyer and Sally" seemed to refer to a scene in *Tom Sawyer,* but when I failed to find it there I realized that the devious—or mistaken —Doyle was referring to Mark Twain's other Tom Sawyer book, *Huckleberry Finn.*

While Huck and Nigger Jim are in hiding, they decide that Huck will have to go into town to learn the lay of the land. Jim dresses Huck Finn in a girl's dress, and Huck goes off to visit the Widow Douglas. But she sees through his crude transvestite performance, and when she asks him/her what his/her name is, Huck answers, "My name is Sarah Williams." The name "Sally" is, of course, the familiar form of "Sarah."

Then, following my research habit of taking nothing for

granted and looking up every name, I consulted several books about the derivation of names and found that the always surprising Conan Doyle seems not to have forgotten the Greek god Dionysus. "Dennis" is a time-eroded version of the Greek Dionysus. The transvestite connection? Robert Graves tells us in his book *The Greek Myths:*

Persephone brought him [Dionysus] to King Athamas and his wife, Ino, whom he persuaded to rear the child in the women's quarters *disguised as a girl.* . . . When he grew to manhood, Hera recognized him as Zeus's son, *despite the effeminacy* to which his education reduced him, and drove him mad also. [One of Conan Doyle's sons was named Denis.]

12.

"Murger" . . . *"Murcher"* . . . *murder*
. . . *merge in* A Study in Scarlet

THE ALLEGORICAL WHEEL of sex and guilt and punishment is kept in motion by the sex-haunted Doyle: While Sherlock Holmes is out foolishly chasing the young transvestite actor ("she is an accomplice, she will lead me to the murderer"), Watson spends three hours reading a naughty French novel, *Scènes de la vie de Bohème* (later adapted by Puccini as *La Bohème*) .

Murger's novel is about the amorous adventures of Rodolphe, the lover of the beautiful and ill-fated Mimi. Like Holmes and Watson, Rodolphe and his best (male) friend share an apartment. But unlike Baker Street's celibate pair (Watson is still a bachelor in this story) , the bohemians have many mistresses.

I read this old novel with the certainty that Doyle had mentioned it because it fitted his *syndromic* scheme. (Why else would Watson choose to read an "immoral" French novel while his friend was out chasing a young actor in women's clothes?) So I was not surprised to read that Rodolphe, imprisoned by his uncle, and his usual clothing taken away, is forced to wear an oriental woman's garment, complete with "petticoats." Later, when a girl-neighbor brings him "masculine apparel" (his words), he emerges from the avuncular prison to find that his beloved Mimi has died. (In the novels of the period, as in Hollywood later on, the immoral woman had to die as punishment for her sexual sins.) Yes, Henri Murger's *La Vie Bohème* was well chosen by Doyle; it fits his scheme perfectly.

But there is another devious, intricate, and fascinating name-clue in Doyle's story, a literary clue that binds Murger's themes of unlicensed heterosexuality and sexual deviance to the similar themes in *A Study in Scarlet:* It is a name buried in a rambling statement made by Constable Rance when he is questioned by Sherlock Holmes.

In the midst of his statement the garrulous constable mentions, with relevant irrelevancy, a fellow constable he talked with shortly before he saw the light in the "two-stoned" empty house and entered to find the dead Drebber:

> I'll tell it to ye from the beginning. My time is from ten at night to six in the morning. . . . At one o'clock it began raining, and I met *Harry Murcher*—him who has the Holland Grove beat—and we stood a'talking . . .

Since "Harry" is a well-known variant of "Henry," and "Murcher" is only a slight variation of "Murger," this gives us a merger of "Murcher" and "Murger" which places Henri Murger and his sexually ambivalent novel at the scene of the murder.

Yes, with the chronic assiduity of Charles Dickens's Mr. Dick, Conan Doyle has brought forth his own "King Charles's head" once more. Probably unconsciously, he associated the name of the book read by Watson, an innocent and playful "Charley's Aunt" charade of hankyheteroandhomosexualpanky, with his monomaniacal theme of murdered lovers.

13.

NOT TOO LONG AGO, while thinking about the story-within-a-story of *A Study in Scarlet,* another of my soliloquacities began in vagueness—and ended in astonishment.

Why does this too seem so familiar: Jefferson Hope, as hansom cab-driver, relentlessly tracks his intended victim Drebber through the intricate maze of London streets. The monstrous Drebber, interested only in getting drunk and laid, is completely unaware that Hope, a man with a sinister ulterior motive, is following him wherever he goes. Hour after hour the unflagging Hope tails Drebber and looks on as he lurches from one liquor-shop to the next, getting more and more soused. A climax is reached when Drebber is thrown out of a saloon and beaten for allegedly "insulting an honest girl." Finally, at one o'clock in the morning, Hope moves in on the helplessly drunk Drebber, takes him in his cab to an empty house for which he has made a key. When they enter, Hope lights a candle, reveals his identity with the wedding ring forced on Lucy Ferrier . . . and, at knife-point, gives his victim his choice of two pills, one of which is poison. Drebber takes the poison and dies.

Came the dawn of recognition: Of course this is familiar! And it should be instantly recognized by anyone who really knows James Joyce's *Ulysses:* The above synopsis of the tracking and murder scene from the inner story of *A Study in Scarlet,* except for the ending, is exactly like the tracking and home-taking sequences of Joyce's masterpiece.

In that great novel, begun about twenty-five years after Doyle's *A Study in Scarlet* was published, we find: On June 16, 1904, Leopold Bloom becomes obsessed with Stephen Dedalus, a descendant of the Daedalus who built the Cretan maze as a prison for the boy-and-girl-eating Minotaur. After seeing Stephen Dedalus, as Hope saw Drebber, from a hansom-cab, Bloom then tracks Dedalus through the maze of Dublin streets* from one saloon to the next and watches him get more and more drunk. The pursuing Bloom continues to follow Dedalus and observes that, exactly like Drebber, Dedalus is beaten by a young man for "insulting a girl." The similarity between pursuit incidents in Doyle's *A Study in Scarlet* and Joyce's *Ulysses* ends with the pursuer Bloom picking up the drunken Dedalus and taking him to his house at about one o'clock in the morning. Drebber is taken to an "empty house," and Bloom takes Dedalus to a house he fears is empty. (Molly, he thinks, may have gone off with "Blazes" Boylan.) He also lights a candle.

There are three Sherlock Holmes and Doyle references in

---

* In his *James Joyce and the Making of Ulysses,* Frank Budgen, to whom Joyce explained his allegorical intentions, writes, "Joyce wrote *Ulysses* with a map of Dublin . . . on which he traced the paths of all his characters. All towns (to Joyce) are labyrinths. . . . Joyce bought a game called "Labyrinth" which he played every evening with his daughter Lucia. (Doyle's "Jefferson Hope," similarly, used a map of London to make his way through the "maze of London.")

Ulysses that prove that James Joyce was consciously aware of Doyle's detective stories when he wrote the book. The first is found in the celebrated "Nighttown" scene staged in Bella Cohen's brothel. In the *Circe* chapter, while in the midst of his homoerotic hallucinations, Bloom says wistfully, "O, I so want to be a mother." When midwife Mrs. Thornton delivers him of eight gold and silver children, Bloom performs many vaudevillian miracles and then, for a fleeting instant, *actually becomes Sherlock Holmes!*

(Bloom walks on a net, covers his left eye with his left ear, passes through several walls, climbs *Nelson's Pillar,* hangs from the top ledge by his eyelids, eats twelve dozen oysters (shells included), heals several sufferers from the king's evil, *contracts his face to resemble . . . Lord Beaconsfield, Lord Byron, Wat Tyler, Moses of Egypt . . . Rip Van Winkle . . . Jean-Jacques Rousseau . . . Robinson Crusoe*—and *Sherlock Holmes.*

The second proof of Joyce's deliberate use of Doyle's *A Study in Scarlet:* When Bloom picks up the helplessly drunk Dedalus, he first takes him to a cafe frequented by hansom-cab drivers (Doyle's Hope was one). In the cafe they become conversationally involved with one Murphy, a talkative sailor. Joyce describes Bloom's reactions to the sailor:

He had meantime been taking stock of the individual before him and *Sherlockholmesing him up,* ever since he clapped eyes on him.

The third proof: After leaving the cafe, Bloom takes the still-spiflicated Stephen to his house. There, unlike Jefferson Hope, who easily enters the empty house with forged keys, Bloom cannot enter the house because he has (Joyce-Freudianly) forgotten his keys. He is forced to enter through a window.

Then James Joyce gives the reader a final indication that he has "borrowed" a Conan Doyle book: During a detailed inventory of the Bloom household, Joyce asks us to look at a bookshelf reflected in a mirror. One of the books is a volume borrowed by Leopold Bloom, Joyce's alter ego:

The Stark-Munro Letters by A. Conan Doyle, property of the City of Dublin Public Library, 106 Capel Street, lent 21 May (Whitsun Eve), due June 4, 1904, 13 days overdue (black cloth binding, bearing white letter number ticket).

Coincidentally, Doyle's story *Cyprian Overbeck Wells,* from which (I believe) Joyce borrowed the "parody of English authors" idea for his *Oxen of the Sun* chapter in *Ulysses,* takes place on the date June 4 (1886)—the same day that the "borrowed" Doyle book was due at the Dublin Public Library.

Together with these proofs of conscious awareness, we see also that Joyce brought Conan Doyle, like himself an "exiled" Dubliner, back to that city—an intricately poetic allegorical action in itself.

14.

Conan Doyle and James Joyce

(I should like to ask that Shedlock Homes person who is out for removing the roofs of our criminal classics by what *deductio ad domunum* he hopes *de tacto* to detect anything unless he happens of himself, *movibile tectu,* to have a slade off.)

—James Joyce, *Finnegans Wake,* pg. 165

My FIRST REACTION to my discovery that the great James Joyce had taken something from Conan Doyle, one of severe intellectual discomfort, was soon dispelled when I remembered that Joyce had cannibalized every kind of profound and even subcultural writing for his *Ulysses* and *Finnegans Wake.* "After all," I thought, "if he could name his last great work after a drunken hod-carrier celebrated in a lowly saloon song, why not base part of his plot for *Ulysses* upon a 'lowly detective story'?"

But, feeling rather lonely with my discovery, I consulted the more than fifty writers of biographical and critical books about James Joyce and found that only Hugh Kenner had recognized the influence of Conan Doyle on the much younger Joyce.

In his formidable and illuminating essay *From Baker Street to Eccles Street,* Professor Kenner* offers many significant philosophical, literary, cultural, and mythic similarities between Doyle and Joyce, between Sherlock Holmes and Stephen Dedalus, and

---

* *Dublin's Joyce,* Chatto & Windus, London, 1955.

between Dr. Watson (whom he equates with Dr. Doyle) and Leopold Bloom.

Though Hugh Kenner does not comment on any similarity between *Ulysses* and any Doylean story about Holmes, he does, in an opening fanfare, write:

The mythology of the nineteenth century is summed up in two stories: the partnership of Sherlock Holmes and Dr. Watson, and the tumble of Alice into a schizoid mathematician's (Carroll) womb-world. The first underlies *Ulysses* and the second *Finnegans Wake*.

Holmes and Watson epitomize humanity dissected into radiocinative violence and sentimental virtue, the latter avid of absorption into the former. So Stephen and Bloom.

Hugh Kenner sees a great resemblance between Sherlock Holmes, whom Watson calls "the most perfect reasoning and observing machine the world has ever seen," and Stephen Dedalus's similar "anarchic aesthetic" addiction to thinking and reasoning. Though Holmes is a defender of the Victorian status quo and Joyce a vehement enemy of all Victorian moral rules, they are in their intellectual habits and methods almost identical twins:

The sleuth's bric-a-brac is notorious. Stephen in the library dialogue achieves an intricate fusion between his own dilemma, Hamlet's, Shakespeare's, and the heresies of the Church, propped with analogies from Milton, Swinburne, Socrates, Maeterlinck, Drummond of Hawthornden, Brunetto Latini, St. Thomas Aquinas, and others.

"In a single novel," adds Kenner, "*The Sign of Four,* Holmes recommends Winwood Reade's *The Martyrdom of Man,* quotes Goethe twice, cites Richter and alludes to his connections with Carlyle, and talks in brilliant succession of miracle plays, medieval poetry, Stradivarius violins, the Buddhism of Ceylon, and the warship of the future, handling each as though he had made a special study of it."

To this I would add that James Joyce, like Sherlock Holmes and therefore Conan Doyle, habitually offered the tiniest objects in his environment as the clues to his greatest profundities.

15.

And his Baskerville Hound
Which, just at a word from his master
Will follow you faster and faster
And tear you limb from limb.
—T. S. Eliot, *Lines to Ralph Hodgson Esquire*

JAMES JOYCE was not the only writer of the first rank to see past the beguiling character of Sherlock Holmes to his remarkably "invisible" creator and then copy profound ideas from Conan Doyle's multileveled stories without acknowledgment.

Yale University's Grover Smith has written:* "Holmes himself would have been pleased that his adventures have several times, and not always in an ordinary manner, been useful to T. S. Eliot."

Professor Smith adds:

It has been the role of previous commentators to point out that the "grimpen where is no secure foothold" reaches Eliot's *East Coker* from the *Hound of the Baskervilles,* and it is the privilege of any reader to recognize the "Baskerville Hound" in Eliot's *Lines to Ralph Hodgson Esquire.*

But, says the professor:

A lengthier example, occurring in Eliot's *Murder in the Cathedral,* shows his debt to Conan Doyle somewhat more elaborately.

Professor Smith's remarks are an understatement. A comparison he himself makes between the "strange catechism" in Conan Doyle's *The Musgrave Ritual* and a "stichomyth" (dialogue) in *Murder in the Cathedral* shows that Eliot took not only Doyle's exact poetic language but his erudite and intricate allegorical ideas as well.

"The Musgrave Ritual," written on a scrap of paper deciphered by Holmes, is "the strange catechism to which each Musgrave had to submit when he came to man's estate." Brunton, the hapless butler-victim of Hurlstone Manor, is the first to understand that it is a clue to the great treasure hidden in the manor:

---

* *Notes and Queries,* Oct. 1948.

the long-lost crown of the decapitated Charles I. (That royal "head" is mentioned in at least six Doylean stories.)

The story of Brunton's divination of the ancient secret and Holmes's solution of the mystery comprises the top layer of *The Musgrave Ritual,* but it is the ritual itself and the courtly symbolism it contains, as revealed by Conan Doyle, that is copied almost verbatim by Eliot:

The "strange catechism" in the Sherlockian story:

"Whose was it?"
"His who is gone."
"Who shall have it?"
"He who will come."
"What was the month?"
"The sixth from the first."

. . . .

"What shall we give for it?"
"All that is ours."
"Why should we give it?"
"For the sake of the trust."

"In Eliot's play," writes Professor Smith, "the temptation of Thomas à Becket takes place immediately upon his arrival at Canterbury. The Tempters are four in number. Of them the Second urges Becket as Archbishop to submit to King Henry's will, and to recover the Chancellorship, and to exercise temporal power for the good of the Kingdom. His stichomythic exchange with Becket concerning that power runs as follows:

THOMAS
Whose was it?
TEMPTER
His who is gone.
THOMAS
Who shall have it?
TEMPTER
He who will come.
THOMAS
What shall be the month?
TEMPTER
The last from the first.
THOMAS
What shall we give for it?

TEMPTER
Pretense of priestly power.
THOMAS
Why should we give it?
TEMPTER
For the power and the glory.

Professor Smith again: "The connection between Doyle's story and *Murder in the Cathedral* is less tenuous than it seems. The 'battered and shapeless diadem' which Brunton finds by obeying the deciphered ritual 'once encircled the brows of the royal Stuarts'; it therefore signifies the secular power and is moreover 'the ancient crown of the kings of England,' so that . . . it must also once have been in the possession of King Henry II. Precisely this crown, or rather vicariously the sovereignty it represents, is offered to Becket by his Tempter. The ritual accordingly stands for the means by which the symbol of dominion is restored; and such is the use that Eliot makes of it."

When several articles like Professor Smith's appeared, all drawing attention to Eliot's seeming plagiarism of Conan Doyle, several scholars, unwilling to believe Eliot could have borrowed from Doyle, wrote to the *London Times Literary Supplement* suggesting (without proof) that both Eliot and Doyle had taken the "strange catechism" from a common literary ancestor. But Mr. Nathan Bengis of New York, a Baker Street Irregular, ended the dispute with a letter that appeared in the *Times Literary Supplement* on September 28, 1951:

CONAN DOYLE AND MR. T. S. ELIOT

Sir,—Early this year a spate of letters appeared in these columns concerning Mr. T. S. Eliot's use of the Musgrave Ritual (from Sir Arthur Conan Doyle's Sherlock Holmes story of that name) in his *Murder in the Cathedral*. There has been much speculation about this, and it has even been suggested that Mr. Eliot and Sir Arthur borrowed the Ritual from a common source.

Remembering Sherlock Holmes's warning about the danger of theorizing before one has all the evidence, I wrote to Mr. Eliot in May of this year and asked him about the matter point-blank. I quote with permission from his reply: ". . . My use of (Doyle's) *Musgrave Ritual* was deliberate and wholly conscious."

This definitive answer should, I think, end the discussion of this

much-mooted point.–Nathan L. Bengis, Keeper of the Crown, The
Musgrave Ritualists of New York.

16.

A third star witness to Doylean allegory

WHILE DEEPLY INVOLVED with Doyle's first detective story, I happened to reread Franz Kafka's *The Trial* and saw that its opening
and closing scenes bore many striking resemblances to scenes in
A Study in Scarlet. I have no direct documentary proof that Kafka
(who admitted copying from Dickens) ever read the Sherlock
Holmes story, but the partial list of similarities below obviates
(for me) any needed proof of access. It speaks for itself:

Study in Scarlet: Dr. Watson, a young bachelor living in lodgings,
awakens one day and finds that for the first time his
landlady has not sent up his breakfast.

The Trial: Joseph K., a young bachelor living in lodgings,
awakens one morning and finds that "his landlady's
cook, who always brought him his breakfast . . .
failed to appear on this occasion."

Study in Scarlet: The time factor is explained: "I arose," says the
bachelor, "somewhat earlier than usual" (but didn't
get breakfast) .

The Trial: The time factor is explained: Joseph K. says that he
arose at his usual time (8 o'clock) but didn't get his
breakfast.

Study in Scarlet: The two bachelors react to this situation with the
same emotion and physical action: Dr. Watson nar-
rates that with the "unreasonable petulance of mankind," he *"rang the bell"* to summon his landlady to
bring him his breakfast.

The Trial: Dr. Kafka, bachelor and narrator, writes that Joseph
K. "feeling put out and hungry . . . *rang the bell"*
to summon the landlady's cook to bring him his
breakfast.

Study in Scarlet: Watson is forced to look on hungrily while detective
Holmes selfishly eats breakfast.

The Trial: When Joseph K.'s breakfast is brought to him, one of
the *plainclothes policemen* (detectives) who has

come to arrest him takes away his food and eats it while the hungry Joseph K. looks on helplessly.

Study in Scarlet: While watching Holmes (*bee-keeper*) eat his "toast" (*bread*), Watson and Holmes enter into a philosophical discussion about the methods for determining guilt or innocence.

The Trial: While watching the detective who came to arrest him "dipping a slice of *bread* and butter into the *honey*-pot," Joseph K. engages the detective in an abstract discussion about Joseph K.'s possible guilt or innocence.

Study in Scarlet: In this discussion the dull-witted Watson takes an inferior intellectual position. He struggles hard but fails to comprehend the detective.

The Trial: In his discussion with the plainclothesman (detective), Joseph K. assumes an inferior position intellectually. He struggles mightily but fails to comprehend the legal situation in which he finds himself.

Study in Scarlet: A letter from *Inspector* Lestrade arrives at the Baker Street flat. Later Holmes, accompanied by Watson, meets Lestrade and discusses the mystery with him.

The Trial: Joseph K. meets and discusses his own mystery with the *Inspector,* who comes to his flat to arrest him.

Study in Scarlet: There is a running verbal conflict in the Sherlock Holmes stories between Holmes and the Inspector, unimaginative upholder of the law.

The Trial: Joseph K. argues strenuously with the Inspector, rigorous and unimaginative upholder of the law.

Study in Scarlet: We learn that the "executioner" (Hope), while forcing his victim (Drebber) to take poison, *pinions him* and holds a *knife to his throat.*

The Trial: At the end of this tragic allegory, one of *Joseph* K.'s executioners *holds him by the throat* while the other kills him with a *knife thrust into his heart.* This repeats exactly the action of Jefferson Hope. After killing Drebber, Hope finds *Joseph* Stangerson and, after a similar confrontation, *stabs him through the heart.* (Both men named *Joseph* are privately *executed in the same way.*)

Study in Scarlet: During this private "execution scene," Hope calls his victim: *"You dog!"* When the terrified Drebber stammers: "Would you murder me?" Hope screams: "There is no murder . . . who talks of murdering a *mad dog?*"

The Trial: During the closing private "execution scene" the victim Joseph K. sees his shameful plight as that of an unwanted animal; his final words are: *"Like a dog!"*

Study in Scarlet: While confronting and accusing his victim for his sexual and moral sins, Hope invokes the name of "the high God *judge*" as the present but unseen justifier of his actions. He then kills him.

The Trial: Immediately before he is killed, Joseph K. invokes the name of the punishing deity whom he has sought in vain: "Where was the *judge* whom he had never seen?"

Thus we see that *A Study in Scarlet* is a mystery (allegory) featuring a detective who goes about ferreting out the guilty and the innocent. In this story Doyle gives us a character (Hope) who, because he is morally innocent but legally guilty, is punished by death.

Compare this with Kafka's *The Trial,* also a mystery (allegory), featuring Joseph K., who is legally innocent but guilty of an unknown moral crime so heinous he must die for it. Like Holmes, described in *A Study in Scarlet* as "an amateur bloodhound," Joseph K. becomes a private sleuth who goes about seeking and interrogating witnesses and seeking clues that will establish the nature of his unknown crime as well as the facts that will free him.

I conclude from all these numerous and exact similarities that, like his contemporaries James Joyce and T. S. Eliot, Franz Kafka also saw the allegories hidden-revealed in Conan Doyle's detective stories and secretly used them as a foundation for his more serious and profound allegorical novel.

CHAPTER FIVE

The Conan Doyle syndrome and allegory in
The Red-Headed League

> *"It's pretty maddening to think that*
> *an important secret may lie here on this*
> *slip of paper and that it is beyond hu-*
> *man power to penetrate it,"* [says Wat-
> son].
> [Sherlock Holmes] . . . "I wonder,"
> said he, ". . . Perhaps there are points
> that have escaped your Machiavellian in-
> tellect. Let us consider the problem in
> the light of pure reason. *This man's ref-*
> *erence is to a book. That is our point of*
> *departure."—The Valley of Fear*
> [my italics]

1.

ALTHOUGH CONAN DOYLE wrote all of his detective stories with a
very light and charming touch, his only Sherlock Holmes comedy
per se is *The Red-Headed League,* a little masterpiece of wit and
ingenuity. It is so funny, in fact, that I assumed it would be entirely exempt from the compulsive tyranny of Conan Doyle's idea-
clusters, which, as we have seen, routinely associate normal and

deviant sexuality with crimes of passion and with murder, especially mass murder.

My assumption was wrong! When my own literary compulsions forced me to apply Conan Doyle's deciphering keys to this
brilliant comedy, I found that he had implanted his personal
allegory of revenge against his characters (and perhaps his
readers) here too, and that he had done so with a degree of
ingenuity matching anything to be found in the other Sherlockian
tales.

In this story there may be seen, also, another facet of Conan
Doyle's personal parable: some strong indications of his self-
detestation for having written the lowly detective stories which he
regarded as obstacles to his high literary ambitions.

Finally, in this same short story we shall see how its compulsive syndromic and allegorical elements offer definite clues to
Conan Doyle's final and literal act of character-assassination: The
murder of that part of himself which he called Sherlock Holmes.

First, however, let us review the manifest or top layer of this
charming little comedy: A man with fiery-red hair (Jabez Wilson)
comes to Holmes with a very bizarre tale. A not-too-successful
pawnbroker, he had recently hired a very energetic young assistant, Vincent Spaulding. Shortly afterward this new employee
brought him a newspaper advertisement offering employment to a
very special group of men:

TO THE RED-HEADED LEAGUE:
On account of the bequest of the late Ezekiah Hopkins, of
Lebanon, Pennsylvania, U.S.A., there is now another vacancy open
which entitles a member of the League to a salary of £4 a week for
purely nominal services. All red-headed men who are sound in body
and mind, and above the age of twenty-one, are eligible. Apply in person on Monday, at eleven o'clock, to Duncan Ross, at the offices of the
League, 7 Pope's Court, Fleet Street.

Needing money, and his greed aroused, Wilson allowed the
persuasive young man to conduct him to the office of "The Red-
Headed League," where a huge crowd of unemployed redheads
jammed the street and fought to get into the office. But, miracu-
lously, after his assistant pushed him through the writhing mob,
he, Jabez Wilson, was the only man hired by Duncan Ross, the
League's director!

Holmes asks Jabez Wilson, "What is he like, this Vincent Spaulding?" The pawnbroker answers, "Small, stout-built, very quick in his ways, *no hair on his face, though he's not short of thirty*. Has a white splash of acid upon his forehead." [my italics]

"Holmes sat up in his chair in considerable excitement. "I thought as much" said he. "Have you observed that *his ears were pierced for earrings?*" [my emphasis]

"Yes, sir. He told me that a gypsy had done it for him when he was a lad." [The character of a "man whose ears were pierced for earrings" appears again in *The Adventure of the Cardboard Box* in a marked context of effeminacy.]

Having duly noted that another of Doyle's effeminate characters had reared his androgynous head, I continued reading, confident that the author's harnessed compulsions would soon resume their indefatigable parade.

When the "not-over-bright" pawnbroker leaves, Sherlock asks John Watson to grant him fifty minutes of silence ("It is quite a three-pipe problem") so that he can focus his great analytical powers upon the fantastic story he has just heard. When his third pipe and fifty minutes are consumed, Holmes leaps to his feet with the air of a man who has solved a baffling problem.

But, instead of commenting on the case, he invites Watson to accompany him to a violin concert by the virtuoso Sarasate. (In my chapter on *A Study in Scarlet* I make much of the woman violinist who has a man's name (Norman Neruda). Can you, alert reader, guess why, in this story, Sherlock Holmes goes to hear Sarasate? If you do make a guess, check with me later in this chapter and see if your guess agrees with mine.)

But before they attend the concert, Holmes has some work to do. Accompanied by his constant companion and chronicler, Holmes travels across London to a mythical "Saxe-Coburg Square" for a sharp look at Mr. Wilson's pawnshop and at "Vincent Spaulding," the mysterious assistant. He stares at "the dingy *two-storied house* . . . with a lawn of weedy grass and a few clumps of faded laurel" . . . and Watson notes the "three gilt balls" over the entrance to the pawnshop.

Then, on the pretext of asking street directions, Holmes knocks on the pawnshop door, and when Spaulding, a "bright, clean-shaven fellow," appears, Holmes gives him the once-over.

As they walk away, Holmes observes: "Smart fellow that. He

is, in my judgment, the fourth smartest man in London, and for daring, I am sure that he has a claim to be third. I have known something of him before."

Watson: "Evidently Mr. Wilson's assistant counts for a good deal in this mystery of the Red-Headed League. I am sure that you inquired your way merely to see him."

"Not him."
"What then?"
"The knees of his trousers."
"And what did you see?"
"What I expected to see."

When, during the preliminary tour of inspection, Holmes discovers that directly behind the pawnshop is the City and Suburban Bank, he strongly suspects that there is a larcenous connection between the pawnshop, the bank that abuts it, and the daring (and effeminate) young Spaulding.

Holmes then invites Watson to return to Saxe-Coburg Square after the Sarasate performance: "This business is serious. . . . A considerable crime is in contemplation. . . . I have every reason to believe that we shall be in time to stop it. . . . I shall want your help tonight."

The climactic scene of this Conan-drum is staged by Doyle in the cellar of the bank,* where Holmes briefs a Scotland Yard inspector, a bank official and Watson. "Vincent Spaulding" is the alias of the notorious John Clay, a black-sheep grandson of a royal duke, a graduate of Eton and Oxford. Clay, explains Holmes, a "murderer, thief, smasher [counterfeiter], and forger," is after the £30,000 pounds of French gold that is stored in the cellar of the bank. It was Clay who planned the entire fantastic caper, created the mythical Red-Headed League, and conceived the idea of putting the gullible pawnbroker into pawn for only "four gold sovereigns a week" while he copied the *Britannica* far away from his shop. It was John Clay who was even now tunneling through the bowels of the earth from the pawnshop cellar into the bottom of the bank to steal its golden cloacal treasure.

After waiting in the pitch-dark room (the syndromic image!), "such a darkness as I have never experienced," writes Watson:

---

* Also "two-storied," main floor and basement.

Suddenly my eyes caught a glint of light. At first it was but a lurid spark upon the stone pavement. Then it lengthened out until it became a yellow line, and then, without a warning or a sound, a gash seemed to open and a hand appeared; a white almost *womanly* hand, which felt about the little area of light. [my emphasis]

I interrupt this dramatic scene to point out the obvious syndromic fact: Once again, the compulsive Doyle has performed his switching of the sexes act. Holmes and his companions sat in the darkened room expecting to see a violent man, but instead they see an effeminate hand. It is the "almost womanly hand" of John Clay, whose "ears are pierced for earrings."

Watson continues:

For a minute or more the hand, with its writhing fingers, protruded from the floor. Then it was withdrawn as suddenly as it appeared . . . its disappearance, however, was but momentary. With a rending, tearing sound, one of the broad white stones turned over on its side and left a square gaping hole. . . . over the edge there peeped a clean-cut boyish face . . . in another instant he stood at the side of the hole and was hauling after him his companion.

When the enterprising young Clay sees that a reception committee is on hand, he shouts a warning to his accomplice, who retreats down the hole, leaving his "skirts" (another transvestite indication) in the hands of the policeman.

As always, Sherlock Holmes overpowers the thief and turns him over to Scotland Yard, but he does so with the use of a very odd and revealing weapon. Before they go to this anticipated showdown with John Clay, Holmes advises Watson: "And, I say, Doctor, there may be some little danger, so kindly put your army revolver in your pocket." But Holmes carries only a peculiar, hardly adequate weapon: a *riding crop* (whip) . When Clay, seeing himself surrounded, pulls out his gun, "Holmes's hunting crop came down on the man's wrist and the pistol clinked to the floor."

With this easy and humiliating victory over the effeminate thief, the supermanly Holmes seems to be expressing a Nietzschean attitude toward women and womanly men (and perhaps to the feminine component that came out of Doyle's "inner room" in the character of John Clay). While writing this scene Conan Doyle seems to have been thinking of the line from Nietzsche: "Thou goes to woman? Do not forget thy whip."

After collaring the would-be bank robber and disposing of him, Conan Doyle's hero ends the story with a syndromic quotation from a letter to *George Sand* written by *Gustave Flaubert:* *"L'homme c'est rien—l'oeuvre c'est tout"* ("The man is nothing —the work is everything"). Later, in a more strategic context, I shall explain my reasons for emphasizing the names of Flaubert and Sand. But I am sure that the well-informed reader will guess, from what has already been said, why Doyle ended his highly ambivalent *The Red-Headed League* with a reference to George Sand.

2.

The Conan Doyle syndrome and allegory: The book-title clue

IN THIS COMEDY the required clue to Conan Doyle's personal parable or allegory is, as always, the printed or written word in the form of a book. It is the *Encyclopaedia Britannica,* itself a library of more than twenty volumes.

Since we know now that the inevitable book-clue is always a key for opening the door to the other associated elements, I carefully scrutinized the context of its first mention, which occurs in the riotous employment scene at the office of the Red-Headed League.

What exactly did I expect to find? Well, in more than a dozen stories I have noted that the first mention of a book is usually accompanied by an automatic allusion to some form of uncontrollable sexual desire, either normal or abnormal, which carries with it the image of individual or mass murder.

So now, as I scanned the frenetic employment scene, I wondered: Which form of unbridled lust or perversity bonded to murder has Conan Doyle woven into this story? But, to my surprise, there seemed to be no reference to either perversity or murder. I persisted, however, and finally found it in another" purloined letter," staring at this and every other reader from the open page.

The recognition of that plainly visible-yet-hidden "letter" came when, after much brain-racking, certain phrases, words, names, and images from the Red-Headed League's newspaper ad and from the pawnbroker's description of the frenzied mob-scene at the League's office began to seem hauntingly familiar.

I thought: The name "Ezekiah" . . . mythical founder of the mythical League . . . from Lebanon, a Biblical place . . . and "Jabez," another Biblical name . . . the dramatic scene of desperate *men and men only* who converge upon a single office where there are two men (Clay and accomplice) masquerading under false names and identities. . . . One of these men turns away the frantic mob of men because *only one is chosen.* . . .

Then a bell of Biblical recall clanged loud and clear: But of course! Doyle has taken this scene, its characters, its details, even some of its imagery and language, from the Biblical story of the destruction of Sodom and Gomorrah!

I had recognized the origin of Doyle's incident because my recently published book* contains an essay which discusses the "suppressed scene of homosexual mass madness" that preceded the annihilation of the "cities of the plain." Now as I compared the scene in *The Red-Headed League* with the awesome scene in Genesis it became quite clear to me that Conan Doyle had, in the midst of his comedy, associated a book (the *Britannica*) with an astonishing example of sexual perversity connected with mass murder. And what an ingenious association it is!

Here, for aid in understanding Doyle's allegorical use of the Biblical story, is my account of the sensational and tragic incident in the book of Genesis:

The story of Sodom and Gomorrah is a brief digressive interlude within the more important history of the patriarch Abraham, Lot's uncle and protector. (Actually, the Lot family was allowed to escape from Sodom because of Abraham's influence. Nepotism!) As God is informing Abraham, aged 99, and Sarah, 90, that a son would be born to them, He suddenly digresses to tell them that He has decided to destroy the "cities of the plain." Horrified, Abraham intercedes on behalf of all the "righteous men" who will perish with the wicked. (Nothing at all is said of the innocent women and children who also live in the doomed cities.)

There then ensues the famous—and peculiar—haggling scene in which Jehovah appears to be ill-informed and vacillating, while Abraham, a mere mortal, displays greater compassion, logic, and bargaining

* *The Confessions of a Trivialist*, Penguin Books, 1972.

skill. It is quite evident from this haggling scene that God, presumably aware of "the fall of every sparrow," did *not* know how many "righteous men" there were in the doomed five cities. This lack of "intelligence" about the condemned populations is compounded by the divine comedy of tragic errors that follows. Abraham finally persuades Him to spare the cities if "only ten good men" are found in them.

The capricious and irresolute Deity (it had to be bad writing on the part of the chroniclers!) then reveals his uncertainty in the manner of all later chief executives: He sends a fact-finding team of angels down to Sodom to look for the required quorum of ten good men.

My essay continues:

The two angels (disguised as men) arrived at the main gate of the city and found Lot, their contact man, waiting for them. He recognized them, bowed low, and brought them to his house as guests. A feast was prepared for them including matzohs specially baked for the occasion. But before the angelic guests could retire for the night, an astonishing scene of homosexual mass-madness was enacted which immediately decided the fate of Sodom, Gomorrah, and the other cities of the plain.

Here is the part of the Biblical story borrowed by Conan Doyle for use in *The Red-Headed League:*

But before they lay down, *the men of the city,* even *the men of Sodom, compassed the house round,* both old and young, all the people *from every quarter.*

And they called out unto Lot and said unto him, Where are the men which came unto you this night? Bring them out so that we may *know* them. [In the *Bible* the word "know" means sexual intercourse.]

The Biblical story then tells us that Lot acted quickly to head off the greatest pederastic gang-bang in all recorded history. He went out, shut the door behind, and faced the mob with these unfatherly words: "I pray you, brethren, do not so wickedly. I have two daughters which have never *known* men; let me, I pray you, bring them forth unto you, and do ye unto them as is good in your eyes; only unto these men do nothing: for therefore came they under the shadow of my roof."

The Biblical legend builds to a very strange climax: When the sex-crazed mob rejects Lot's dreadful and unfatherly offer (they madly desire only the beautiful androgynous angels within) and insanely surge up to the door of Lot's house to smash their way in, the angels belatedly take action. In a masterly pioneering demonstration of mob control they stop the onrushing stampede of Sodomites by blinding all of them.

The rest of the legendary story is fairly well known. The besieged, beleaguered and almost buggered angels of God take Lot and his family by the hand and lead them out of the doomed city, then leave them to find their way to the spared city of Zoar. God then issues his famous order, "Look not behind thee," and proceeds to the genocidal act: "Then the Lord rained upon Sodom and Gomorrah brimstone and fire. . . . and He overthrew those cities, and all the plain, and all the inhabitants of the cities, and that which grew upon the ground." Then, after the angels of God take Lot and his family out of Sodom, the celebrated passage: "But his wife looked back from behind him and she became a pillar of salt."

That Conan Doyle had this story clearly in mind when he wrote the employment scene in his *The Red-Headed League* becomes obvious when we read that the pawnbroker "looks back" in anguish at his experience. He tells the great detective:

I never hope to see such a sight again, Mr. Holmes. From *north, south, east and west, every man* . . . had tramped *into the city.* . . . Fleet Street was *choked with red-headed men* and Pope's Court looked like a coster's orange barrow. I would not have thought there were so many in the whole country as were brought together by that single advertisement.

When his words are compared with those from Genesis, "The *men from the city of Sodom compassed the house,* both young and old, *from every quarter,*" we see that the scenes and verbal imagery are identical. In both Sodom and London masses of desperate *men* and *men only* arrive from the four corners of the city to converge upon a single house, where they strive to "know" two disguised men within the house.

When placed side by side, the resemblances are even more striking:

Genesis: "*from every quarter.*"
Doyle: "*from north, south, east, and west.*"

Genesis: "*the men of the city* . . . *all* the people."
Doyle: "*Every man* . . . tramped *into the city.*"

Genesis: The pederastic men of Sodom fight through the crowd desiring to forcibly enter the *orifices* of the angels within, who are disguised as men.

Doyle: Similarly, the men of London fight their way through crowds seeking to enter the *office,* or as the old medical joke has it, the *orifice,* where two disguised men sit.

Genesis: *Only one man* is saved, the rest are condemned.

Doyle: *Only one man* is chosen, the rest are turned away.

3.

Scribe, n., one who serves as a penman or a copyist. One of the Palestinean scholars and teachers of Jewish law and tradition from the 5th Century B.C. to the 1st Century A.D. who transcribed, edited, and interpreted the law.

—*Random House Dictionary*

CONAN DOYLE's astounding travesty of the Old Testament story of Sodom and Gomorrah and his habitual use of proper names to convey multiple meanings suggest that he probably chose the Biblical name "Ezekiah" (Hopkins) for the mythical founder of the mythical Red-Headed League, and the name "Jabez" (Wilson), the copyist, with careful allegorical intent. A glance into William Smith's *Bible Dictionary* (1865) has verified this guess. Doyle selected the name "Ezekiah" because the Biblical King Ezekiah, or Hezekiah, employed a large corps of rabbinical scribes to make the first accurate, definitive copies of the written and oral Talmudic commentaries on the Bible.

The name "Jabez" (Wilson), whom the thief John Clay hired with "Ezekiah Hopkins's bequest" to serve as a copyist (scribe), is also Biblical. Mr. Smith tells us that "Jabez" was the "town where dwelt the scribes" (of King Ezekiah).

These facts suggest that in Doyle's original conception of this story, the pawnbroker was probably hired by the totally immoral John Clay to copy the Holy Bible (which begins with Genesis) and that Doyle changed it to the *Britannica* to avoid offending his pious Victorian readers.

4.

CONAN DOYLE's pawnbroker-turned-copyist reminds one of the three great victim-copyist clerks of nineteenth-century fiction: Akaky Akakyevich, the doomed copyist in Gogol's masterpiece *The Overcoat* (1842) ; Nemo, the sorrow- and drug-destroyed copyist in Dickens's *Bleak House* (1852), near whose body pawn tickets were found; and Herman Melville's great *Bartleby the Scrivener* (scribe) (1853), who dies of voluntary starvation after refusing to copy or proofread his employer's law briefs.

5.

Three friends of Oscar Wilde in The Red-Headed League

AFTER TELLING SHERLOCK HOLMES how he came to be hired by the fantastic but generous League, the bewildered pawnbroker says, unhappily, "And then suddenly the whole business came to an end."

"To an end?"
"Yes, sir. And no later than this morning. I went to my work as usual at ten o'clock, but the door was shut and locked, with a little square of cardboard hammered to the middle of the panel with a tack. Here it is, and you can read it for yourselves:

THE RED-HEADED LEAGUE
IS
DISSOLVED
October 9, 1890

Jabez Wilson then says that, "staggered" by this sudden, unexplained loss of his sinecure, he searched for "Duncan Ross," the League's director, but could find no trace of him. "Finally I went to the landlord . . . to ask him if he could tell me what had become of the Red-Headed League. He said that he had never heard of such a body. Then I asked him who Duncan Ross was. He said the name was new to him."

" 'Well,' I said, 'the gentleman in No 4.' "

"What, the red-headed man?"

" 'Oh,' said he, 'his name was *William Morris* . . . he moved out
yesterday.' "   [my italics]

The names Duncan Ross and William Morris, especially the
latter, mentioned in the context of what I had already discovered
in this story, sent me into an analytical reverie, which followed
this approximate line:

This time the printed or written syndrome indicator is a sign,
probably hand-lettered by John Clay or Duncan Ross. Therefore,
what follows this sign, the rigid formula insists, will be one or
more allusions to some form of forbidden sexuality linked to
images of mass murder. Well, we already have that, since the sign
is posted on the door of the Red-Headed League's office, where
the employment scene, a parody of the thwarted angel-rape incident at Sodom (mass murders), was staged by Clay and Ross
. . . who certainly resemble the androgynous angels nearly buggered by the Sodomites. This Duncan Ross, a red-head, not only
is the "gunsel" of John Clay, but also calls himself "William Morris." There *was* a William Morris, a famous Pre-Raphaelite painter,
publisher of the Kelmscott Press books, weaver, inventor of the
Morris chair . . . a friend of Oscar Wilde's, I think. Some advertising cards in my collection show Oscar Wilde during his lecture
tour of the United States in 1882. He was sent by D'Oyly Carte as
advance man for Gilbert and Sullivan's *Patience,* said to be based
on Oscar Wilde's gay "aestheticism" at Oxford University. The
connection between Wilde and Morris? Oscar had a wonderful gag
he pulled whenever he entered the ugly homes of the American
nouveau riche. He would pretend to swoon, then pull out of his
pocket a swatch of exquisite brocade woven by William Morris
and gaze at it until its great beauty overcame the ugliness of the
American surroundings. He called it his aesthetic antidote. And
the name Duncan Ross sounds quite like Robert Ross, the intimate friend of Oscar Wilde involved in Wilde's disastrous scandal.

"Did Conan Doyle know of Oscar Wilde? Did he use the names
of Wilde's friends as an inside joke to tip off his contemporary
readers to the effeminacy of Clay and Ross in his *The Red-Headed
League*—as he used the prejudicial Victorian image of Friedrich
Nietzsche in the creation of his villains Moriarty and Moran? But

of course Doyle knew about Oscar Wilde! When he wrote *The Red-Headed League* in 1891, everyone knew about Wilde. He was the most talked-about personality in England! . . .

My curiosity and Doyle-hunting suspicions aroused to a high pitch, off I went to the library for some biographies of Oscar Wilde. Within minutes they informed me that Conan Doyle's "William Morris" (alias "Duncan Ross") and "John Clay" referred to two of Oscar Wilde's most intimate friends.

Doyle's red-headed William Morris was undoubtedly based on the William Morris who gave Wilde his "aesthetic antidote" when Oscar became an aesthetic champion of the Pre-Raphaelite group led by Morris. The extremely close friendship between Morris and Wilde is described in a letter written by George Bernard Shaw to Frank Harris. Shaw, referring to Oscar's conversational genius and great personal charm, says, "I can understand why William Morris, when he was dying slowly, enjoyed a visit from Wilde more than anyone else." (William Morris was a contributor to the *Encyclopaedia Britannica*.)

Duncan Ross? His name is, I believe, Conan Doyle's cunning reference to Robert Ross, who was, as St. John Ervine writes,* "Wilde's closest friend until he was superseded by Lord Alfred Douglas." Ervine also identifies Robert Ross as the "original" of Lord Henry Wotton, the Mephisto of Wilde's Faustian novel, *The Picture of Dorian Gray*.

After calling Robert Ross, whom he hates, a "smooth effeminate man," and a "small bunched-up sodomite," St. John Ervine climaxes his attack with this remarkable and revolting Freudian metaphor: "It must suffice to say that when he (Wilde) stepped up to the swill-tub, full of husks that swine do eat, it was Robert Ross who showed him the way." (Remember the phallic corn husks in William Faulkner's *Sanctuary?*)

But Robert Ross and William Morris are not the only intimate friends of Oscar Wilde employed by Conan Doyle as shadowy exemplars for the saucy villains of *The Red-Headed League*. In Frank Harris's biography of Wilde, I found that the name bestowed by Doyle on the "fourth smartest man in London," John Clay, is almost identical with that of John Gray, another intimate friend of Wilde's, and the man supposed by many to be the origi-

---

* Biography of Wilde.

nal of Dorian, the perverse central character in *The Picture of Dorian Gray*. Frank Harris, who knew all of the members of Wilde's circle, reports:

> One day I met a handsome youth in [Wilde's] company named John Gray, and I could not wonder that Oscar found him interesting, for Gray not only had great personal distinction, but charming manners and a marked poetic gift, a much greater gift than Oscar possessed. He had, besides, an eager, curious mind, and of course found extraordinary stimulus in Oscar's talk.
>
> But no sooner did Oscar publish *Dorian Gray* than ill-informed and worse-minded persons went about saying that the eponymous hero of the book was John Gray, though *Dorian Gray* was written before Oscar had met or heard of John Gray. One cannot help admitting that this was partly Oscar's fault. In talk he often alluded to John Gray as his hero "Dorian." It is just another instance of the challenging contempt he began to use about this time in answer to the inventions of hatred.

The possibility that Conan Doyle may have been thinking of the intimate friends of Oscar Wilde when he created John Clay, Duncan Ross, and William Morris seemed to me quite unbelievable until I continued to read the biographies of both men and found that shortly before he wrote *The Red-Headed League,* Conan Doyle actually met Oscar Wilde!

The two entirely dissimilar authors (and men) met several years before Wilde was attacked for his flaunted homosexuality, and Doyle, though respectful of Wilde's great talents, carefully and tactfully emphasizes that their two meetings and brief correspondence were entirely impersonal and professional.*

In his excellent biography of Wilde, Hesketh Pearson describes their meetings: "A curious conjunction in the history of English literature is recorded by Conan Doyle, then an unsuccessful doctor and almost unknown writer who traveled from Southsea to London in order to dine with a representative from Lippincott, the American publisher. His fellow guests were an Irish M.P. named Gill and Oscar Wilde, who immediately put Doyle at ease

---

* Though Doyle describes his meetings with Wilde, John Dickson Carr does not mention them in his biography of Doyle. Furthermore, Wilde's name is not included in a list of Doyle's correspondents. Carr indicates that he wrote his biography with the helpful cooperation of Conan Doyle's son Adrian.

by praising Doyle's first historical romance, *Micah Clark*. Wilde's conversation left an indelible impression on Doyle. In his *Memories and Adventures,* written forty years later (1924) Doyle wrote, "It was a golden evening for me. [Wilde] towered above us all, and yet had the art of seeming to be interested in all that we could say. He took as well as gave, but what he gave was unique."

Hesketh Pearson continues:

Doyle gives us one of Wilde's impromptus. They were discussing the commonly held view that the good fortune of one's friends makes one discontented. Said Wilde: "The devil was once crossing the Libyan desert, and he came upon a spot where a number of small fiends were tormenting a holy hermit. The sainted man easily shook off their evil suggestions. The devil watched their failure, and then stepped forward to give them a lesson. "What you do is too crude," he said. "Permit me for a moment." With that he whispered to the holy man: "Your brother has just been made the Bishop of Alexandria." A scowl of malignant jealousy at once clouded the serene face of the hermit. "That," said the devil to his imps, "is the sort of thing I should recommend." As a result of that meeting, Doyle wrote the second Sherlock Holmes story *The Sign of Four* for Lippincott's, and Wilde, *The Picture of Dorian Gray.*

In his autobiography Doyle recalls: "When his little book [*Dorian Gray*] came out, I wrote telling him what I thought of it. His letter is worth reproducing as showing the *true* Wilde. I omit the early part in which he comments on my work in too generous terms:"

Between me and life there is a mist of words always. I throw probability out the window for the sake of a phrase, and the chance of an epigram makes me desert the truth. Still I do aim at making a work of art, and I am really delighted that you think my treatment subtle and artistically good. The newspapers seem to me written by the prurient for the Philistines. I cannot understand how they treat *Dorian Gray* as immoral. My difficulty was to keep the inherent moral subordinate to the artistic and dramatic effect, and it seems to me that the moral is too obvious.

I have included all the above Conan Doyle–Oscar Wilde material for its great intrinsic value, to show the fairness and objectivity of Conan Doyle, and because, as Hesketh Pearson puts it, it shows the "indelible impression" left by Oscar Wilde on his bedazzled dinner-partner—an impression that found its literary expression in three Sherlock Holmes stories. First, in the story commissioned at the "historic" dinner, *The Sign of Four,* in which Oscar Wilde, his aestheticism, a couple of his epigrams, and even a salient facial feature, reappear in one of its most amusing characters. In *The Red-Headed League,* as we have seen, two of Wilde's closest friends may be glimpsed as gay criminals. In the third, *The Adventure of the Empty House,* the "ghost" of Oscar Wilde (he died three years before the story was published) returns to associate itself with the famous "wax dummy" of Holmes shot at by Sebastian Moran and to merge its ectoplasmic self with that of the reincarnated spirit of Nietzsche-Dionysus!

6.

Oscar Wilde as Thaddeus Sholto in The Sign of Four

The Sign of Four, commissioned during the same Lippincottian meeting that also gave birth to *The Picture of Dorian Gray* and written later, begins with the arrival at Holmes's consulting room of the lovely Mary Morstan, later the wife of Dr. Watson.

She tells him that each year since her father's death six years before, she has received a single pearl of great value from an unknown benefactor. Now, she has received a very frightening anonymous letter, probably from the same unknown person:

Be at the third pillar from the left outside the Lyceum Theatre tonight at seven o'clock. If you are distrustful bring two friends. You are a wronged woman and shall have justice. Do not bring police. If you do all will be in vain. Your unknown friend.

At the Lyceum Theatre Miss Morstan, Holmes, and Watson are met by a man who takes them on a long cab ride through London's West End and out to a suburban street of abandoned two-storied houses. (With this mention of a letter and two-storied houses Conan Doyle is signaling: Syndrome! Allegory!)

The mysterious guide takes Miss Morstan and her invited "two friends" to the only occupied house on that desolate street. They are admitted by a "Hindoo servant, clad in a yellow turban, white loose-fitting clothes and a yellow sash." This highly exotic oriental leads them "down a sordid and common passage, ill-lit and worse furnished" into a magnificent apartment which, as Watson says: "In that sorry house looked as out of place as a diamond of the first water in a setting of brass."

In that *Arabian Nights* setting they meet the author of the anonymous note sent to Mary Morstan: He is Thaddeus Sholto, a superaesthete who talks like Oscar Wilde and who even has several physical features which clearly identify him as the man whom Conan Doyle called "the champion of aestheticism."

The obviously effeminate and effete Sholto reveals himself as a caricature of Wilde with his opening remarks:

Pray step into my sanctum. A small place, miss, but furnished to my liking, *an oasis of art in the howling desert* of London. [my italics]

This is an obvious parody of a widely quoted epigram uttered by Oscar Wilde during his 1882 lecture tour of the United States: "The American woman? She is *a charming oasis in the bewildering desert* of commonsense." [my italics]

Sholto then apologizes to his visitors for his devious method of bringing them to his palace of exquisiteness: "You will excuse these precautions, but I am a man of retiring, and I might say refined, tastes, and *there is nothing more unaesthetic than a policeman.*" [my italics]

This is pure Wilde! It is probably Doyle's sly and ribald reference to the perennial joke about Oscar Wilde's visit to a brothel, first heard by me in Cleveland, Ohio's Glenville High School:

Oscar Wilde went to this joint. The madame said: "Do you want a blonde?" Oscar Wilde said: "No, thank you, I'm so *bored* with blondes." So the madame said: "How about a red-head?" "No," said Oscar, "I'm so *bored* with red-heads." "Well, then," said the madame, "can I bring you a brunette?" When Oscar said: "But I'm so *bored* with brunettes," she got mad and said: "Oh, I know what *you* want! Well, I don't run *that* kind of house! If you don't get the hell out of here, I'll call a policeman!" And Oscar Wilde said: "But I'm so *bored with policemen!*"

After his self-as-Wilde identifications, the garrulous Sholto ends his monologue with some remarks about his painting collection, remarks that seem pointless until one realizes that the entire parody of Wilde was written by Doyle for the sake of his final jokes about Wilde's well-known sexual preferences:

I may call myself a patron of the arts. *That is my weakness.* That landscape is a genuine Corot (core-oh), and though a connoisseur might perhaps throw a doubt upon that Salvatore Rosa, *there cannot be the slightest doubt about the Bouguereau* (bugger-oh). I am partial to the *French* (orogenital, fellatio) *school.*

[my emphases and interpolations]

All of this reminds me of the sadder joke about the tragic Wilde that also circulated in Cleveland during the 1940s:

After Oscar Wilde was released from prison, he left England on the channel boat, and, as the boat sailed away from the shore, Wilde looked back (like Lot's wife) and said: "I sure hate to leave my friends' behind."

In *The Red-Headed League,* we find another Wildean character who disdainfully rejects a physical contact with a policeman. When Peter Jones, described by Holmes as "official police agent . . . an absolute imbecile, but brave in his profession," steps forward to arrest the gay John Clay (John Gray), he is told: "I beg that you will not touch me with your filthy hands."

After reading the detailed inventory of Sholto's too, too utterly Wildean furnishings, we return to the author's description of Sholto and find that the mischievous Doyle has given him several of Oscar Wilde's best-known facial features: his "Hapsburg lip," his noticeably bad teeth, and his habit of trying to conceal them.

In Hesketh Pearson's biography of Wilde, we read: "[Wilde] had *thick, purple-tinged sensual lips, uneven discoloured teeth.* . . . it was noticed that when talking *he frequently put a bent finger over his mouth* which showed that he was *conscious of his unattractive teeth."* [my italics]

When this is compared with Conan Doyle's description of Thaddeus Sholto, it becomes quite obvious that Doyle was thinking of the Wilde he spent an evening with shortly before he wrote, in *The Sign of Four:* "Nature had given him [Sholto] a *pendulous lip,* and a too-visible line of *yellow and irregular teeth,* which *he feebly strove to conceal by constantly passing his hand over the lower part of his face."* [my italics]

7.

Herman Melville's Redburn (*1849*)
and Doyle's The Sign of Four (*1890*)

MY MAIN CONCERN while thinking and writing about Sherlock Holmes's visit to Thaddeus Sholto was the discovered Oscar Wilde resemblances. But as I reviewed that humorous incident for perhaps the tenth time I found that it closely resembled the chapter "A Mysterious Night in London" in Melville's early sea story, *Redburn.**

Wellingborough Redburn, an American sailor lad, meets a gay young Englishman, Harry Bolton, in Liverpool. While Redburn's ship is being loaded with emigrants and supplies for the westward voyage, Harry Bolton persuades Redburn to go to London with him on a very secretive, never-explained errand. Upon arrival in London at night, Bolton hires a cab and orders the driver to a mysterious and luxurious "Aladdin's Palace."

When the two visits are placed side by side, it soon becomes obvious that Conan Doyle copied many of the details, major and minor, of his incident from *Redburn,* along with some of Melville's exact descriptive language.

Some of the similarities: In both stories we have a *naive narrator* (Redburn and Dr. Watson) who is *taken on a mysterious cab-ride* at night through *London's West End* to an *unknown destination*. In both instances the narrator is unfamiliar with the streets and neighborhoods he traverses, but a *companion knows exactly where they are and where they are going*. In both stories several similar details of the cab-ride are similarly described: In *Redburn,* for example, the *cab* "rattled . . . *through sumptuous squares*"; and in Doyle's story the *cab* "*rattled through squares*."

Upon arrival at the "unknown place" the naive narrator in each story fails to see that it is a gay residence or establishment. In *Redburn* the rendezvous is obviously (obvious to all but Redburn) a gay club, or house of assignation for men only. Redburn describes the brilliant apartment in detail. A table supported by

---

* In his *Through the Magic Door,* Doyle expresses his great admiration for Melville's novels.

carved "turbaned servants," a *"man* in charge" *whose head resembles an* "almond *tree* in blossom," and a *collection of pictures* are described in detail as being *of a homoerotic nature.* Redburn is offered *"yellow wine."*

We find the same elements in Doyle's *The Sign of Four:* Sholto's *"apartment"* (the same word) contains the images of a *"turbaned . . . servant,"* the *offer of* "Tokay" *(yellow wine)* ; a *man* (Sholto) who is *compared,* not to an *"almond tree,"* but *to a "fir tree,"* and who *describes a collection of pictures* using lewd puns like "Bouguereau" (bugger-oh) to remind the reader of Oscar Wilde's perversity.

The strong resemblance between Melville's Bolton and Doyle's Sholto (an odd name) is increased when the two names are placed side by side:

B O L T O N
S H O L T O

The literary and nautical links between Herman Melville and Conan Doyle are most interesting. Herman Melville gained his knowledge of the sea as a sailor on a transatlantic passenger ship and then aboard a whaler and a military frigate. Conan Doyle worked as a ship's doctor on an Arctic whaler and then on a passenger ship to Africa; he based several of his early non-Sherlockian stories on these experiences.

The reader interested in the genesis of literary ideas might wish to read Conan Doyle's early story *J. Habakuk Jephson's Statement* and see that Doyle has joined the true-life story of the famous derelict ship *Marie Celeste* to a flagrant copy of another Melville sea story forgotten at that time (1880s) by the public but well-remembered by Doyle: *Benito Cereno.*

8.

Oscar Wilde in The Adventure of the Empty House *(1903)*

IN THIS STORY, written three years after Wilde's death and about fifteen years after he had met Wilde and the editor who commissioned his *The Sign of Four* and Wilde's *Picture of Dorian Gray,* I have found that Conan Doyle still had Wilde and his novel vividly in mind when he created the famous "wax portrait" of

Sherlock Holmes and its assailant, the new character, Colonel Sebastian Moran. (*The Sign of Four* appeared a year later than the first publication of *Dorian Gray* in *Lippincott's Magazine*.)

But first, to set the stage for this "discovery," we must return to the moment after Holmes's resurrection and joyous reunion with his old friend. He explains that he had been forced into his prolonged (and secret) exile because Moran, Professor Moriarty's "bosom friend," henchman, and successor, had witnessed Moriarty's death in the Reichenbach Falls and had been trying to kill Holmes ever since. But now, says Sherlock, he has returned to London to face an inevitable showdown with this terrible enemy.

He then invites his own bosom friend to join him in a mysterious "piece of work for us tonight . . . at half past nine, when we start the adventure of the empty house."

En route to that scene of anticipated crime, Watson, excited by this resumption of his life of adventure with Holmes, reflects: "I know not what *wild beast* we are to hunt down." (I have drawn attention to the words *wild* and *beast* because, though meaningless in themselves, they are the first links in the chain of verbal clues that reveal the presence of Oscar Wilde in this adventure.)

Upon their arrival at the unoccupied house Holmes explains that they have come to set up an ambush for Moran. "That is the man who is after me, Watson, and that is the man who is unaware that I am after him."

Now we come to the molded-wax portrait of Sherlock Holmes: As they crouch in the darkest corner of the *dark room* (the usual allegorical setting for Conan Doyle's psychotheater) Holmes whispers:

"Do you know where we are?"

"Surely that is Baker Street," I answered, staring through the dim window.

"Exactly. We are in Camden House, which stands opposite our old quarters."

"But why are we here?"

"Because it commands so excellent a view of that old pile."

Sherlock Holmes then dramatically presents his wax portrait. "May I trouble you, my dear Watson, to draw a little closer to the window, taking every precaution not to show yourself, and then to look up at our old rooms—the starting point of so many of your fairy-tales? We will see if my three years of absence have taken away my power to surprise you."

(I believe that Conan Doyle makes this disparaging reference to his Sherlock Holmes stories as "fairy-tales" for several reasons related to his decision to quit writing them. He saw them as "dream-stories" or "fairy-tales," far inferior to his historical novels. Also, Oscar Wilde wrote *The Happy Prince,* a book of fairy-tales.)

As the master of ceremonies in this suspenseful scene, Holmes continues his rather boastful presentation of the wax portrait, and Watson writes:

I crept forward and looked across to the familiar window. As my eyes fell upon it, I gave a gasp and cry of amazement. The blind was down, and a strong light was burning in the room. The shadow of the man who was seated in a chair within was thrown in hard, black outline upon the luminous screen of the window.

There was no mistaking the poise of the head, the squareness of the shoulders, the sharpness of the features. The face was turned half-round and the effect was that of one of the black silhouettes which our grandparents loved to frame. It was a perfect reproduction of Holmes. So amazed was I that I threw out my hand to make sure that the man himself was standing beside me. He was quivering with silent laughter.

"Well?" said he.

"Good heavens!" I cried. "It is marvelous!"

"The credit [says Holmes later] is due to *Oscar* Meunier, of Grenoble, who spent some days in doing the moulding. It is a bust in wax."

I have stressed the name *Oscar* for reasons that must be obvious by now. When added to the previous mention of Sebastian Moran as a "wild beast,"* we have "Oscar" "wild beast." But that is only the beginning: the subsequent references to Oscar Wilde are the clinchers.

Later, after they have waited in the syndromically dark room for a very long time, the expected man of violence enters, and, unaware that Holmes and Watson are lying in ambush, he assembles an airgun and fires at the shadow cast upon the window by the wax bust of Holmes. There is a "tinkle of glass" as the window shatters; and then, with the help of Watson, Holmes overpowers Moran and hands him over to the police.

---

* As we shall see, the word "beast," in this context, implies bestiality or sodomy.

Now, confident that the recurring image of men waiting in the dark for a murderer to arrive would be harnessed to one or more references to some form of sexual deviation, I looked for and found it in the person of a transmogrified Oscar Wilde.

This account of Sebastian Moran's futile and funny attack upon the decoy wax portrait of the foxy Holmes reminded me vaguely of Oscar Wilde's *The Picture of Dorian Gray*. Then further thoughts about the historic meeting of Doyle and Wilde, their brief correspondence, and the actual presence of Wilde and his friends in Conan Doyle's *The Red-Headed League* and *The Sign of Four* led me to a comparative study of *The Picture of Dorian Gray* and *The Adventure of the Empty House*.

As I read Wilde's compelling neo-Gothic tale of the accursed oil portrait and compared it with the incident of the molded-wax portrait in Doyle's story, the two portrait images, as in a film montage, began to dissolve into each other to form an almost perfect single image.

The resemblances are truly remarkable. It was the literary artist named *Oscar* Wilde—who died in *France* three years before Doyle wrote his story—who created *The Picture of Dorian Gray,* and it is an *Oscar* Meunier, an artist of Grenoble, *France,* who "moulds" (a copying method) the *portrait of Sherlock Holmes.*

These two Oscarian portraits serve identical purposes: They are used in both stories as *surrogate artistic targets which accept the murderous attacks intended for the man they portray.* The exact similarity continues: In both stories *the attack upon the surrogate portrait fails and boomerangs upon the attacker.* Dorian Gray is killed by his own knife-thrust when he attacks the portrait. In Doyle's *The Adventure of the Empty House,* the would-be killer Moran is caught and presumably executed, not for his attempted murder of Holmes but for his slaying of Robert Adair. As in *Dorian Gray,* the portrait of Holmes, "a perfect facsimile," is undamaged except for a little hole through its "brain."

Afterthought: Actually, like Dorian Gray, Sherlock Holmes attacked his own image. *He* posed for the "perfect facsimile" of himself, *he* bought it, *he* set it up as a decoy, and it was *he* who tricked Moran into shooting at the deceptive image.

The readers who have chosen to join me in the ferreting out of Conan Doyle's allegorical game will, I'm sure, now look for the printed- or written-word mention which invariably accompanies the sex and murder elements contained in Wilde's *Dorian Gray*. (Dorian is responsible for the death of a beautiful girl, and he murders an obviously homosexual man, the painter Hallward.) If they do look for such a clue, they will find it stated by Holmes immediately before Watson gazes at the "Oscarian wax portrait."

The ever-revealing Sherlock, referring to the fact that Watson is the chronicler of all but two of his adventures, offers the signaling words:

May I trouble you, my dear Watson, taking every precaution not to show yourself . . . to *look up at our old rooms—the starting point of so many of your fairy-tales?*

This syndromic allusion to the previous twenty-four Sherlock Holmes tales as "fairy-tales" is, I need hardly say, a fitting prelude to the images which cluster around *The Picture of Dorian Gray* and its crucified "fairy" author.

9.

Oscar Wilde as Sebastian Moran

I HAVE SHOWN EARLIER that Conan Doyle borrowed the exact imagery, words and opera costume from Shuré's description of Nietzsche for his own description of Colonel Sebastian Moran. Now, after due consideration, I offer the evidence for my belief that Doyle patterned the biography of Sebastian Moran on some facts in the life of Wilde—and for my belief that Moran's first name was also borrowed from Wilde. No, not from Oscar Fingal O'Flahertie Wills Wilde. Doyle borrowed it from Wilde's self-pitying *nom du exile*.

Six years before Doyle thought of calling the villainous Moran "Sebastian," Oscar Wilde emerged from prison and said that henceforth he wished to be called Sebastian Melmoth. He took the surname from *Melmoth the Wanderer*, the Gothic tale of horror written by his great-uncle Robert Maturin. Melmoth, whose ancient portrait reveals that he was the possessor of eternal youth (as was the later Dorian Gray!), is doomed to wander until he can find someone to assume his burden of eternal suffering.

Several of his biographers surmise that Wilde took the name Sebastian from the Christian martyr who is usually depicted as naked and shot full of arrows. Did the self-dramatizing Wilde see himself as a Sebastian martyred by a flight of Cupid's deviant arrows? As a man fatally wounded by the venereally infected arrows of Eros? I sadly think so. As his friend Frank Harris and the more modern biographies tell us, Oscar Wilde died of the complications of paresis.

A comparison between the composite Oscar Wilde–Sebastian Melmoth and Sebastian Moran, as he is described by Holmes, yields these exact similarities:

1. Both have the same initials: S. M.
2. Both are Irish: Moran and Wilde.
3. Both are sons of Irish noblemen: Wilde was the son of Sir William Wilde. Sebastian Moran was the son of Sir Augustus Moran.
4. Both Wilde and Moran are graduates of Oxford University.
5. Wilde was born in Dublin but spent the last half of his life in London. Moran's Irish family came to London, where Sebastian was born. (Doyle's family left Dublin in 1818 for Scotland and never returned.)
6. Wilde-Melmoth and Sebastian Moran were both authors. Moran, says Holmes, wrote two books about hunting in the Himalayas.
7. Both Sebastians were outcasts from society.
8. Both lived underground criminal lives.
9. Both were imprisoned as a result of their involvement in a scandal arising from a relationship with a nobleman's son: Wilde with Lord Alfred Douglas, son of the Marquess of Queensberry. And, as Watson narrates, Sebastian Moran killed Robert Adair, son of the Earl of Maynooth, because Adair threatened to ruin him for cheating at cards.

Also, Conan Doyle, former eye doctor, may have identified with Wilde, not only because he met him and admired his work, but because he knew, as everyone did, that Oscar's father, Sir William Wilde, was also an eye doctor and the author of an authoritative textbook on the diseases of the eye.

10.

Conan Doyle himself as a character in
The Red-Headed League, *etc.*

> . . . and [Judas] said unto [the high
> priests], What will ye give me, and I de-
> liver him unto you? And they cove-
> nanted him *thirty pieces of silver.* And
> from that time he sought the oppor-
> tunity to betray him.   [my italics]
> —*Matthew*, 26:14

THE REALIZATION THAT CONAN DOYLE had offered an option to
the reader to enjoy his brilliant detective stories as bright entertainment or as portals to his hidden personal parables has led me
to many new discoveries, all of which, in turn, have verified the
author's allegorical intentions.

Recently, with these alternatives in mind, I reviewed all the
stories written by Doyle *before* the great encounter at Reichenbach Falls. I found, when halfway through *The Red-Headed
League,* that one of its characters was a disguised self-portrait of
Conan Doyle!

At the moment of this recognition I had already believed
Doyle's confessions that he had cast personified fractions of his
inner psyche as actors in his Sherlockian dramas, but this was
different. In this comedy he had cast himself, the entire Conan
Doyle, struggling young doctor and writer, in the self-satirizing
role of Jabez Wilson, the gullible pawnbroker.

Doyle's situation as a young man and budding author has
already been described; but now, because my strategy of disclosure
requires it, I will repeat some of it in a rearranged form to set the
stage for an explanation of how and why Conan Doyle cast himself
in such an unflattering role.

In 1886, after a meager career as a general practitioner, young
Dr. Doyle opened an office in Southsea as an eye specialist, but
failed to attract any patients. Desperately in need of an activity
that would earn some money and take his mind off his humiliating
failure, he wrote a story (*J. Habakuk Jephson's Statement*) and
sold it for twenty-nine guineas, or about £30.

Encouraged by the sale of this and other stories to small magazines, he began a lengthy and ambitious historical novel. But, needing immediate cash for supporting his small family and large literary ambitions, he dashed off his first Sherlock Holmes adventure—much of it lifted (as he later admitted) from the detective tales of Poe—and sold it for only £25.

He then forgot about Holmes and resumed work on his big novel. But then the combined miracle and curse descended on him. To his astonishment, delight, and utter chagrin, the entire world declared its adoration of "that wonderful new detective Sherlock Holmes" and clamored for more of his adventures.

The young author suddenly found himself in a luxurious dilemma. Though grateful for the recognition (and the money), he soon resented and then grew to *hate* the detective stories because (his publicly stated reason) "They keep me from better things." (I accept this as a partial explanation, but believe that certain psychosexual elements within the stories copied from Poe entrapped him in a deep psychological dilemma that he could solve only by killing his hero.)

But Doyle was still hard-up and continued grudgingly with Sherlock Holmes until his economic position and the success of *Micah Clarke* and *The White Company* and other writings made it possible for him to "slay Holmes for good and all." It is significant that Doyle doesn't use more neutral words like stop, quit, cease, or discontinue: the word he *did* use expresses his homicidal rage against a mere figment of his imagination.

When we return to *The Red-Headed League,* written during this period, to ask which character in this bizarre comedy resembles the Doyle we've described, the answer has to be Jabez Wilson, the gullible pawnbroker.

Like his literary parent, Wilson has a business that yields a meager income. Needing money badly, he allows himself to be gulled into leaving his business to become a menial clerk who copies (writes) the work of others in the *Britannica,* a loss of social status he accepts because the undemanding work pays him £30.

Doyle does not make it convincingly clear why the pawnbroker, who obviously cannot afford a detective like Holmes, tried to hire him. As Holmes points out to him: "As far as you are personally concerned, I do not see that you have any grievance against this extraordinary league. On the contrary, you are, as I understand it, richer by some £30, to say nothing of the minute knowledge which you have gained on every subject which comes under the letter A."

The clue to Wilson's unexpressed feelings and to the feelings and thoughts of Doyle when he created Wilson is the precise amount of money mentioned by Sherlock Holmes: "some £30." Though portrayed as "not-too-bright," the pawnbroker understood that he had actually benefited from this inverse swindle. What really griped him, I think, was the humiliation he suffered when he realized that he had abandoned (betrayed) his middle-class position to become a lowly copying clerk for only thirty pounds, an amount probably chosen by Doyle because it recalls the Biblical "thirty pieces of silver" paid to Judas for his act of betrayal. It also recalled to Doyle (I deduce) the payment of thirty pounds (twenty-nine guineas) he received for one of his first published stories: *J. Habakuk Jephson's Statement.**

This view of Wilson's situation, his outward reactions and inner feelings, provides a two-way mirror of resemblance between this schlemielian character and his chameleon creator. In this double mirror we now see Doyle as a guilt-stricken young man who felt that he had abandoned (betrayed) his prestigious but unrewarding professions as a doctor and potential author of lofty literature to sell himself as a writer of lowly detective stories he had copied from another writer. The price of this family- and self-betrayal? Hesketh Pearson, after studying Doyle's accounts, informs us that "the average payment for each of the first six *Adventures* to appear in *The Strand* was just over £30." The second of these "thirty-pound" *Adventures* was *The Red-Headed League,* in which a silly little man sells his soul for thirty pounds.

As I reconstruct the situation: The uncanny and frequent repetition of this numerical symbol of betrayal during his period of humiliating failure and rejection may have created in Doyle a feeling of Judas-like self-betrayal, a very nasty feeling he then tried to purge by foisting it onto his invented scapegoat character, Jabez Wilson. Yes, *The Red-Headed League* is psychotheater from beginning to end.

---

* The symbolic number "30" is also used in connection with John Clay, betrayer, who is thirty years old. When he wrote this story Doyle was about thirty.

I first encountered the symbolic "thirty pieces of silver" as literary cliché during my first assignment as a literary consultant on plagiarism cases for Warner Brothers—a lawsuit involving Frank Capra's film *Meet John Doe,* starring Gary Cooper and Barbara Stanwyck. In this strange movie Cooper plays the part of John Doe, a former baseball player who is persuaded to become a secular Christ who will save all of mankind by a sacrificial leap off the top of a skyscraper on Christmas eve!

The Judas-figure in this epic is the cynical Barbara Stanwyck, who not only dreams up this gimmick as a publicity stunt for selling newspapers, but then "fingers" John Doe for the cops by giving him a Judas kiss. When her evil Pontius Pilate boss (Edward Arnold) praises Barbara for her efficient betrayals and asks, "How much am I paying you now?" she answers, "Thirty bucks a week and gimme a raise!" But, you will be glad to hear, Barbara becomes converted by her own evocation of the Christ parallel, quits her job and Judas role, falls in love with Gary, and persuades him not to sacrifice himself for us.

11.

IN FEODOR DOSTOYEVSKY's *The Gambler* (1867) , the theme of self-destruction (self-betrayal) is expressed throughout by the constant repetition of the number "thirty" as the losing number.

Only two games are played by Dostoyevsky's character: roulette, which is equated with the suicidal game, Russian roulette; and *trente et quarante,* or thirty and forty. Thus in the latter game, the number thirty is actually the game-arena of the Christ- and self-betraying activity.

Madame Tarasyetichev (Granny) loses a fortune at roulette, including the money she had pledged for the *building of a church* (the betrayal of Christ): "The wheel rotated, and the number thirty came up. She had lost."

When the narrator concludes the tragic tale of compulsive gambling, he says:

I have ruined myself . . . after coming out of prison [for debts incurred in gambling]. I was a lackey . . . a valet for Gintse at *thirty* gulden a month.

The second amount of money repeatedly associated with self-and-other-betrayal in *The Gambler* is 1200 francs, which is not only a multiple of thirty (30 × 40), but is also associated with Judas. In the New Testament book of Matthew, chapter 26, it is written: "one of the twelve, Judas Iscariot, etc."

12.

IN HERMAN MELVILLE's great allegory *Moby Dick,* the ubiquitous "thirty pieces of silver" are mentioned first in the context of Captain Ahab's sacrilegious hunt for the white whale, which some scholars see as a symbol of Jehovah. Others, including D. H. Lawrence (and I), see the omni-symbolical *Moby Dick* as a surrogate of Christ.

But before Ishmael and Queequeg embark upon this Satanic expedition to seek out and kill God or Christ, they become "husband and wife" in a bedroom ceremony described by the incredibly naive Ishmael:

"He [Queequeg] pressed his forehead against mine, clasped me about the waist, and said that henceforth we were married; meaning, in his country's phrase, that we were bosom friends, and he would gladly die for me, if need be . . . [Later in the same scene] . . . thus, then, in our heart's honeymoon, lay I and Queequeg, a cosy, loving pair."

But this "marriage," performed on the eve of their embarkation upon the voyage that will kill all but Ishmael, is not as innocent and humorous as it seems. In the next breath the hermeneutic Herman Melville has Ishmael, happy "bride," describe the wedding gifts given him by his awesome "bridegroom":

"He made me a present of his embalmed [shrunken] head; took out his enormous tobacco wallet, and groping under the tobacco, drew out some *thirty dollars in silver* . . . mechanically *divided them into two equal portions,* pushed one of them towards me, and said it was mine. I was going to remonstrate, but he silenced me by pouring them into my trousers pocket." [my italics]

Thus we see that the perennially accursed "thirty pieces of silver" are mockingly associated by Melville with (a) the murder-betrayal of God, and (b) with the parody-betrayal of heterosexual love and marriage. (Even the punishment of death for Queequeg is implied in the wedding gift of the shrunken human head: a man must be murdered and decapitated before his head can be shrunk.)

13.

In *The Man with the Twisted Lip,* written shortly after *The Red-Headed League,* we find that the compulsive Conan Doyle has written a part for himself that is far from comic. This time he is Neville St. Clair, the man with the twisted lip.

A former actor and expert of disguise (Doyle loved to wear disguises to fool his friends), St. Clair, again like Doyle, is a writer. When his editor assigns him to investigate London's beggars, St. Clair disguises himself as a "crippled wretch of hideous aspect," complete with deep scars that twist his lip, and finds that as a beggar he can easily earn more in a single day than in a week of hard work as a serious writer.

Later, when he desperately needs £25 to pay an unrelenting creditor, he "takes a holiday from work," resumes his begging, and in ten days earns the needed £25. (Doyle left his work as doctor and serious writer to write *A Study in Scarlet* for which he received exactly £25. When he asked, hat-in-hand, for more money, he was turned down. Even the "ten days" is taken by Doyle from his own experience. Hesketh Pearson informs us that the average time required by Doyle, a prodigiously fast writer, for his £30 Sherlock Holmes short stories was ten days.)

Then, like the real-life Doyle and the fictional Jabez Wilson, Neville St. Clair abandons his respected £2-a-week profession to lead a secret double life. During the day he is Hugh Boone, the loathsome crippled beggar who earns a yearly £700 or $3500, about $25,000 equivalent in modern value. At night, after removing his disguises in his dressing room in an "opium den," he entrains for a suburb where he is once again Neville St. Clair, a respected "investor in various companies." Confident in his deception, he marries the daughter of a prominent brewer, becomes the father of two children and continues to lead his double life for many years.

But one day when his wife is in London she accidentally sees

St. Clair in the second-story window (symbolic place) of the opium den. He sees her too and makes agitated motions that lead her to assume he is the victim of foul play. She runs off and finds some constables, who enter the "dressing room" and find Hugh Boone, the beggar, but no trace of Neville St. Clair. When they find St. Clair's clothes (which he has thrown) in the Thames, they assume that the "beggar" killed St. Clair and threw him and his clothes into the water. (This is a forecast of the later struggle between two other Doylean doppelganger characters, which ended with their presumed death in the waters of Reichenbach Falls.)

When he is first hired by Mrs. St. Clair, Sherlock Holmes is baffled by this mystery. But soon his near-clairvoyant brain sorts things out. He goes to the jail, washes the grimy face of Hugh Boone with a large wet sponge, and reveals the missing St. Clair. When it becomes clear that no legal crime has been committed and that it would be best for the now-penitent St. Clair and his family if his story remained secret, Holmes uses his influence with the police and helps the man to give up his life as a beggar. (I wonder: Did he ever get back his £2-a-week job on the newspaper?)

We may deduce from this story—and the preceding *The Red-Headed League*—that Neville St. Clair is a projection of the self-flagellating Conan Doyle who is saying, in effect, "As a doctor and literary pretender I have earned practically nothing. But as a literary beggar who exploits the emotions of the passing throng, I have become respected and prosperous. I am no better than a beggar who abandons his station in life for the pennies thrown to him."

Here, as in every other Sherlock Holmes story, we find an internecine struggle (psychomachy) between two personified fractions of Doyle's imagination. One denizen of Doyle's "inner room" emerges to perpetrate a fraud against himself, his family, and society; but once again Doyle's relentless superego, Sherlock Holmes, exposes the imaginational alter ego of Conan Doyle and forces him to return to respectability.

14

ALMOST EVERY NAME invented by Conan Doyle, when simply *stared at,* reveals his ironical, satirical mind and his inveterate allegorizing. Recently, while checking the names in *The Man with the Twisted Lip,* I, remembering that Doyle was a "renegade" Catholic, consulted a standard *Lives of the Saints.* In it I found that even before Neville St. Clair became a professional beggar named Hugh Boone, which means "huge gift," he was nominally predestined by Doyle to become a beggar. The only St. Clare (or Claire) in the hagiographic dictionary was the twelfth-century lady who renounced her upper-class status to become the founder of the first order of nuns authorized *to live entirely by begging.*

In the same fascinating book, I looked for John Clay's alias (Red-Headed League), and found that as Vincent Spaulding he shared a unique altruistic urge with St. Vincent de Paul. While waiting in the bank cellar for John Clay (Vincent Spaulding) to break in, Holmes offers his companions a brief biographical sketch of the thief. Included in the briefing is the sentence: "He'll crack a crib (bank) in Scotland one week, and be raising money for an orphanage in Cornwall the next."

The similarity? Well, apart from the resemblance between

ST. *VINCENT DE PAUL*
and *VINCENT SPAULDING,*

I find that if the pawnbroker Jabez Wilson had continued to copy the *Encyclopaedia Britannica,* he would have arrived eventually at the "Vs" and learned, as I did, that St. Vincent de Paul raised money for and built two orphanages in Paris.

The reader who wishes to inspect a third example of the self-punishing Conan Doyle as a gullible victim-character in one of his own stories will find him as Victor Hatherley in *The Adventure of the Engineer's Thumb,* said to be one of Conan Doyle's favorites. Like Doyle, young Hatherley opens an office as a consultant, but fails to find a single client. Finally he accepts a job from a visibly shady client, a job that takes him away from his office to a weird house in the country. When he discovers that his client is a counterfeiter, the crazy man first tries to kill the hapless young engineer in a huge press, but then attacks him with a meat cleaver and (symbolic castration) cuts off his thumb! And, of course, he never does get the 50-pound fee promised him. (This is the same story in which we discovered Friedrich Nietzsche [the mad German client] and his sister as "Fritz" und "Elise.")

15.

The Red-Headed League *as a Freudian parable*

Had there been women in the house, I should have suspected a mere vulgar intrigue. That, however, was out of the question. [my italics]
—*The Red-Headed League*

THE VITAL QUESTION of why, in this comedy, Conan Doyle inserted his parody of the "thwarted pederasty" incident from the story of the destruction of Sodom and Gomorrah may be answered: He did so because, below its comedic surface, *The Red-Headed League* contains a parable of *fantasized pederastic rape that is thwarted by Sherlock Holmes!*

This is a startling statement, I admit, but one that can be substantiated through a fairly simple exploration of the classical Freudian situations and symbols displayed in the story.

The visible story of *The Red-Headed League* may be summarized as one in which Sherlock Holmes uses his great analytical powers to anticipate and then prevent a brilliant and daring thief from breaking into a bank to steal the gold stored in its cellar. The less-visible psychological parable interwoven with the surface narrative is, as we shall see, entirely, surprisingly different.

The hypothetical parable of thwarted pederastic rape within *The Red-Headed League* became visible and partly understood through my Freudian analysis of the pawnbroker and his shop; the "cover stories" and personality of the thief; the bank and its golden treasure; the nature of the attempted burglary and its modus operandi; and, lastly, Sherlock Holmes's role as the ruthless detective who prevents and punishes the crime.

The pawnbroker and his shop: From the outset I found Doyle's choice of pawnbroking an odd trade for the gullible Wilson, since that business *per se* has nothing whatever to do with the story or plot. Any business next to any bank would have done just as well. Moreover, the pawnbroker is never seen or heard from after he brings Holmes into the mystery. We may deduce, therefore, that Doyle had other reasons for making his man a pawnbroker.

The pawnshop as a symbolic arena of unhappy heterosexuality is first made known to the reader by the pawnbroker's reference to himself as "a widower with no family" who lives a lonely, loveless, and impoverished life. This is followed by Watson's description of the shop and its neighborhood as a mythic place of dismal failure:

> We travelled by the *Underground* [the unconscious mind] . . . to Saxe-Coburg Square [no such place in London] to the scene of the singular story we listened to in the morning. . . . It was a pokey, little, shabby-genteel place, where four lines of *two-storied* brick houses [as in other adventures the houses tell *stories on two levels of meaning*] looked out on a small railed-in enclosure, where a lawn of weedy grass and a few faded laurel-bushes made a hard fight against a smoke-filled and uncongenial atmosphere. [my italics]

The first of the Freudian symbols that confirms the idea of the pawnshop as a place of heterosexuality is the most obvious: the balls and cross-section of penis that hang in front of the shop.

I call the pawnshop an arena or theater of unhappy heterosexuality because it has always been regarded as a dismal purgatory of pawned (sacrificed) tokens of failed domesticity and marriage (wedding rings, etc.) which all too often die unransomed. Seen in this context the balls out front may be interpreted as the pawnbroker's trophy of castration. The archetypal image? That of the racist image of the moneylender Shylock, circumcisional knife in hand, demanding his well-known pound of gentile genital fleisch.

But perhaps the most remarkable of the Freudian clues to *The Red-Headed League*'s parable of perversity is Spaulding's pretended interest in amateur photography as it is described to Holmes by the pawnbroker: "Oh . . . never such a fellow for photography. Snapping away, and then diving into the cellar like a rabbit in its hole to develop his pictures." (Suddenly Spaulding reminds us of the rabbit which the immortal Alice followed down the hole into the allegorical Wonderland. Is this Doyle's subtle hint of the allegory awaiting the reader who follows Spaulding down into the cellar and through the underground tunnel into the bank? The similarity between Spaulding and Alice is heightened when we recall that Holmes and Watson, who almost always travel by cab, go to look at the thief and the scene of the intended crime by Underground. When Lewis Carroll's masterpiece was first published (1886), five years before Doyle wrote this story, it was entitled *Alice's Adventure Under Ground.*

Photography is a technical process of image reproduction. It also, I have found, happens to be a nearly perfect paradigm of sexual reproduction: desire, penetration, fertilization, gestation, and birth.

As an amateur (from the Latin *amare,* meaning *to love*), Spaulding acquired a box camera (also from the Latin: *camera obscura,* a *dark room*). He then loaded it with sensitized film, called *virgin plate* by its makers, and pointed it at a human subject. After focusing, he then opened the shutter and allowed the sunlight (source of all life on earth) reflecting off the subject to penetrate through the tiny *hole* in the camera (vagina) and expose (impregnate) the "virgin" film. This created an invisible *latent image* (embryo in its earliest stage) which he then transferred to the *cellar-dark room* (womb) where it was placed in liquid developers (amniotic fluid) for a predetermined length of time (gestation). Spaulding then brought the fully developed little image (baby) into the light (birth) where, after washing (baptism), it was dried and presented for inspection. (In our American slang, a vagina is sometimes called a "box" or "mailbox." The *Oxford Unabridged Dictionary* gives one definition of a letterbox as "a receptacle where unwanted babies are left at an orphanage.")

16.

THE GERMINAL IDEA of photography may have been planted in the fertile mind of man by the Greek myth told several millennia before either little Louis Daguerre or tiny Sigmund Freud emerged from his mother's "obscure camera."

When the oracles told Acrisius, king of Argos, that any son born to his daughter Danae was destined to kill him, he cruelly sentenced Danae to life imprisonment in a secret sealed and darkened room where no man could ever see her or get to her. But when the raunchy Zeus learned of her plight, he transformed himself into a golden beam of light, entered her dark room through a tiny hole, penetrated her virgin aperture (F64) and impregnated her. (The child born of this pioneer "flash-shot" was Perseus, who later slew Acrisius.)

To understand the symbolic meaning of the bank and the gold stored in its cellar, it is helpful to keep in mind all of the homoerotic images that cluster about the character of John Clay. It is also helpful to think of him as the author of the scheme to steal the bank's gold, the creator of the fictitious organization that lured Wilson away from his shop, and as the writer of the ad which resulted in the strange reenactment of the Biblical incident in which the angels disguised as men were almost raped by the crazed mob of Sodomites.

With these elements firmly in mind, we now seek to interpret the allegorical meaning of John Clay's labyrinthine quest for the gold stored in the bank cellar.

When Freud first attempted to understand the hidden meaning of the gold that was seen in a great many dreams, he turned to a study of the symbolic language and metaphors in ancient mythology, folklore, slang, dirty stories, limericks, poetry, and pornography. He found that people had always referred to gold in two opposing ways. When freely circulated, used constructively, or given as a token of affection or love, gold was a symbol of love; but when hoarded by misers or soulless corporations, or when used destructively, gold was frequently referred to as an evil substance—in scatological terms as "filthy lucre."

The ancient Babylonians called gold "the dung of hell." Hieronymus Bosch, in his *The Garden of Earthly Delight* in The Prado, paints a demon who swallows naked sinners and voids gold coins; Shakespeare speaks of the "cankered heaps of strangely achieved gold," and adds the sexual image of "saint-seducing gold."

In his classic essay *Anal Erotic Character Traits,** Ernest Jones, Sigmund Freud's intimate friend and biographer, offers many literary examples of "precious gold as excrement." One taken from John Milton's lofty *Paradise Lost* reads:

> On princes with their retinues long
> of horses led by grooms besmeared with gold.

Dr. Jones then adds:

---

* *Selected Essays in Psychoanalysis,* London, 1948.

The association between gold and excrement is common enough in erotic art. Two examples may be cited from Broadley's *Napoleon in Caricature* (1911) : One by *Fores,* depicts *Napoleon* and *George III* as "The Rival Gardeners." At the side is a wheelbarrow filled with gold coins and labelled "Manure from Italy and Switzerland." The other, "The Blessings of Paper Money," is by *George Cruikshank:* there is a figure of *Napoleon* withdrawing a large chamberpot filled with gold coins from under John Bull, who is being dosed with paper money.

These caricature-attacks on Napoleon probably had an additional punning significance to his English enemies based on their undoubted knowledge that all of the gold coins minted during his regime bore his image and were called "napoleons." This gives us the possible equation: If Napoleon is a gold piece and a gold piece is a piece of manure or chamberpotted *merde,* it follows then that a whole wheelbarrow or large chamberpot is filled with napoleon-*merdes.* Or simply: "Napoleon is a big shit!"

But far more relevant to the sexual parable of *The Red-Headed League* are two Victorian toy banks on my desk. One of them is a jolly black man who tosses brown copper pennies into his mouth and stores them in his lower innards. The second bank is "The Tammany Banker" ("Boss" Tweed) who drops the coins put into his hand into his great belly (corporation), from which they fall into his lower colon. Ironically, "Boss" Tweed, like Doyle's John Clay, was a thief and looter of banks who was jugged for stealing millions of dollars from the City of New York.

In each of these personified banks, the metallic money is transformed into food, which then, through the inner logic of such things, becomes precious excrement temporarily deposited in the "bowels" of the bank. When the bank is full, a key must be inserted into the little man's bottom before he can be persuaded to give up his anal-erotic hoard.

Recently, in an effort to visualize it more clearly, I drew a rough cross-sectional floor plan of John Clay's intended bank robbery. On one side I sketched the pawnshop with its various symbols of male genitality; then, directly behind it, the bank with its cloacal cellar filled with fecal gold. Then, as I stared at this diagram, it became obvious that it could also be read as a cross-sectional diagram of the lower male torso—with the reproductive organs in front, and directly behind them the bowels and other plumbing organs. "Well," I thought, "John Clay could have robbed the bank in many ways, but he chose to *force* his way out of the pawnshop world of heterosexuality and then *penetrate* the bank's rectum from underneath. This was an act of *fantasized pederastic rape!*"

The unconscious sexual and moral symbolism of this parable checks out in even the smallest details. We are told by the author that John Clay lured the pawnbroker away from his shop by paying him four gold sovereigns a week. This left the field clear for the theft of the French gold worth some thirty thousand pounds. The difference? The English gold pieces paid to the heterosexual Wilson were stamped with the portrait of Queen Victoria and therefore *female,* but the French (salacious) gold pieces coveted by Clay were *masculine* "gold napoleons."

Curious about this enormous amount of French gold which illogically rested in a branch bank in London, I consulted *The Annotated Sherlock Holmes* (vol. I, pg. 344) and a book about French coins and learned that though they were still called "napoleons," the coins minted after the fall of the Second Empire (1870) bore only the image of a standing angel.

If my analysis is accurate, then I conclude that *The Red-Headed League,* which began with a parody of the incident at Sodom (the thwarted attempt of the Sodomites to break into Lot's house so that they might "know" the angels hidden within), ends with a similar fantasy: John Clay's aborted attempt to break into the bank so that he could "know" the golden angels hidden there.

The great revealer Sherlock Holmes informs Watson (and us) that the value of the French gold is "some thirty thousand pounds," another evocation of the Biblical thirty pieces of silver. One interpretation of this repeated figure (Wilson received only thirty pounds, and Doyle was paid about thirty pounds for this story) : ergo, Conan Doyle believed that John Clay's betrayal of himself and his ducal family and of the Victorian moral code was a thousand times worse than the self-betrayal of "Wilson-Doyle." (Judas returned the accursed "30 pieces" to the high priests, who buried it *in the ground.)*

A tentative summary: Though, on its conscious level, *The Red-Headed League* is a fantasy about a man who is prevented by Sherlock Holmes from stealing real money from a real bank, on its subconscious level it may be read as the parable of a man who is acting out his passionate desire to perform an act of sodomy; and, as we have seen, both the real and the subconscious schemes are thwarted simultaneously by the relentless Sherlock Holmes, the resident detective and superego (censor) in Conan Doyle's psychic inner room and in the outer world of England.

Sherlock Holmes, a Doylean character who has converted all of his own erotic desires and most of his emotions into cold logical analysis and hot bounty-hunting, stands guard at the scene of intended crime conceived by the perverse "criminal" within Doyle's psyche and imagination and prevents its consummation.

17.

". . . Gustave Flaubert wrote to George Sand"

AFTER SHERLOCK HOLMES performs his double fictional duty of preventing a real bank robbery and a surreal act of unconscious pederastic rape, he sums up the case for his friend; and Watson responds with "unfeigned admiration":

"You reasoned it out beautifully. It is so long a chain, yet every link rings true. . . . You are a *benefactor to the race.*"   [my italics]

To this glowing praise Holmes answers:

"Well, perhaps, after all, it is of some little use. '*L'homme c'est rien—l'oeuvre c'est tout,*' as Gustave Flaubert wrote to George Sand." ["The man is nothing, the work is everything."]

I find that Gustave Flaubert qualified for membership in Doyle's syndromic club in several ways. First, as the writer of "immoral" heterosexual novels. When his best-known novel, *Madame Bovary,* was published in 1856–57, both he and his publisher were put on trial for "offending public morality and religion." (They were acquitted, and, as always, the scandal made the book a best-seller.) The second: *Madame Bovary* is the tragic story of a romantic woman whose great desire for love drove her to adultery and suicide. A third possible reason for Doyle's mention of Flaubert is a nice example of verbal confusion of the sexes. When he was asked upon whom he had based the character of Madame Bovary, Flaubert wittily answered, "Madame Bovary? C'est moi!" ("I am Madame Bovary!")

When asked the similar question about the "origin" of Sherlock Holmes, Conan Doyle, echoing Flaubert's famous remark, answered similarly: "If anyone is Sherlock Holmes, I must confess that it is I."

The fact that Conan Doyle's interest in Flaubert led him to read and quote from his letters to George Sand indicates that he knew a great deal about the man—enough perhaps to know that Flaubert's attitude toward *Madame Bovary* was exactly like that of Doyle toward his Sherlock Holmes adventures.

The great success of *Bovary* overshadowed Flaubert's later work and plagued him bitterly. He preferred his *Salammbo, Sentimental Education,* and *Bouvard and Pecuchet* and grew to hate the story of Emma Bovary. "I wish that I could buy up all the copies, throw them into the flames, and never hear of it again!"

These words, as we know, express the hostile feelings of Doyle toward Sherlock Holmes exactly. In his memoirs, Doyle wrote: "If I had never touched Sherlock Holmes, who has tended to obscure my higher works, my present position in literature would be a more commanding one."

Yes, Gustave Flaubert fulfills the Doylean imperatives (heterosexual department) very nicely, and George Sand is just right for the compulsory reference to some form of sexual deviation. She was, of course, the world-renowned cigar-smoking author who shocked the public when she appeared in men's clothing. Though her novels were heterosexual, and she had many well-publicized affairs with men—Chopin, Alfred de Musset, Franz Liszt, among others—she seems also to have been associated with gay liberation as well. In his authoritative *The Romantic Agony,* Professor Mario Praz has written, "During the years just after 1830, thanks especially to George Sand, the vice of Lesbianism became extremely popular."

18.

. . . and let's not forget Sarasate

WHILE PROFOUNDLY INVOLVED in pursuing the "scarlet thread" through the labyrinth of *A Study in Scarlet,* Sherlock Holmes

suddenly, and with seeming irrelevance, mentions the name
Norman Neruda, a woman (Madame Norman-Neruda) whom he
magically transformed into a man (Norman Neruda) by simply
omitting the "Madame" and the hyphen. He did so, we recall, in
the context of murders arising from the unbridled heterosexual
tragedies which began in a far-off time and place. Doyle's compulsive reasons are also known to us. He felt compelled to fulfill his
strange need to mention some form of switching of the sexes in
that context of heterosexually motivated murder.

Now, in *The Red-Headed League,* Doyle does the same compulsive thing, but in reverse. Immediately, after listening to the
pawnbroker's parody of the destruction of the Sodomites in the
Book of Genesis and immediately before his first face-to-face
meeting with the deviant John Clay, Holmes mentions the name
of the violinist Sarasate—a man (Signor Pablo Sarasate) whom he
verbally transforms into a woman named Sara Sate by simply
omitting "Signor" and "Pablo."

Trivial? Perhaps. But no more trivial than Sherlock Holmes's
reminder that he had solved "the dreadful business of the Aber-
netty family" by observing the "depth to which the parsley had
sunk into the butter upon a hot day."

19.

. . . as Gustave Flaubert wrote to
George Sand.
—Sherlock Holmes, *The Red-Headed League*

I CONCLUDE THIS DISCUSSION of *The Red-Headed League* with an
amusing verbal discovery based on the spoofing words above (the
last seven words of the comedy), the implications of which are so
mind-boggling that I can express it only in the following order-
imposing form:

  I: Conan Doyle admitted many times that he patterned Sher-
lock Holmes upon Edgar Allan Poe's detective "A. Dupin."
  II: In his *A Study in Scarlet* Doyle writes a scene in which
Holmes, his fictional character based on *A. Dupin,* discusses
Poe's fictional *A. Dupin* with Watson, also a fictional char-
acter.

III: At the end of his summation of *The Red-Headed League* Holmes mentions *George Sand*. She is given the last two words of the story.

IV: *George Sand* was the pseudonym of *Madame Dudevant* whose baptismal name was *A*mandine Lucille *A*urore Dupin. Before her first marriage she called herself Aurore Dupin. Therefore *George Sand* equals *A. Dupin.*

V: In the late 1830s Edgar Allan Poe reviewed several novels written by George Sand, whom he also refers to as Madame Dudevant.

VI: In 1841 Edgar Allan Poe created the detective story whose hero he named Auguste Dupin, upon whom

VII: Conan Doyle patterned Sherlock Holmes, who then discusses A. Dupin and gives the last two words of his summation in *The Red-Headed League* to George Sand, who was really A. Dupin. . . .

VIII: ad infinitum. . . .

CHAPTER SIX

Porlock, Watson, is a *nom-de-plume,* a
mere identification mark; *but behind it
lies a shifty and evasive personality.*
—Sherlock Holmes, *The Valley of Fear*

1.

The Adventure of the Cardboard Box

How was it that Dr. Watson hap-
pened to cherish a portrait of Henry
Ward Beecher?
—Christopher Morley

FIRST, A SYNOPSIS of the story: Holmes and Watson, together in a
darkened room (always the presage of an allegorical scene to follow), are reading: Holmes, a letter; and Watson, a newspaper.
Finally, Watson tosses his paper away, and Holmes breaks the long
silence to tell his companion that he has been reading his mind.
He has deduced that Watson has been thinking about the American Civil War.

When the always amazed Watson admits that the great detective has indeed correctly read one of his inmost thoughts, and asks
him for a complete reading and explanation, Holmes says:

"After throwing down your paper . . . your eyes fixed themselves
on your newly framed portrait of *General Gordon.* . . . Then your
eyes flashed across the unframed portrait of *Henry Ward Beecher* . . .

which stands upon the top of your books [the book clue again!] . . .
you were recalling the incidents of Beecher's career . . . of the mission
he undertook on behalf of the North during the Civil War. . . ."

[my emphases]

When I read the above, my own inmost thoughts were these:
"Henry Ward Beecher? I can understand why Watson would have
a framed picture of the English general 'Chinese' Gordon, who was
decapitated at Khartoum shortly before Doyle wrote this story.
But why would Watson, not at all a religious man, want a picture
of Beecher, an American clergyman and brother of Harriet
Beecher Stowe? Some very obscure thoughts being read here!"

I continued reading Holmes's explanation but found no
immediate answer to my questions:

"Then, your mind turned to the Civil War. . . . You were thinking of the gallantry displayed on both sides. . . . You were dwelling
on the sadness and the horror and the useless waste of lives."

When this mind-reading exhibition ends ("Amazing!" "No,
superficial!"), Holmes then draws Watson's attention to a newspaper story about a Miss Susan Cushing of Croyden whose post-
man delivered to her a cardboard melon box containing "two
freshly severed human ears." After Watson reads this account of
the peculiarly revolting practical joke played upon Miss Cushing,
Holmes tells him that Scotland Yard has asked him to help them
solve this "earie" mystery.

In Croyden, Susan Cushing insists that the package must have
been sent to her by mistake since she has no enemies. Holmes
believes her and turns his attention to Susan's two sisters, Mary
and Sarah. Mary, he learns, is the wife of Jim Browner, a ship's
steward. The other sister, Sarah, unmarried, proves to be the
Jezebel of this story. When Jim Browner coldly rejects her sexual
advances, she proceeds to poison the mind of her sister against him
and then turns her own lover loose on her sister Mary. Doyle
depicts the caddish lover, Alec Fairbairn, as an effeminate rotter
who curls his hair and wears earrings; once again the Doylean
effeminate man rears his marcelled, earringed (and doomed)
head.

In his confession written after Holmes catches him, Jim, yet
another Doylean man destroyed by heterosexual love, explains
that he came home unexpectedly, found his wife and lover to-

gether, killed them, lopped off an ear from each body and mailed them to the highly immoral Sarah, the instigator of the sexual crimes that led to murder. (Susan *did* get them by mistake.) The fate of the sex-crazed husband is left—uh—hanging, but we assume that he will die on the gallows.

Here we have a part of the Doylean syndrome. Two men and a woman (Sarah becomes irrevocably mad) all become victims of their sexual desires. But, as we shall see, this tragedy born of love is what merchants call "merely an introductory offer." Later in this very short story Conan Doyle associates much more bloodshed with the forbidden erotic activities of its male and female characters.

The reader has undoubtedly noticed the resemblance between the fictional Jim Browner and Vincent Van Gogh. Four years before Doyle wrote *The Cardboard Box,* Van Gogh cut off the lobe of his left ear and gave or sent it to a prostitute of Arles with the Biblical name Rachel because, as the story goes, he blamed her for causing the dissension between himself and his house-guest Paul Gauguin. Similarly, Jim Browner sent his present of ears to a highly immoral woman with the Biblical name Sarah. The Old Testament Sarah was the grandmother-in-law of Rachel and, since Sarah lived to be almost a hundred, probably lived in the same house with her. Did Doyle know of the Vincent Van Gogh ear incident?

Later, in this same story, we shall see that the image of the severed ears sent to a woman as a reminder of her guilt and responsibility for murder is repeated in a truly remarkable if round-about manner.

2.

CONAN DOYLE MUST BE complimented for the marvelous ingenuity with which he implanted his personal syndrome-allegory in this *Cardboard Box* adventure. Even with my present knowledge of the intricate workings of his hidden-visible formula, it still took a lot of digging, thinking, and luck before I finally understood Doyle's cunning reasons for hanging the "purloined letter" portraits of General Gordon and Reverend Beecher upon the walls of 221B Baker Street for everyone to see—and totally ignore.

To jog the reader into seeing the plainly visible but inscrutable icons he presents, Doyle even (in earlier stories) mentions Poe's Dupin, the original finder of the purloined letter. But even with the several clues provided by Doyle, no one has accepted his challenge to read the obvious picture-clues which, when deciphered, tell us what Doyle thought about detectives and the criminals they hunt, about detective stories, and, perhaps, about the polymorphously perverse readers who loved Sherlock Holmes and forced his creator to resurrect him.

Now as a result of my decoding of the Gordon-Beecher picture clues, which here again unfold dense clusters of guilt-laden ideas, I have succeeded, I think, in seeing the contents of Doyle's *Cardboard Box*, a Pandora's box if ever there was one. In this story I have found that he has clearly associated two very famous contemporaries with his obsessive theme: the disasters which befall those who engage in either normal or abnormal sexuality. One of these men embodies the fate of illicit heterosexuals; the other personifies Conan Doyle's haunting theme of the punishments inflicted upon individual men and vast multitudes because of one individual's love for a person of the same sex. After noting, for the fifteenth time in as many stories, that this set of harnessed images was always linked to the mention of the printed or written word, I searched here for such mentions and found them stashed away in the most unexpected places.

Now I shall proceed to a most presumptuous act: I will attempt to read Conan Doyle's inmost thoughts, using the very same portraits and books used by Sherlock Holmes to read the inmost thoughts of Dr. Watson.

I shall begin this thought-reading with the first book clue mentioned by Holmes when he is asked by Watson to explain how he knew that the doctor was thinking about the American Civil War: "Your eyes," says Sherlock, "flashed across the portrait of Henry Ward Beecher which stands upon the top of your books." I understood at once that Doyle was once again challenging the reader to find the connection between those books and some form of erotic behavior forbidden and severely punished by the repressive Victorian society of the 1890s.

And, since Doyle points so directly to the unframed "portrait of Henry Ward Beecher which stands upon" the row of books, it seems obvious that he is asking us to gaze into the face, personality and career of the famous American whom many of his contemporaries believed to be the greatest preacher since Saint Paul.

Now, after learning more about him, I see that Doyle's reference to Beecher is most revealing, not for what Doyle says about him, but for what he leaves unsaid. Speaking through Holmes, Doyle refers to the American preacher only as "an emissary [to England] during the Civil War." That surprised me, because I knew that Doyle knew—as every person of his generation knew—that Reverend Beecher barely escaped being ruined by the juiciest sexual scandal of the nineteenth century.

As described by the *Britannica:* "Beecher's favorite theme was love . . . love of man, the love of God . . . and religion as a life of liberty in love." But, ironically, it was another form of love, that of an overheated man for a woman of similar temperature, which almost destroyed him. "The later years of his life," says the encyclopedia, "were darkened by the charges brought against him by Theodore Tilton of improper relations with Tilton's wife, and before and during the lawsuit which involved him, his reputation as a man of honour and as a clergyman suffered."

(Conan Doyle's repeated use of the words "framed" and "unframed" in juxtaposition with his mention of the picture of Reverend Beecher is amusing. During the sensational and prolonged lawsuit [which Beecher won by a close split-jury decision] his lawyers insisted that he had been framed.)

In strict obedience to the rigid Doyle syndrome, Doyle links Beecher and his unmentioned but well-known sex scandal to the mass murders of the Civil War: "the sadness and horror and useless waste of lives" (says Holmes) . But the theme of unbridled sex linked to murder and the severed ears mailed to a woman is further tied to the Beecher reference in a most devious yet direct manner—through the knowledge common in Doyle's day that the nearly unfrocked Beecher was the brother of Harriet Beecher Stowe, the world-famous author of *Uncle Tom's Cabin,* whom everyone always associates with the slavery issue of the Civil War. (President Lincoln invited her to the White House and said, "Why, Mrs. Stowe, I'm right glad to meet you! So you're the little woman who wrote the book that started this great war!")

I wonder if Conan Doyle knew of the fascinating, almost occult, connection between Beecher's sister Harriet and the "immoral" sister Sarah in *The Cardboard Box* who is mailed a

package containing severed human ears as an accusative reminder
of her guilt and responsibility for the murders resulting from her
poisonous words?

Few biographers of Harriet Beecher Stowe fail to mention
that she received a mailed package containing the *severed ear* of a
black man and an obscenely offensive note blaming her "love of
niggers" and her impassioned words for all the deaths of the Civil
War! Perhaps Conan Doyle did know of this Beecherian incident,
so remarkably similar to the fictional "ear" incident involving
Sarah Cushing in his *Cardboard Box.* If he didn't it is one hell of a
coincidence!

But still alert to the automatic features of the singular syndrome, I looked for and found the inevitable mention of the
companion hang-up—some form of sexual deviation. And, as expected, this new mention of perversity was heralded by the mention of a literary work, this time an article written by Holmes
himself.

Before he applies his uncanny prophylactic eye to the contents of the very Freudian cardboard box, Sherlock says: "As a
medical man, you are aware, Watson, that no part of the human
body varies as much as the human ear. . . . In last year's *Anthro-
pological Journal* you will find two short *monographs from my
pen* upon the subject."   [my italics]

The detective then reveals an important fact unnoticed by
the incompetent police: The two ears in the cardboard box did
not come from the same head. One is a woman's ear, but the other
is a "man's ear pierced for earrings." Thus we see that once again
a reference to a written and printed article is followed by a reference to a confusion of the sexes, and also to an effeminate man
(Alec Fairbairn) who wears earrings and who also curls his hair.
The sissy!

Fairbairn is Doyle's second earringed man: In the brilliant
story, *The Red-Headed League,* Holmes (it is almost always
Holmes who exposes these things) asks the gullible pawnbroker,
"Have you observed that he" (Vincent Spaulding) "had his ears
pierced for earrings?" This bank robber with "almost womanly
hands," who travels with a "beskirted gunsel," is the gay John
Clay, whose entire bank caper, as I've explained in the previous
chapter, is an almost perfect paradigm of perverse (symbolic)
sexuality.

But interesting and telling as these "pierced earring" descriptives are, they seemed inadequate, not at all like the melodramatic examples of the other adventures. I felt there *had* to be something far more theatrical than "male earrings" and "womanly hands." But repeated readings failed to divulge the predictable dramatic "gay" ingredient.

Then, finally, after a Holmesian elimination of all the "impossibles," I found myself staring at a highly "improbable" residual: Dr. Watson's "recently framed portrait of General Gordon," which Doyle had hung on the wall like that certain unfindable letter in Poe's famous story.

The thought that the general lately played by the utterly masculine Charlton Heston might be the deviant male for the Doyle syndrome stunned me: "No! *Not* General Gordon, the hero and martyr of Khartoum! There couldn't be anything 'perverse' about *him!*" But then I remembered and reread Lytton Strachey's brilliant essay about General Gordon* and learned that in Doyle's insistent scheme, Gordon was a perfect candidate for punished perversity.

According to Strachey, Gordon had two great private passions. The first was for the Holy Bible which he read incessantly. The second and far less sanctimonious passion is described by the always ironic Mr. Strachey:

He was particularly fond of boys. Ragged street arabs and rough sailor lads. They made free of his house and garden: they visited him in the evenings for lessons and advice; he helped them, found them employment, and corresponded with them when they went out into the world. They were, he said, his *Wangs*. It was only through a singular austerity that he was able to afford such a variety of charitable expenses.

To underscore Gordon's sexual preference, Strachey—who certainly knew one when he saw one because he was one himself—says, delicately: "The presence of ladies . . . filled him with uneasiness." Strachey also describes the telling traumatic incident that occurred in Khartoum during an early visit:

[During a party in Gordon's honor], "the function ended in a prolonged banquet, followed by a mixed ballet of soldiers and completely naked young women. At last the Austrian consul, overcome by the exhilaration of the scene, flung himself among the dancers: the Governor

---

* *Eminent Victorians*, London, 1918.

General, shouting with delight, was about to follow suit, when Gordon abruptly left the room, and the party broke up in confusion."

The framed portrait of this deviant general, hung in Holmes's study so very close to the syndromic row of books, tragically fulfills its Doylean purposes when we learn from Strachey that after Gordon was cut to shreds by the Arabs, his severed head was stuck in a tree. All who passed were ordered to throw stones at it as a punitive expression of disgust for his well-known "unnatural vices."

(General Gordon's contemporaries were sometimes even more ambiguously ambivalent than Strachey. In his *Heroes of the Dark Continent,* written shortly after Gordon's death, J. W. Buehl begins: "He was a Peter the Hermit in pious devotion, a Lancelot in skill, a Barbarossa in impetuous courage." Then in sentences that seem never to get to the point, Buehl confirms Strachey's hint that the general's interest in "ragged street arabs and rough sailor lads" was not entirely philanthropic or philadelphian:

But though he was one of the gods of war, if that metaphor be not too florid [it is, Mr. Buehl, it is!]; though he was a very thunderbolt in battle and was as anxious on the eve of battle as a warhorse that is held in curb when he hears the rattle of musketry [go, man, go!], he was in quiet scenes a babe of peace, thus within him were those warring elements that, like torrid and frigid currents of air that come together to produce a cyclone, swept him into the most furious actions and left upon his brow the marks of heroic struggle. While Nature seems to have made him a great military leader, endowing him with Napoleonic sagacity and almost unexampled courage, yet his heart was so gentle that it may well have served the most pious nun. And with the woman's sweetest sympathy there was joined the greatest charity, devotion, loyalty and all the holy attributes of a truly generous nature. But with all this he was adapted to command an army.)

3.

General Gordon rides again!

WHEN I READ LYTTON STRACHEY's "insinuendoes" about the general's "ragged street arabs," I thought at once—as many Sherlockians probably have—of Sherlock Holmes's own similar group of "ragged street arabs."

We first meet them syndromically in *A Study in Scarlet* when Holmes and Watson are talking about Enoch J. Drebber. This allusion to the heterosexual murderer of Lucy Ferrier elicits from Holmes a quotation from *L'Arte Poetique,* an obscure seventeenth-century *book* written by Nicolas Boileau-Despreaux: *"Un sot trouve toujour un plus sot qui l'admire"* (A fool always finds a greater fool to admire him) .

Immediately after this quotation Dr. Watson exclaims: " 'What on earth is this?' For at that moment there came the pattering of many steps in the hall and on the stairs *accompanied by audible expressions of disgust on the part of our landlady."*

[my emphases]

"It's the Baker Street division of the detective police force," said my companion gravely; and as he spoke there rushed into the room half a dozen of the dirtiest and most ragged street arabs that ever I clapped [!] eyes on."

After noting that Holmes hastily and ambiguously explains they may not be his own little boys but an auxiliary of the official detective police force (Scotland Yard) , we see that Holmes assumes the Gordonesque role of military commander:

" 'Tention! cried Holmes in a sharp tone, and the six *dirty* little *scoundrels* (who *disgusted* Mrs. Hudson, the landlady) stood in line like so many *disreputable statuettes."*   [my emphases]

Then, to show that *he* is no boy-loving General Gordon (who died at Khartoum the year before Doyle wrote this story introducing the "ragged street arabs") , Sherlock bawls out these boys for entering his home unbidden: "In the future you shall send up Wiggins alone to report, and the rest of you shall wait in the street."

Sherlock Holmes is saying: "You ragged street arabs may have been General Gordon's house (and bed) guests, but I forbid you to enter my home. Wait in the street!"

Here, as in every other story, Sherlock Holmes performs his role as the incorruptible censor who nullifies, prevents, forcibly stops any lascivious act of intrusion. The culprit within Doyle's imagination who thinks, "I'll bring the dirty, disreputable, disgusting little scoundrels into Holmes's inner sanctum," is immediately overruled by Doyle's incarnate superego-detective-judge. (Like so many of Doyle's names, Sherlock Holmes is allegorical and suggests the protective and censorious "sure locker of homes."

In a personal note [journal] about Friedrich Nietzsche, Doyle, commenting on his insanity and insane philosophy, uses the image: "We must put our shoulder to the door and keep out insanity all we can.") In *Finnegans Wake*, James Joyce calls him "Shedlock Homes."

Incidentally, after his resurrection from the baptismal waters of Reichenbach Falls in 1903, Sherlock Holmes is a different man. He never again uses morphine and cocaine and General Gordon's "ragged street arabs" never reappear.

4.

IN MY EARLIER DISCUSSION of *A Study in Scarlet,* I offered my data which showed that Conan Doyle was probably thinking of the actress Rachel when he wrote the amusing scene in which Lestrade fantasized a "Rachel" as the scribbler of the bloody word "RACHE."*

Now, in this story, the repetition of the names Sarah and Rachel (Van Gogh) suggests that Conan Doyle, repetitive man, may have used a part of Racine's *Phèdre* in *The Cardboard Box* as well. (The timing checks: In the *same year* this Holmesian story appeared, Doyle also published his novel *The Refugees* in which Racine actually reads a scene from his *Phèdre* to Louis XIV.)

And the two stories are quite similar: In Racine's tragedy, Phèdre, sexually rejected by her stepson Hippolytus, retaliates by poisoning the mind of his father Theseus against him, an action that ends in the deaths of Hippolytus and the sex-maddened Phèdre.† In the nearly identical plot of *The Cardboard Box*, we repeat, Sarah Cushing is rejected by her sister's husband Jim, poisons her sister's mind against Jim, an act that ends with the deaths of her sister, her lover and Jim Browner, and in Sarah's fall into incurable madness.

* The two most famous actresses who ever performed in Racine's *Phèdre* were *Rachel* and her sister *Sarah* Felix.
† Conan Doyle's use of the Theseus myth has already been noted: In *The Final Problem* Sherlock Holmes clearly identifies himself as a Theseus who threads London's underworld maze to find the secret lair of the Minotaur known as Moriarty.

CHAPTER SEVEN

A man's life of any worth is a continual
allegory. . . . His works are the comments.

—John Keats, *Letters*

1.

The Adventure of the Empty House

IN THIS, the "resurrection" story, we have thus far, with the help
of Doyle's printed and written word clues, uncovered some of his
allegorical preoccupations with Friedrich Nietzsche, Dionysus,
Oscar Wilde (and friends) : In the pitch-dark "empty house" we
found Sebastian Moran to be an amalgam of Nietzsche and Wilde.
We saw there also the "Oscarian wax portrait of Sherlock
Holmes," the duplicate image of Wilde's Dorian Gray, become an
artistic facsimile-target for an attempted murder that boomer-
anged to kill the killer.

But now, with the new vision given us by Conan Doyle, we
return to this far from "Empty House" to take a longer and harder
look at the dozen books syndromically dropped by the disguised
Holmes at the scene of Robert Adair's murder, the same books
which Holmes—cruel prankster!—later tried to sell to the unsus-
pecting Watson.

Until very recently I have assumed that these books were

random Stanislavskian props chosen by Holmes for his impersonation of the elderly bibliophile; but now as a seasoned Doyle-watcher I reasoned: He has mentioned books, bookseller, precious volumes, bookshelf, eighteen times in a few short paragraphs. In other stories the mention of many books has been accompanied by catastrophic happenings. In *The Red-Headed League* the multivolumed *Britannica* was linked to the annihilation of the entire sinful populations of Sodom and Gomorrah. The row of books in *The Cardboard Box* was tied first to General Gordon and the mass murders at Khartoum, and then, through Reverend Beecher, to the slaughter of hundreds of thousands in the Civil War. If the unvarying Doyle imperatives are still operating in this story, then the dozen volumes Holmes carried to the scene of murder, and made so much of, indicate we are in the presence of a sexual allusion that is a blockbuster.

It is! The anticipated high sexplosive is contained in one of the twelve books offered by the play-acting Holmes to Watson in the instant before Watson fainted. It is the volume of poems by Catullus.

Ignorant of Catullus as man or poet (paradoxically my encyclopedic ignorance has been one of my best research tools. Sometimes it enables me to avoid preconceptions which lead me to think I know about something when I don't) , I procured all the available translations and several critical studies. The critics quickly informed me that Catullus is regarded as the greatest lyrical poet of ancient Rome and as a great influence on later poets.

His poems wasted no time in telling me that he was also Rome's most explicitly "obscene" writer and that, to the adjectives I'd applied to Conan Doyle—"captivating," "compulsive," "brilliant," "insistent," and "devious"—I would now have to add "filthy"!

"Filthy," I hasten to add, not to Catullus's own Roman audience, or to the liberated reader of the 1970s, but unspeakably so to those among Doyle's readers in 1903 who had also read the complete Catullus in Latin. (Until 1967, when C. H. Sisson first translated all the words relating to vaginal, oral, and rectal intercourse, all other translations of Catullus dealt with them by pretending they didn't exist, by falsifying them through mistranslation, or by leaving them in the original Latin. The logic of the last is beautiful: "If the reader knows Latin well enough to understand the forbidden words, he can, of course, be trusted with them!'')

For the shockproof reader—or for the reader who enjoys being shocked—here are two poems originally written on flameproof parchment by ancient Rome's Lenny Bruce, Gaius Valerius Catullus:

XVI

Pedicabo ego vos et irrumabo,
Aureli pathice et cinaede Furi,
qui me ex versiculis meis putastis,
quod sunt moliculi, parum pudicum.
nam castum esse decet pium poetam
ipsum, versiculos nihil necessest.

As translated by C. H. Sisson:*

All right I'll bugger you and suck your pricks,
Aurelius, you pair of sodomites
Who imagine, on the strength of my verses
That I am as lacking in reserve as they are.
But though the sacred poet ought to be chaste
It does not follow that his verses should be.

And:

XCVII

Non (ita me di ament) quicquam referre putavi,
    utrumne os an culum olfacerem Aemilio.
nilo mundius hoc, nilque immundius, illud,
    verum etiam culusmundior et melior:
nam sine dentibus est: os dentis sequipedalis,
    gingivas vero ploxeni habet veteris,
praeterea rictum qualem difussis in aestu
    meientis mulae cunnus habere solet.
hic futuit multas et se facit esse venustum
    et no pistrino traduitur atque asino?
quem siqua attingit, non iliam posse putemus
    aegroti culum lingere carn ific?

Sisson's translation:

So help me gods, I didn't think it mattered
Whether I smelt Aemilius's mouth or his arse:
One is no cleaner or dirtier than the other.

---

* *The Poetry of Catullus,* Orion Press, London and New York, 1967

As a matter of fact the arse-hole is cleaner and pleasanter
Because it has no teeth. The mouth has teeth eighteen inches long,
Gums like an old wagonbox,
And gapes like the cunt of a pissing mule in summer.
This man fucks a lot of women and thinks himself charming:
He would better be employed driving a donkey round a millstone.
Any woman who touches him would be capable
Of licking the arse of a sick executioner.

Wow! And *this* is one of the "precious volumes" pre-Freudianly offered by the elderly bibliophile as phallic filler for the "untidy gap" in the bookshelf behind Watson!

But before leaping to the erroneous conclusion, as I confess I did, that it was Sherlock Holmes who made this doubly homoerotic offer, let us first apply the syndromic test to see who really made that offer.

We have found thus far that a great many Sherlockian stories have followed the same allegorical line: a personified fraction of Doyle's multiplex personality emerges from his psychic inner room to commit a forbidden, sexual, antisocial act. But in every story, that other psychic component named Sherlock Holmes arrives to prevent its consummation or to punish his sibling malefactor.

When we apply this psychological Rosetta Stone to this Catullus incident we find that it fits Doyle's compulsive pattern perfectly. (a) The unnamed disguised book-lover (was it the part of Doyle which loved to don disguise to fool people?) offers the books, one of which is bisexual in the extreme, as an insert in Watson's bookshelf, but (b) when the undisguised Holmes, detective and censor appears, (c) the "dirty old man" disappears forever and (d) the volume of Catullus is never mentioned again.

Yes, in this story Doyle has remained loyal to his fixations and kept his Galahad character unsullied. Holmes, a Victorian gentleman, sublimates all of his erotic drives in logical analysis, fiddling, criminal detection, research, personal combat with male criminals, the making of scrapbooks, and (auto-erotic) self-needling with hard drugs known to be anti-aphrodisiacal. He never makes a single lewd suggestion to his platonic friend, Watson. Later, however, Doyle does write several very puzzling ambivalent remarks for Sherlock, one directed by Holmes at himself, the other to Colonel Sebastian Moran. This characterization of Sherlock

Holmes as a completely sublimated man is supported by Holmes's own acute self-appraisal. When at the end of *The Red-Headed League,* Watson exclaims "in unfeigned admiration": "You reasoned it out beautifully, it is so long a chain, and yet every link rings true. . . . And you are a benefactor to the race," Holmes answers with the line from Flaubert, "The man is nothing. The work is everything."

2.

NOW, LIKE THE HAUNTING CHARACTERS in the film *Last Year at Marienbad* who revisit the same rooms over and over again, we return to haunt the allegory-filled empty house, this time to hear Doyle's unmasker Holmes recite two more syndromic lines—written by William Shakespeare.

The first of these printed-word clues is uttered by Holmes while waiting in the dark room for the expected man of violence: When Watson, amazed by the shadow cast upon the window of their flat by the decoy wax dummy of Holmes, exclaims, "Good heavens! It's marvelous!" Holmes says proudly:

I trust that age doth not wither, nor custom stale my infinite variety
. . . it really is rather like me, is it not?   [my emphases]

The underlined words, from *Antony and Cleopatra,* are spoken by Enobarbus when he and Maecenas and Agrippa, friends of Mark Antony, voice their fear that his great passion for Cleopatra will destroy him, his army, and Rome's occupation of Egypt. When Agrippa reminds his companions of Cleopatra's ruination of Caesar, her former lover:

> Royal wench!
> She made great Caesar lay his sword to bed;
> He ploughed her and she cropped . . .

the frightened Maecenas exclaims, "Now Antony must leave her utterly." Enobarbus answers despairingly:

> Never; she will not;
> *Age cannot wither her, nor custom stale*
> *Her infinite variety:* other women cloy
> The appetite they feed, but she makes hungry
> Where most she satisfies. For vilest things

> Become themselves in her, that the holy priests
> Bless her when she is riggish.* [my emphases]

Syndromically speaking, Doyle had two reasons for giving his "actor" the italicized words from the printed play. It is a perfect example of the required images of the switching or confusion of the sexes (Doyle identifies Holmes with Cleopatra) in tandem with the other compulsive images. Also, as every fellow allegory-spotter now recognizes, there could be no better example of heterosexual love linked to the slaughter of masses of men and the companion image of punished lovers than that of Antony and Cleopatra. As his friends feared, Antony's army was annihilated, he committed suicide, and who does not know how Cleopatra killed herself?

In one of the most moving of death-scenes, Cleopatra puts the fatal asp to her breast, and, addressing it contemptuously as if it were a man or a death-impregnating penis: "O venomous fool!" she commands it to "unty at once . . . the knot intrinsicate of life." The well-educated asp instantly obeys her pedantic command, the Queen's attendant cries aloud in grief, and, in perhaps the most surrealistic simile to be found in Shakespeare, Cleopatra sweetly asks the girl to desist from disturbing the biting snake:

> Peace, peace!
> Dost thou not see my baby at my breast,
> that sucks the nurse asleep?

3.

Such was the remarkable narrative to which I listened on that *April evening,* a narrative which would have been utterly incredible had it not been confirmed for me by [Holmes] who I had never expected to see again.
—Dr. Watson, *Adventure of the Empty House*

Nothing that is so is so.
—Festus, *Twelfth Night*

UNSEEN, WE READER-VOYEURS stand once again in the darkest corner of the dark, abandoned house with Holmes and Watson as

---

* Horny.

they anxiously await the syndrome arrival of the murderous Sebastian Moran. Finally, he enters stealthily and, as Watson later recalls:

I saw that he held in his hand a gun . . . then crouching down he rested the end of the barrel upon the ledge of the open window . . . then his finger tighten on the trigger. There was a strange loud whiz and a long silvery tinkle of glass. At that moment Holmes sprang like a tiger upon the marksman's back, and hurled him flat upon his face . . . with convulsive strength he seized Holmes by the throat, but I struck him on the head with the butt of my revolver, and he dropped to the floor. I fell upon him and as I held him my comrade blew a shrill call upon a whistle . . . two policemen in uniform, with one plain-clothes detective, rushed into the room. . . .

Then, while Sebastian Moran is being firmly held by the "stalwart policemen," he gazes at Holmes "with an expression in which hatred and amazement were equally blended." "You fiend!" he keeps on muttering. "You clever, clever fiend!"

Holmes answers this compliment with one of the most remarkable of syndromic signals in all the sixty stories. Walking up to the villain who has just recently tried to strangle him, who had tried to kill him in Switzerland, who is the successor to the fiendish Professor Moriarty, he says, teasingly, ironically, seductively: "Ah, Colonel, *'Journeys end in lovers' meetings,'* as the old play says. I don't think I've had the *pleasure* of seeing you since *you favoured me with those attentions as I lay on the ledge above Reichenbach Falls.*" [my emphases]

When I read this extraordinary remark in presyndromic days I thought: What a *queer* thing for Sherlock Holmes to say! and, assuming it to be a Doylean mistake or aberration, I promptly forgot or suppressed it.

Recently, however, while comparing this quotation with all of the others which trigger or accompany the Doylean images and which link deviant or normal sex with murder, I saw that once again the pattern is perfectly stated. Then, curious as to the form Doyle's obsession would take this time (the syndrome is repetitive, but it always finds new material for its expression), I traced the quotation and found it in the love song performed by the clown Festus in Shakespeare's *Twelfth Night:*

Clown sings.
O mistress mine, where are you roaming?
O, stay and hear! your true-love's coming,
    That can sing both high and low,
Trip no further, pretty sweeting;
Journeys end in lovers' meetings,
    Every wise man's son doth know.   [my italics]

After Andrew and Toby praise him, Festus continues:

What is love? 'Tis not hereafter;
Present mirth hath present laughter;
    What's to come is still unsure:
In delay there lies no plenty:
Then come kiss me, sweet and twenty,
    Youth's a stuff will not endure.
            (II, iii, 35-50)

The allegorist strikes again! Conan Doyle's decidedly devious and deviant comparison between the Holmicidal Moran's three-year pursuit of Sherlock and the "journeys" that "end in lovers' meetings" is, of course, another of Doyle's compulsive irrelevancies, associating sexual images with murder. Like all the rest, it follows immediately a written-word clue—offered this time by Dr. Watson (Dr. Doyle).

When the superego policemen end the symbolic darkness of the empty house with candles and lanterns held near Sebastian Moran, we are asked to "have a good look at the prisoner," to read the murderer's face:

But *one could not look* upon his cruel blue eyes, with their drooping, cynical lids, or upon the fierce aggressive nose and the threatening, deep-lined brow, *without reading Nature's plainest danger signals.*
            [my italics]

When we add this face-reading image to those of the previous messages left by the sex-murderers upon the walls and floors (*A Study in Scarlet*) ; in the books dropped at the scene of murder (this same *Adventure of the Empty House*); the sex-murder images tied to the *Britannica* (*The Red-Headed League*) ; and the row of books in *The Cardboard Box;* and all the many other similar images I leave for the reader to find . . .

4.

> Wherefore, right curteous gentilwomen,
> if it please you with pacience to peruse
> this historie following, you shall see
> Dame Errour so play her parte with a
> leishe of lovers, a male and two femalles,
> as shalle woorke a wonder to your wise
> judgement, in notying the effects of their
> amorous devises . . .
> —Barnabe Riche, *Riche his Farewell to Militarie
> Profession* (1581)*

A RUMINATION: Yes, Conan Doyle habitually makes these irrelevant references to acts of forbidden sexuality tied to murder . . . his own "King Charles's head" . . . this time in the form of a subtle, "inside" reference to the multiple transvestism of *Twelfth Night*. As I remember the play . . . saw it in Rome in 1951 with Edith Johnson as Viola and with a marvelous Chaplinesque Malvolio. . . . it's about the twins, a boy (Sebastian) and girl (Viola) who become separated during a shipwreck. After much wandering twin Viola arrives in Illyria, where, to gain employment with Duke Orsino, she disguises herself as a boy. Orsino sends her as his love-ambassador to Olivia, but she falls in love with the disguised Viola. When we remember that in Shakespeare's theater all the women's roles were played by pretty men, we see here the farcical spectacle of an Olivia, a boy dressed as a girl, falling in love with Viola, a boy dressed as a girl who visits her dressed as a boy! How the Elizabethan audiences must have loved these high-camp variations on the transvestic theme.

But Conan Doyle may have been thinking not only of Shakespeare's comedy of innocent sexual confusion, but also of the festival of Twelfth Night. . . .

---

* Quoted by Charles H. Prouty, introduction to *Twelfth Night*, Penguin Books, as source of Shakespeare's play.

5.

ONE IMPLICATION of the Shakespearean quotation: By comparing Holmes and Sebastian Moran with the twins Viola and Sebastian who finally find each other, Doyle may be saying: "Though the rules of the detective-criminal confrontation require these classical antagonists to seek each other's destruction, Sherlock Holmes is saying to Moran confidentially, 'We are characters in a fantasy. We are perhaps similarly motivated psychosocial twins conceived and carried in the imaginational womb of Conan Doyle.' "

(This interpretation is suggested to me by Ambrose Bierce's dazzling epigram: "The world is full of murderers and their victims—and how hungrily do they seek each other!" It is suggested also by *The Captain Had Bad Dreams,** Nelson Algren's brilliant story about a very tough Chicago police captain who stage-manages a daily lineup of recividist thieves, addicts, hookers, drunks, muggers, etc. He grows unconsciously to identify with and love even the worst of them. If they are absent from his lineup he misses them. When they show up again he scolds them, half-seriously, for neglecting him. Finally the captain has bad dreams in which he himself stands guiltily in the daily lineup among his beloved enemies of society, his symbiotic partners in sin and punishment.)

6.

I SHALL ASSUME THAT since very few readers in 1903—and even fewer readers in 1974—would be likely to recognize "journeys end in lovers' meetings" as a line from *Twelfth Night,* it must then have been an "inside" practical joke played by Doyle for himself and for the rare reader who might understand the esoteric reference.

Because the festival of Twelfth Night plays no part in Shakespeare's comedy, scholars agree that the playwright used that title and its subtitle *Or What You Will* as an easily understood

---

* *The Neon Wilderness,* New York, 1947.

allusion to the permitted anarchy then still practiced during the twelve days between Christmas and Epiphany (January 6) : It was Shakespeare's invitation to his audience to react to the play's licentiousness in the carnival spirit. I believe that Conan Doyle, a keen student of medievalism, knew all this and made *his* Twelfth Night allusion in the same spirit.

The festival of Twelfth Night followed closely the Saturnalia of ancient Rome, described in *The Golden Bough* of Sir James Frazer as: "an annual period of license, when the customary restraints of law and order are thrown aside, when the whole population gives itself to extravagant mirth and jollity, and *when the darker passions find a vent which would never be allowed them in the more staid and sober course of ordinary life.*" I have emphasized the last sentence to draw attention to the mingling of jocularity and "darker passions" implicit in (Doyle's) Holmes's "erotic" remark to the captured Moran. I also wish to draw attention to the fact that the very first meeting between Holmes and Moran's predecessor Moriarty* takes place on January 4th, a day well within the saturnalian twelve days. It is another indication of Doyle's allegorizing and, of course, the mention of "January 4th" was consciously deliberate.

In "this carnival of antiquity," continues Frazer, "a young man disguised as Saturn, as 'master of the revels,' went about in public with full license to indulge his passions and taste of every pleasure, however base or shameful.

"The saturnalian Twelfth Night, or Feast of Fools, in medieval Europe was similarly presided over by a King of Misrule or Bishop of Fools, whose every whim had to be obeyed."

Frazer adds:

In France a Pope of Folly reigned over a round of grotesque and sometimes impious masquerades, merry and often disgusting scenes, furious orgies, dances, profane songs, and impudent parodies of the Catholic liturgy.

At these parodies of the most solemn rites of the church, the *priests* wore grotesque masks and *sometimes dressed as women,* danced in the choir and *sang obscene chants: laymen dressed as monks and nuns* mingled with the clergy: the altar was transformed into a tavern where deacons and subdeacons ate sausages and played dice and cards under the noses of the celebrants: and the censers smoked with old

* *The Final Problem.*

shoes, filling the church with a foul stench. After playing these pranks and running, leaping, and cutting capers through the whole church, they rode about the town in mean carts, exchanging scurrilities with the crowds of laughing and peering spectators.   [my italics]

Sherlock Holmes, who returned from death in the disguise of a lewd old practical joker who offers his friend a volume of Catullus and another about Dionysian resurrection, began his flight from the Satanic Professor Moriarty in a disguise that is—when thought about in the context of the Catholic Twelfth Night—most revealing.

In the "death of Sherlock Holmes" story (*The Final Problem*) Holmes asks Watson to join him in his flight from certain death. Following Holmes's precise instructions, Watson arrives at Victoria Station on time to find that Holmes has been delayed and will not catch the departing train. Only a "venerable Italian priest" is in the train's compartment. Watson is now certain that Holmes has been caught and killed by Moriarty, when suddenly the "venerable Italian priest" speaks in a very familiar English voice and sheds his priestly robe. It is, of course, Sherlock Holmes!

Yes, Conan Doyle was indeed thinking of the Shakespearean play and the Festival of Fools called Twelfth Night when he played these cruel practical jokes on the trusting and gullible Watson—and upon the vast public that demanded and rejoiced in the resurrection of Sherlock Holmes.

7.

I MORE THAN SUSPECT THAT the playful Conan Doyle, who most reluctantly resumed the writing of the detective stories he regarded as "inferior" stuff about a hero he loathed, meant his "resurrection of Holmes" story to be an elaborate spoof.

Because: The actual "return to life," staged as a practical joke; the fainting incident; Holmes's long and incredible rigmarole about his escape from Reichenbach Falls; his second escape from the rock-throwing Moran; his story about the three-year journey to Tibet and back—all occur on April Fool's Day!

This is clearly revealed by the glaring "mistake" in Watson's narration. According to him, the story begins when "death came to the easy-going young aristocrat (Adair) . . . on the night of

182 : NAKED IS THE BEST DISGUISE

March 30, 1894." Watson then goes on to say that he read about it on the next day, March 31st, and, after thinking about it all that day, he visited the scene of the crime that afternoon. There, after bumping into Watson, Holmes followed him home, caused him to faint, and then told him how he escaped from his presumptive death in Switzerland, and related his subsequent adventure.

The "glaring mistake" occurs when, after listening to this long monologue on "March 31st," Watson writes: "such was the remarkable narrative I listened to on *that April evening* . . ."

[my italics]

Watson adds illogically: ". . . a narrative which would have been utterly incredible to me had it not been confirmed by the tall spare figure, and the keen, eager face, which I had never thought to see again."

By this act of "mistakenly" pushing forward by one day after March 31st Watson's gullible reaction to Holmes's practical joke and fantastic explanation, it all takes place on All Fool's Day. And who is better suited to play the part of the fool than the lovable, trusting, gullible and unbrilliant Watson? (Doyle, who knew German fluently—he quotes Goethe in German several times—may have been thinking in that language when he juxtaposed the words "April," "incredible," and "narrative," since *narr* in German means "fool.")

8.

> When I turned again, Sherlock Holmes was standing smiling at me across the study table . . . and I fainted for the first and last time in my life.
> —Dr. Watson, *The Adventure of the Empty House*

LIKE OTHER READERS, I've always assumed that Watson fainted because Sherlock Holmes's Lazaruslike return was so shocking. But now, along with that most obvious of reasons, I can suggest several other causes: First, Watson may have lost consciousness because of the highly inconsiderate, even sadistic charade perpetrated by Doyle at such a serious moment. Also, like one of Dr. Pavlov's multisignaled experimental dogs, Watson may have fainted because of the utterly opposing nature of the books simultaneously offered to him in the instant before Holmes's resurrection—the bisexual poems of Catullus and John Bunyan's Puritan allegory entitled:

THE HOLY WAR; made by King Shaddai (Jehovah) *upon Diabolus* (Satan) *for the regaining of the Metropolis of the World; or the Losing and Regaining again of the town of Mansoul.* (Man's soul).

It seems that Dr. Doyle, appalled by his audacity in even mentioning Catullus, followed it immediately with the mention of Bunyan's pious Holy War as a Mithridate (antidote) powerful enough to neutralize the Catullian "poison."

From the moment Holmes reveals the existence of Professor Moriarty he quits his role as a worldly detective who solves the random mysteries brought him by mainly random clients. Instead, as his acts and words reveal, Sherlock Holmes becomes a Bunyanesque Emmanuel (King Shaddai's earthly champion of virtue) who wages a selfless Christlike war against Diabolus or Satan (Moriarty) for the spiritual and moral control of the Metropolis of the World. (In 1893, London was called "the metropolis of the world.")

This reading of Doyle's mention of The Holy War arises from my new insight into Doyle's allegorical processes and from the words and images found in Holmes's various descriptions of the evil ex-professor.

Invented by Doyle for the sole purpose of killing the detective whom he loathed, the expendable Moriarty is altogether different from the villains of the previous twenty-four stories. While they are all-too-humanly motivated by greed, sadism, or desire for revenge, Moriarty is portrayed by Holmes as an invisible, almost-supernatural Satanic Prince of Darkness:*

"You have never heard of Professor Moriarty?" said he.
"[Watson] Never."
"Ay, there's the genius and the wonder of the thing!" he cried. "[Moriarty] has tendencies of the most *diabolical* kind . . . for years past I have been conscious of some *power behind the malefactor,* some *deep organizing power which forever stands in the way of the law.* . . . A veil shrouds it. . . ." [my emphases]

---

* In *The Valley of Fear,* Moriarty is called "this king-devil."

Then, describing London as a Bunyanesque metropolis, Holmes adds:

"Moriarty is the *organizer of half that is evil,* and nearly all that is undetected *in this great city.* . . . He sits motionless at the centre of its web, but that web has a thousand radiations. . . . *He does little himself. He only plans.* . . . The agent may be caught, *but the central power* . . . *is never caught—never so much as suspected* . . . at last I had met an antagonist who was my intellectual equal." [my emphases]

The final transformation of this superhuman yet mortal London detective into an allegorical sacrificial hero who resembles Theseus, Dionysus, and Jesus Christ (especially Jesus Christ) is revealed in the "death" story (*The Final Problem*) and in *The Adventure of the Empty House,* the "resurrection" story.

In what is probably the coolest, most understated "farewell speech" ever delivered by a hero facing death in combat, Sherlock Holmes becomes a secular Christ who willingly gives his life for mankind:

MY DEAR WATSON [it said]:

I write these lines through the courtesy of Mr. Moriarty, who awaits my convenience for the final discussion of those questions which lie between us. . . . *I am pleased to think* that *I shall* be able to *free society from* the further effects of *his presence,* though I fear it is at a cost which will give pain to my friends, and especially to you, my dear Watson. I have already explained to you, however, that my career had in any case reached its crisis and that no possible conclusion to it could be more congenial to me than this. . . . Pray give my greetings to Mrs. Watson, and believe me, my dear fellow,

Very sincerely yours,
SHERLOCK HOLMES
[my italics]

Sherlock Holmes attains apotheosis when Watson, lured away from the final showdown between Holmes and Moriarty by a forged note (written by Moriarty), returns to find Sherlock's farewell note. After realizing that Moriarty and Holmes had fallen over the cliff "locked in each other's arms," and that "any attempt at recovering the bodies was absolutely hopeless . . . deep down in that dreadful cauldron of swirling water and seething foam, will lie forever the most dangerous criminal and the foremost champion of the law in their generation," Watson eulogizes his great friend as: "him whom I shall ever regard as the best and wisest man whom ever I have known."

9.

Sherlock Holmes and Socrates

> Frank . . . do you remember how Socrates felt when the *chlamys* blew aside and showed him the limbs of [the youth] Charmides? How the blood throbbed in his veins? How he grew blind with desire?
>
> —Oscar Wilde in Frank Harris, *Oscar Wilde*

As GEORGE ORWELL and others have noted, the last words of Watson's beautiful and lofty eulogy to Sherlock Holmes: ". . . him whom I shall ever regard as the best and wisest man whom I have ever known," is taken without quotation marks from Benjamin Jowett's great translation of Plato's *Phaedo,* the account of Socrates's noble death.

An eyewitness to that celebrated death-by-hemlock forced upon Socrates, Phaedo says:

> Such was the end, Echecrates, of our friend; concerning whom I may truly say, that *of all the men who I have ever known, he was the wisest and the justest and the best.* [my italics]

If any readers assume, as well they might, that by using the exact words of Phaedo's (Plato's) eulogy to the (homosexual) Socrates, Watson is implying that along with being the "best and wisest man," Sherlock is also *Holmosexual*—I disagree emphatically and offer the Doylean syndrome as my argument to the contrary.

As we have seen thus far, in every story Sherlock Holmes is the incorruptible and relentless guardian of the Victorian criminal and moral code. He almost always prevents or tries to prevent any crime—on both the conscious and unconscious levels of the story—from being consummated. When a sexual or other crime has been committed, he stops a repetition. Or, as a combined detective-judge-policeman, he is an auxiliary to the punishment of the malefactor.

Understanding his precise role in the syndrome as the super-ego-in-residence from Conan Doyle's schizoid "inner room," we return to the Socratic last paragraph of *The Final Problem* to note that Sherlock Holmes is already dead when Dr. Watson (Dr. Doyle) uses the words that subtly raise the specter of homosexuality. The last word is given to this mistaken suggestion because obviously Sherlock Holmes is no longer there to act as the censorious nullifier of the posthumous fantasy staged by the tireless deviant devil also resident in Conan Doyle's psychic inner room.

10.

> What is truth? said jesting Pilate, and
> would not stay for an answer.
>
> —Francis Bacon, *On Truth*

THE FULL SIGNIFICANCE of the "elderly bibliophile's" offer to Watson of *The Holy War,* John Bunyan's allegory of the war between Emmanuel and Satan for the possession of Metropolis and Man's Soul, is revealed by the more than twenty-five similarities between Doyle's death and resurrection stories—*The Final Problem* and *The Adventure of the Empty House*—and the Catholic liturgy of Easter, commemorating the Death and Resurrection of Jesus Christ.

These astonishing similarities were first noticed by me when, after learning that the jesting Doyle had reluctantly resurrected the detective he hated (but whom the world adored) on April Fool's Day, I glanced at the current calendar (1972) and saw that March 30, the day of Robert Adair's murder, was Good Friday and that through Watson's "glaring mistake" Sherlock Holmes had been resurrected, two days later, on Easter Sunday! (The *World Almanac* shows that Easter Sunday, a movable feast which date-varies each year, has fallen on April 1st six times since the 1880s.)

Confounded by the strange confusion among the images of All Fools' Day, resurrection of Holmes, Resurrection of Christ, and Easter Sunday, I read the *Britannica* (11th edit.) article on April Fool's Day and was further confounded to read that it was

. . . the name given to the 1st of April in allusion to the custom of playing practical jokes on friends and neighbors by sending them on fool's errands. The origin of this custom has been much disputed, and many ludicrous solutions have been suggested, *e.g.,* that it is a farcical commemoration of Christ being sent from Annas to Caiaphas, from Caiaphas to Pilate, from Pilate to Herod, and from Herod back to Pilate again, *the crucifixion having taken place about the 1st of April.*

[my italics]

11.

> But over the whole [Sherlock Holmes] epic there hangs an air of irresponsible comedy, like that of some father's rigmarole for children.
>
> —Edmund Wilson, *Classics and Commercials*

MY STARTLED INNER REACTION: I know that Conan Doyle was an irrepressible practical joker and that to mock his readers he might have staged the Christlike return of Holmes on the first of April— as his way of sending the reader on a fool's errand. But are there any facts, images, ideas, words, anything to support my hunch that he had also written the "return" of Sherlock Holmes as a travesty of the great Christian drama?

In "serious" literature . . . in Herman Melville's allegorical *Moby Dick,* mad Captain Ahab assembles the *Pequod*'s crew to celebrate a Black Mass. After plunging the God-and-Christ-killing harpoon into savage blood (on Good Friday the Catholic priest plunges the Paschal candle into the blessed baptismal water), Ahab howls the Satanic "blessing": "I baptize thee not in the name of the father, but in the name of the devil!" And in *Ulysses,* James Joyce staged a similar profanation in Bella Cohen's brothel, an obscene travesty of the Catholic mass conducted by the Satanic ecumenical team: Father Malachi O'Flynn and the Reverend Haines Love.

But *Doyle!* Would *Doyle* of all people ever be capable, even unconsciously, of thinking of and then actually writing in such diabolical terms?

But come to think of it, Conan Doyle, like James Joyce, attended Jesuit schools until he was seventeen. He was offered but rejected priesthood along with Catholicism to become a parlor necromancer . . . Yes, the psychological and intellectual possibilities do exist in this man for the writing of a serio-comic travesty of the Death and Resurrection of Jesus.

Alerted now to so fascinating and important a possibility, I read the stories in question along with various Catholic encyclopedias and found that Conan Doyle had indeed woven into *The Final Problem* and *The Adventure of the Empty House* an unmistakable and sacrilegious travesty of the Easter festival commemorating the last three days of Jesus's life: Good Friday, Holy Saturday, and Easter Sunday as well.

But quite aware that as a non-Catholic layman I might easily misunderstand the intricacies of their liturgy, I contacted Sister Mary Dotto, the educational director of a neighborhood church. After hearing my reasons for calling, she arranged a conference with Father Robert Dacian Ferand, who verified my list of Doylean quotations as direct allusions to precise details of the Easter liturgy.

12.

IN NON-SEQUENTIAL ORDER, here are the most important parallels between Doyle's death and resurrection stories and the New Testament drama of Jesus as it is seen in the various Easter services:

(a)

New Testament: Jesus voluntarily died for mankind.

The Final Problem: In his farewell note left at Reinchenbach Falls for Watson, Sherlock Holmes announces modestly that after serious deliberation (his *Gethsemane*) , he is *"pleased" to sacrifice his life* if it will rid "society" (mankind) of Professor Moriarty, the fictional avatar of the "Anti-Christ" Nietzsche.

(b)

New Testament: Jesus, the Son of the Lord, was murdered by *Roman soldiers.*

The Empty House: This adventure begins with the *murder of* the Honorable Robert Adair, *the son of a lord* (the Earl of Maynooth) by *Colonel* Sebastian Moran, late of the Indian *army.*

Moran, Holmes tells us, was the son of Sir *Augustus* Moran: Augustus was a *Roman* emperor. Also: St. Sebastian, says *Lives of the Saints,* was a *soldier* in the *Roman* Imperial Guard under Diocletian.

Note: When sharp-shooter Moran tries to kill Holmes in the exact same way he killed Adair, *Holmes replaces Adair as the "son of a lord"* to become the target of Anti-Christ Nietzsche-Moran. (Doyle had to invent Adair as a victim as his device for bringing back Holmes—to provide a crime for which the expendable Moran could be executed.)

(c)

New Testament: Jesus was crucified between two thieves.

The Empty House: During his recapitulation of his escape from Reichenbach Falls and the rock-throwing Moran, Holmes says that after Watson and the police had left the scene (they thought he was drowned) , he remained in hiding—alone with the dead Moriarty on one side (in the waters below) , and the very alive Moran above and behind him. Thus, at the time of his "death," *Holmes, a self-proclaimed secular Christ, was left alone on a hill (Calvary) between two thieves.*

(d)

Catholic Liturgy: One of the high points of the Easter *Holy Saturday* Mass is the blessing of the holy font and its *baptismal water.* "Its general theme," explains the *Catholic Encyclopedia,* "is that the *water,* made productive by the Spirit, *gives birth to the divine life* of men. The Font is compared to a Womb: it is the womb of the Holy Church producing a heavenly offspring and *reborn as a new creation."*   [my italics]

The Empty House: Sherlock Holmes is *reborn* out of the waters of Reichenbach Falls after *three* years of immersion in what Doyle called his "worthy tomb." This corresponds to the *three* days in which Jesus lay in His tomb before his Resurrection. (This is the *internal* time of the stories as told by Watson. Actually Holmes was not revived until 1902 (*The Hound of the Baskervilles*) and did not tell his story until 1903 (*The Adventure of the Empty House*) .

(As previously noted, Sherlock Holmes is a different man

after his "rebirth"; *e.g.,* he drops his only physical vice: addiction to morphine and cocaine.)

(*e*)

Good Friday: The Prostration of the Priest: During the *Good Friday* service, according to a book loaned me by Sister Mary Dotto, *"Priests appear in black* and *lie prostrate* at the altar stairs; this powerless prostration expresses the desolate state of man before redemption."

The Empty House: After first disguising himself as a *black-cassocked Italian priest* Sherlock Holmes undergoes the ordeal of combat with Moriarty and then finds that he cannot climb the rocks (altar steps) because Moran is above him throwing down rocks. *Powerless* against this attack *he lies prostrate* on a ledge for some time. Later under the cover of darkness he makes his *ascension* and finds freedom (*redemption*) from his (*Roman*) persecutor.

(*f*)

Holy Saturday: The Night Vigil: On Holy Saturday, which looks back to the preceding day of Crucifixion (Good Friday), and forward expectantly to Easter Sunday, a *"night vigil"* is held in the dark and empty (of decorations) church.

The Empty House: On "Saturday, March 31st, 1894," Holmes and Watson maintain a long *night-vigil in the dark and empty house* while awaiting the arrival of the Satanic Moran.

(*g*)

New Testament: Jesus engages in hand-to-hand combat with Satan. In his *Theological Dimensions of the Liturgy,** Father Cyprian Vagaggini writes, "Christ's activity appears as a victorious struggle against Satan. . . . Christ comes to free mankind of the Devil's power. *Immediately after his Baptism* Jesus was led to the desert where he engaged the devil in hand-to-hand combat."

The Empty House: During his account of his symbolical rebirth from the baptismal waters of Reichenbach Falls, Holmes recounts his earlier *hand-to-hand combat* with the *diabolical Moriarty* and his later (one-sided) fight with the Satanic Moran.

---

* *Theological Dimensions of the Liturgy,* Minnesota, 1959.

(h)

The Paschal candle: On Holy Saturday, the Easter vigil service begins with the church in almost total darkness to symbolize the spiritual darkness and gloom that prevailed before Christ, the Light of the World, was resurrected. Finally, after the night vigil, a dramatic scene is enacted. A deacon heading a procession enters the church *carrying a candle* which symbolizes the Risen Savior who, radiant with heavenly light, has left the grave. At the appropriate moment, the *deacon lights the candle,* and the church lamps are lit. By word and symbol the Moment of Resurrection is solemnly proclaimed.

The Empty House: This is perhaps the most ingenious detail of Conan Doyle's entire travesty of the Easter Liturgy. After Holmes and Watson hold their *night-vigil* and Holmes conquers Satan (Moran) in personal combat, Holmes blows a whistle and there comes running into the dark and empty house Inspector Lestrade and two uniformed policemen. The policemen carry bright lanterns, but *Lestrade enters carrying two candles!*

As the two *cops* (acolytes!) uncover their lanterns and hold Moran, Lestrade *lights his candles* to illuminate the dark room and reveal the face and identity of Moran. At that moment it becomes bright and clear that the only threat to Sherlock Holmes's life has been eliminated. His resurrection has been fully accomplished. (From that moment, as all Sherlockeans know, Holmes attains immortality.) Since the policemen bring in powerful lanterns, "deacon" Lestrade's supererogatory act of lighting two weak candles is obviously intended by Doyle to be a parody of the symbolical lighting of the Paschal candle.

(i)

New Testament: The Lamb of God: Because Jesus was crucified at the exact time that the daily Passover lamb was sacrificed (three hours after noon), *the sacrificed lamb* has come to symbolize the sacrificed Jesus. (Sherlock Holmes also "dies" in the afternoon.)

The Empty House: This one is amazing! While the captured Moran is being firmly held by the policemen, Holmes explains to this captive audience of one that just as he (Moran) used to tether a kid as a *sacrificial bait* to lure a tiger into ambush, he, Sherlock

Holmes, had *set himself up as a sacrificial kid* for Moran (the wax "icon").

With this gratuitous explanation (Moran is a bad listener) Sherlock Holmes equates himself with Jesus, the Easter *Paschal lamb.*

(j)

The New Testament: The "Smiting on the Head": In *The Gospel According to St. Matthew* it is said: ". . . they [the Romans] smote him on the head . . . and they led him away to be crucified." The words "Matthew," "smote," and "crucified" (cross) are found in

The Empty House: After the drama in the empty house ends, Holmes and Watson return to 221B Baker Street where the great man takes down his "M" scrapbook to read its "Moran" entry to Watson. Digressively, he mentions: *"Mathews, who knocked out my left canine in the waiting room at Charing Cross."*

Thus we see that (as in *The Gospel According to St. Matthew*) Christ was struck on the head before being led to the Cross, so Sherlock Holmes (secular Christ) is *also hit on the head* (his tooth is knocked out) in the *waiting room at Charing Cross* station.

Why "waiting room at Charing Cross station"? The *Britannica* informs us that Charing Cross takes its name from the huge crucifix erected there in 1209 by King Edward to commemorate the death of his wife Eleanore. The cross was destroyed in 1657 and replaced by a statue of Charles I; Charing Cross became the place of execution for political and other criminals.

But a substitute cross was later installed in the *waiting room* of the *Charing Cross railroad station,* and it was there that Holmes, as secular Christ (like Jesus Christ), was smitten on the head!

The "M" scrapbook compiled by Sherlock Holmes is syndromic. The image of a beloved dead wife (sexual partner) is associated with the murder of Jesus and of untold thousands of early Christians; the Charing Cross also associates that emotional-sexual partnership with the legal murder of a great many English men, women and children and repeats the image-pattern we have seen so many times in Doyle's detective and other stories.

(k)

New Testament: Matthew (16:1) ". . . Jesus appeared to Mary."

The Final Problem: The farewell note read by Watson after Sherlock's disappearance in the waterfall contains the penultimate sentence: "Pray give my greetings to Mrs. Watson." Mrs. Watson's first name was, of course, Mary. Mary was also the name of Conan Doyle's mother.

13.

New Testament: The Empty Tomb of Jesus Christ

THE LAST PARALLEL between Conan Doyle's travesty of the New Testament drama of Jesus's Death, Disappearance, and Resurrection is one of the most poetic. In *The Gospel According to St. John,* the Disciple narrates Mary Magdalene's discovery that the tomb of Jesus is empty:

. . . she runneth to Simon Peter and the other disciple whom Jesus loved, and saith unto them, They have taken the Lord out of the sepulchre, and we know not where they have laid him.

This recalls the Jehovah-like words used by Sir Arthur Conan Doyle in his memoirs, "I decided to end the life of my hero [and when] we saw the wonderful falls of Reichenbach, a terrible place, and one which I thought would make a worthy *tomb* for Sherlock . . ."

But the tomb of Doyle's sacrificed fictional son is empty now, for he was taken out of that watery sepulchre by the man who was in turn his father-creator, his Judas, his Pilate, his Herod, his crucifying Roman soldier. But, happy ending, the man who was also his redeemer: who resurrected Holmes and transfigured him as an undying Dionysian keeper of bees.

14.

We "poisson d'avril" (*fish of April*)

The *fish that you have tattooed* immediately *above your right wrist* could only have been done in China.

—Holmes to the pawnbroker, *The Red-Headed League*

AFTER READING (and believing) the *Britannica*'s "ludicrous" explanation: "April Fool's Day . . . is a farcical commemoration of Christ being sent from Annas to Caiaphas, from Caiaphas to Pilate, from Pilate to Herod, and from Herod back to Pilate, the crucifixion having taken place about the 1st of April," I continued to read the article and learned that "it has been plausibly suggested that Europe derived its April-fooling from the French" because of the wild and funny confusion that resulted in 1564 when the King changed the year's beginning from the 1st of April to the 1st of January. "In France," says the *Britannica*, "the person befooled is known as a 'poisson d'avril.' This has been explained from the association of ideas arising from the fact that in April the sun quits the zodiacal sign of the fish. A far more plausible explanation would be that the April fish would be young fish and more easily caught."

All of this fishy information may explain the curious symbol noticed by the eagle-eyed Sherlock Holmes on the person of the red-headed pawnbroker who had been sent on the great fool's errand by the thief John Clay: ". . . he takes snuff, that he is a Freemason, that he has been to China."

When challenged to explain the "China" deduction, Sherlock Holmes tells the red-headed *schlemiel:* "The *fish you have tattooed* immediately above your right wrist could only have been done in China."

I deduce from this, as Sherlock might say, that as another of his serious allegorical jokes, Conan Doyle tattooed the foolish man who copied the *Britannica* "in longhand on *fools*cap paper" [my italics] with the stigmatic *fish* (also the early symbol of Christ) to show that he was a "fish of April," and, I daresay, if Sir Arthur Conan Doyle could have managed it, every one of the millions of

readers who demanded and rejoiced in the resurrection of the
Sherlock Holmes whom they adored and he hated would have
been similarly tattooed.

15.

> I flatter myself that I can distinguish at
> a glance the ash of any known brand
> either of cigar or of tobacco.
> —Sherlock Holmes, *A Study in Scarlet*

As THE NUMEROUS dramatic parallels between Doyle's two detective stories and the details of the Easter liturgy unfolded, more
questions arose: Did Doyle, who repeated his personal sexual
allegory for about forty years, also cling to his religious allegory
with a similar tenacity? And, if *The Final Problem* (1893) and
The Adventure of the Empty House, written ten years later, mock
the solemn liturgy of the last three days of Easter, are there any
Doylean travesties of the previous thirty-seven days of Easter in
any of the earlier stories?

Suspecting that he had remained faithful in his fixations, I
reread *A Study in Scarlet* and found that its amazingly persistent
author had staged his first Sherlock Holmes adventure on Ash
Wednesday, the first day of Easter and of the fast of Lent! And, as
always, it is the ventriloquial Doyle himself, speaking through his
"puppet"-narrator John Watson, who offers the multiple proofs of
his deliberate use of that holy day.

The first proof: Dr. Watson's words: "It was upon the 4th of
March . . ." sent me to the same Catholic calendar which had
identified the "March 30th" of *The Empty House* as Good Friday.
Like all the other Easter holy days, *Ash Wednesday* is a movable
feast and falls in some years upon the 4th of March.

The second proof: Recalling the very high density of other
Doylean idea-clusters, I pursued the matter and found that the
mischievous man had identified and underscored the *Ash Wednesday*-ness of the "4th of March" with a lengthy and odd explanation:

It was upon the 4th of March, as I have good reason to remember,
that I rose somewhat earlier than usual, and found that Sherlock
Holmes had not yet finished his breakfast. The landlady had become so

accustomed to my late habits that my place had not been laid nor my coffee prepared. With the unreasonable petulance of mankind I rang the bell and gave a curt intimation that I was ready. Then I picked up a magazine from the table and attempted to while away the time with it, while my companion munched silently at his toast. One of the articles had a pencil mark at the heading, and I naturally began to run my eye through it.

Its somewhat ambitious title was "The Book of Life." . . .

This rather trivial, unconvincing, even tedious explanation as to *why* John Watson happened to remember that particular date, of no importance whatever to the story, remains puzzling until one extracts its essential point: On the "4th of March," the first day of *Ash Wednesday* and of the *fast of Lent,* John Watson remembers that he was forced to *fast* for a few minutes!

The anonymous "magazine article" picked up and read by the petulant Watson while he waited for his break-*fast* becomes a bone of contention. Watson thinks it's all "twaddle," but Holmes reveals that he is its hidden author and defends his thesis that no one can hide a concealed truth from a scientific observer (like himself) who knows how to read even the tiniest of clues. "All of life," he insists, "is a great chain, the nature of which is known whenever we ('observant men') are shown only a single link."

Taking his words as gospel, I gazed at the title of Holmes's article as a possible single link that might reveal a great chain. Then, because it seemed vaguely Biblical, I looked into a *Concordance* and found that the words "book of life" are mentioned only in the New Testament *Book of Revelations*—the revelations given by Jesus to his disciple and chronicler, St. John. In one of the six mentions of this phrase Jesus is ambiguously associated only in the New Testament *Book of Revelation*—the revelations with "the book of life": as its author or as the book of life itself.

I mused: This is amusing. And illuminating. And the suspected religious allegory is gathering force. First Doyle's "secular Christ" Holmes reveals himself to his disciple and chronicler as the secret author of a "Book of Life," a book of scientific *revelations* explaining his methods for unraveling mundane mysteries. Then, after a short inquiry into the words "book of life," we find ourselves in the New Testament chapter in which the prototypical Christ offers His disciple and chronicler, also named John (of Patmos) , his mystical revelations. Is this conscious parody?

The analytical meditation continued: Ash Wednesday . . . The fast of Lent . . . the Book of Life, meaning either scientific or mystical revelations. When we add these to the symbols of the Paschal lamb, the Paschal candle, and all the rest of the Easter rituals deployed in depth by Conan Doyle, we see that a religious allegory is indeed raising its anointed head. But how far will Doyle carry this? I'm now willing to bet that the well-known penitential ashes of Ash Wednesday will show up in *A Study in Scarlet.* Syndromically.

Conan Doyle did not fail me. The stigmatic ashes with which each Catholic is "signed" on that holy day *are* exhibited in the story. They are found by Sherlock Holmes not far from the corpse of the sex-motivated beast and murderer Enoch Drebber, whom ironical Doyle calls a "Latter-Day Saint."

The awe-stricken Watson, as he watches Sherlock Holmes at work for the first time, writes: ". . . I was irresistibly reminded of a fox-hound, whining in its eagerness, until it comes across the lost scent." Then, he continues, Holmes concludes his twenty-minute "researches" by gathering "up carefully a little pile of grey dust from the floor, and packed it away in an envelope."

Holmes then explains to Watson that the "grey dust" he'd gathered and "read" was the ash of a "Trichinopoly cigar" smoked by the then unknown murderer (Jefferson Hope).

I find it hard to believe that a fanatical Monte Cristo avenger like Hope would, after catching up with Drebber after a twenty-year-long chase, smoke a cigar while maniacally confronting him, haranguing him, and holding a knife to his throat while he forced him to take poison! The illogic of all this suggests that Doyle introduced the cigar and its ashes mainly as a clue to his continuing travesty of Easter, this time of Ash Wednesday and its rite of "the signing with ashes."

A *Bible Missal,* copies of which may be seen in every Catholic Church, helps reveal Doyle's religious allegory. After stating that the stigmatic ashes were borrowed from the ancient Hebrew custom of wearing sackcloth and ashes as a sign of mourning and penance, the *Missal* instructs:

The ashes stand for the dust of the earth to which, because of the *sin of Adam,* we must all return.

The Missal then adds:

In the ashes we see not only our death with Christ in sin, but also our resurrection from the earth to glory with the new Adam, our redeemer.

From this we may deduce the obvious meaning of the stigmatic ashes rubbed upon the faces of our Catholic neighbors. Because Adam and Eve once performed the forbidden act of sexual union, they and all of us, their descendants, were meted out the worst of all punishments by a wrathful god: mortality.

Thus we see that the ash of an ordinary cigar smoked by a fictional mortal man, *ash* which was found and "read" by the Paracletean Sherlock Holmes, becomes the resurrectional materialistic-mystical substance that binds together in unity the sexual and religious allegories concealed and revealed within the Cretan maze of Conan Doyle's marvelous detective stories.

16.

I have found that the Doylean allegory discovered and unfolded here was once anticipated and perfectly stated by John Donne in his *Hymn to God in My Sickness:*

> We think that Paradise and Calvary,
>   Christ's cross and Adam's tree, stood in one place:
> Look, Lord, and find that both Adams met in me.

INDEX